Thomas D. Hooks

S0-ARN-033

Independence Hall in 1776. Here the Continental Congress adopted
and signed the Declaration of Independence.

Signers of the Declaration

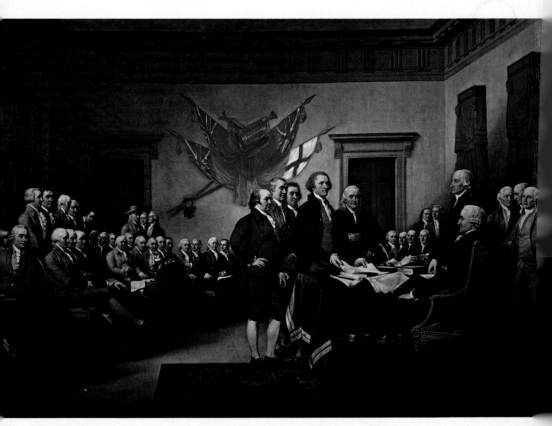

John Trumbull's "The Declaration of Independence" hangs in the rotunda of the U.S. Capitol. Depicting the drafting committee presenting the document to the Continental Congress, the painting commemorates the signers.

Signers

OF THE DECLARATION

Historic Places Commemorating the Signing
of the Declaration of Independence

ROBERT G. FERRIS
Series Editor

UNITED STATES DEPARTMENT OF THE INTERIOR
NATIONAL PARK SERVICE

Washington, D.C. Rev. Ed. 1975

ASSOCIATE DIRECTOR FOR PROFESSIONAL SERVICES
Ernest A. Connally

OFFICE OF ARCHEOLOGY AND HISTORIC PRESERVATION
Robert M. Utley, *Director*

DIVISION OF HISTORY
A. Russell Mortensen, *Chief*

HISTORIC SITES SURVEY
Horace J. Sheely, Jr., *Chief*

This volume incorporates a comprehensive survey of sites and buildings associated with the signers accomplished by Charles W. Snell and the late John O. Littleton. Also utilized were survey and evaluation reports authored by the following individuals: S. Sydney Bradford, Charles E. Hatch, Jr., W. Brown Morton III, Denys Peter Myers, John D. R. Platt, Frank B. Sarles, Jr., Charles E. Shedd, Jr., Horace J. Sheely, Jr., and Martin I. Yoelson. These surveys and reports were reviewed by the Advisory Board on National Parks, Historic Sites, Buildings, and Monuments. Members of this group are listed in the Acknowledgments. Directly involved in all aspects of the preparation of this book were Assistant Editor Richard E. Morris and Editorial Assistant James H. Charleton. It was designed by Gary Gore.

THIS BOOK IS ISSUED AS PART OF THE NATIONAL PARK SERVICE OBSERVANCE OF OUR NATION'S BICENTENNIAL.

As the Nation's principal conservation agency, the Department of the Interior has basic responsibilities for water, fish, wildlife, mineral, land, park, and recreational resources. Indian and Territorial affairs are other major concerns of America's "Department of Natural Resources." The Department works to assure the wisest choice in managing all our resources so each will make its full contribution to a better United States—now and in the future.

LIBRARY OF CONGRESS CATALOG CARD NUMBER: 73-600028

For sale by the Superintendent of Documents, U.S. Government Printing Office, Washington, D.C. 20402 - Price $6.85
Stock Number 024-005-00593-5

Foreword

As we approach the two hundredth anniversary of the signing of the Declaration of Independence, each of us is stirred by the memory of those who framed the future of our country.

In the coming years we will have many opportunities to refresh our understanding of what America means, but none can mean more than personal visits to the sites where freedom was forged and our founding fathers actually made the decisions which have stood the severest tests of time.

I remember my reactions, for example, when I visited Independence Hall in Philadelphia in 1972 to sign the new revenue sharing legislation. Walking into the building where that small group of patriots gathered some two centuries ago, I thought back to what it must have been like when the giants of our American heritage solemnly committed themselves and their children to liberty. The dilemmas they faced, the uncertainties they felt, the ideals they cherished—all seemed more alive to me than ever before, and I came away with an even stronger appreciation for their courage and their vision.

As people from all over the world visit the places described in this valuable book, they, too, will feel the excitement of history and relive in their minds the beginnings of a great Nation.

I commend this book to your attention and encourage all people, Americans and foreigners alike, to make a special effort to visit our historic sites during these Bicentennial years.

The White House
Washington, D.C.

Richard Nixon

Preface

Nearly two hundred years have passed since America proclaimed her independence. Yet this action and the beliefs and hopes motivating those responsible for it are as central to us as a people today as they were to Abraham Lincoln, whose words still remind us that ". . . our fathers brought forth upon this continent, a new nation, conceived in Liberty, and dedicated to the proposition that all men are created equal. . . ."

To understand what we have become, we must know what we have been. This volume illuminates the role of those who framed the Declaration of Independence and took the bold risk of putting their signatures to it, thus bringing into being a new Nation on a new model of stated principle. It will stimulate our visual memory of the persons and events that cast this Nation upon its course, and I commend it to all who would more fully appreciate that heritage.

ROGERS C. B. MORTON
Secretary of the Interior

It is my hope that this volume will not only increase popular knowledge of the Declaration of Independence and its signers, but that it will also undergird the efforts of historic preservationists to protect sites and buildings associated with them. Written records alone cannot convey the appreciation and understanding that come from personal acquaintance with historic places. Thus, while we preserve and study the documents of the American Revolution, we must also save and experience what physical evidences remain to illustrate the lives of those who so boldly brought it about. With the assistance of this book, many more Americans may come to know the sites and structures frequented by the signers of the Declaration, to visit them personally, and to appreciate more deeply the importance of their preservation.

Credit for the preparation of this volume is shared widely by persons both in and out of the National Park Service. The historic preservation activities of the Service have particularly benefited from the assistance of the National Trust for Historic Preservation in the United States, cosponsor of the National Survey of Historic Sites and Buildings. The Survey is authorized by the Historic Sites Act of 1935.

RONALD H. WALKER
Director
National Park Service

Contents

Part III

Signers of the Declaration:
Survey of Historic Sites and Buildings

Appendix

All photographs are indexed.

Part One

Signers of the Declaration:
Historical Background

$\mathcal{A}$T PHILADELPHIA in the summer of 1776, the Delegates to the Continental Congress courageously signed a document declaring the independence of the Thirteen American Colonies from Great Britain. Not only did the Declaration of Independence create a Nation, but it also pronounced timeless democratic principles. Enshrined today in the National Archives Building at Washington, D.C., it memorializes the founding of the United States and symbolizes the eternal freedom and dignity of Man.

BY the time the Continental Congress adopted the Declaration in July 1776, the War for Independence had been underway for more than a year. Failing to obtain satisfactory redress from the mother country for their economic and political grievances during the previous decade, the colonists had finally resorted to armed conflict. These grievances had come to a head shortly after the French and Indian War (1754-63). Long and costly, the war depleted the royal treasury and added the financial burden of administering the vast territory acquired from France. Britain levied new, direct taxes in the Colonies and tightened customs controls.

The colonists, accustomed to considerable economic freedom, resented these measures. A number of Americans also felt that some

George III, King of England during the War for Independence,
was the focus of colonial hatred.

sort of conspiracy existed in England to destroy their liberties and
self-government. They believed that the mission of the large force of
redcoats assigned to the Colonies actually was internal suppression
rather than protection from a nonexistent external threat, especially
since the French had been expelled. Particularly aggravating was the
realization that the new tax levies supported the force. Some of the
discontent was regional in nature. Indebtedness to British creditors
irritated Southern planters. Commercial interests in the Middle Colonies disliked the prohibition on manufacturing certain products. Frontier settlers and speculators were irked at restrictions on westward
expansion and the Indian trade.

In various places, peaceful protest and harassment of tax and cus-

The Revolutionaries utilized this exaggerated version of the Boston Massacre (1770) by Paul Revere to nourish resentment of British troops.

toms collectors gave way to rioting and mob violence. In New York and Massachusetts, clashes with British troops culminated in bloodshed. Realizing that some of these disturbances stemmed from agitation in the colonial assemblies, which had enjoyed wide autonomy,

"The Bostonians Paying the Excise-Man or Tarring & Feathering,"
a British cartoon satirizing colonial methods of protest.

the Crown tightened its control over them. Disputes between legislators and the King's officials, once spasmodic, became commonplace. In some instances, notably in Virginia and Massachusetts, the Royal Governors dissolved the assemblies. In these and a few other provinces the Whigs separated from their Tory, or Loyalist, colleagues, met extralegally, and adopted retaliatory measures. Nearly all the Colonies formed special "committees of correspondence" to communicate with each other—the first step toward unified action.

In May 1774, in retaliation for the "Boston Tea Party," Parliament closed the port of Boston and virtually abolished provincial self-government in Massachusetts. These actions stimulated resistance across the land. That summer, the Massachusetts lower house, through the committees of correspondence, secretly invited all 13

In retaliation for the Boston Tea Party (1773), the Crown imposed rigid limitations on the freedom of Massachusetts citizens.

A rare contemporary engraving of the British-American clash
in 1775 at North Bridge, near Concord, Mass.

Colonies to attend a convention. In response, on the fifth of September,
55 Delegates representing 12 Colonies, Georgia excepted, assembled
at Philadelphia. They convened at Carpenters' Hall and organized
the First Continental Congress.

Sharing though they did common complaints against the Crown,
the Delegates propounded a wide variety of political opinions. Most
of them agreed that Parliament had no right to control the internal
affairs of the Colonies. Moderates, stressing trade benefits with the
mother country, believed Parliament should continue to regulate commerce. Others questioned the extent of its authority. A handful of
Delegates felt the answer to the problem lay in parliamentary representation. Most suggested legislative autonomy for the Colonies.
Reluctant to sever ties of blood, language, trade, and cultural heritage, none yet openly entertained the idea of complete independence
from Great Britain.

After weeks of debate and compromise, Congress adopted two
significant measures. The first declared that the American colonists

were entitled to the same rights as Englishmen everywhere and denounced any infringement of those rights. The second, the Continental Association, provided for an embargo on all trade with Britain. To enforce the embargo and punish violators, at the behest of Congress counties, cities, and towns formed councils, or committees, of safety—many of which later became wartime governing or administrative bodies. When Congress adjourned in late October, the Delegates resolved to reconvene in May 1775 if the Crown had not responded by then.

In a sense the Continental Congress acted with restraint, for while it was in session the situation in Massachusetts verged on war. In September, just before Congress met, British troops from Boston had seized ordnance supplies at Charlestown and Cambridge and almost clashed with the local militia. The next month, Massachusetts patriots, openly defying royal authority, organized a Revolutionary provincial assembly as well as a military defense committee. Whigs in three other colonies—Maryland, Virginia, and New Hampshire—had earlier that year formed governments. By the end of the year, all the Colonies except Georgia and New York had either set up new ones or taken control of those already in existence. During the winter of 1774-75, while Parliament mulled over conciliatory measures, colonial militia units prepared for war.

Headlines of a broadside showing American alarm over the Battle of Concord. The two rows of coffins at the top represent slain militiamen.

TO ALL BRAVE, HEALTHY, ABLE BODIED, AND WELL
DISPOSED YOUNG MEN,
IN THIS NEIGHBOURHOOD, WHO HAVE ANY INCLINATION TO JOIN THE TROOPS,
NOW RAISING UNDER
GENERAL WASHINGTON,
FOR THE DEFENCE OF THE
LIBERTIES AND INDEPENDENCE
OF THE UNITED STATES,
Against the hostile designs of foreign enemies,

TAKE NOTICE,

Continental Army recruiting poster.

The crisis came in the spring of 1775, predictably in Massachusetts.
Late on the night of April 18 the Royal Governor, Gen. Thomas
Gage, alarmed at the militancy of the rebels, dispatched 600 troops
from Boston to seize a major supply depot at Concord. Almost simultaneously the Boston council of safety, aware of Gage's intentions,
directed Paul Revere and William Dawes to ride ahead to warn militia units and citizens along the way of the British approach, as well

COMMON SENSE;

ADDRESSED TO THE

INHABITANTS

O F

A M E R I C A,

On the following interesting

S U B J E C T S.

I. Of the Origin and Design of Government in general, with concise Remarks on the English Constitution.

II. Of Monarchy and Hereditary Succession.

III. Thoughts on the present State of American Affairs.

IV. Of the present Ability of America, with some miscellaneous Reflections.

Man knows no Master save creating HEAVEN,
Or those whom choice and common good ordain.

THOMSON.

PHILADELPHIA;

Printed, and Sold, by R. BELL, in Third-Street.

MDCCLXXVI.

Title page of *Common Sense,* the anonymously written and widely distributed pamphlet that converted thousands of colonists to the Revolutionary cause.

as John Hancock and Samuel Adams, who were staying at nearby Lexington. Forewarned, the two men went into hiding.

About 77 militiamen confronted the redcoats when they plodded into Lexington at dawn. After some tense moments, as the sorely outnumbered colonials were dispersing, blood was shed. More flowed at Concord and much more along the route of the British as they retreated to Boston, harassed most of the way by an aroused citizenry. What had once been merely protest had evolved into open warfare; the War for Independence had begun.

Thomas Paine, author of *Common Sense,* did not emigrate to America from England until 1774, but he became an ardent patriot.

Sir William Howe, British commander in chief in America from 1776 until 1778.

Robert R. Livingston of New York, the most conservative member of the drafting committee, neither voted on independence nor signed the Declaration.

THE Second Continental Congress convened in the Pennsylvania State House at Philadelphia on May 10, 1775. Burdened by wartime realities and the need to prepare a unified defense, it created a Continental Army, unanimously elected George Washington as commander in chief, appointed other generals, and tackled problems of military finance and supply. Yet, despite these warlike actions, many Delegates still hoped for a peaceful reconciliation.

In July Congress adopted the Olive Branch Petition, a final attempt to achieve an understanding with the Crown. The petition appealed directly to King George III to cease hostilities and restore harmony. But, unwilling to challenge the supremacy of Parliament, he refused to acknowledge the plea and proclaimed the Colonies to be in a state of rebellion.

During the winter of 1775-76, as the war intensified, all chance for accommodation vanished. Congress, for the first time representing all Thirteen Colonies because Georgia had sent Delegates in the fall, disclaimed allegiance to Parliament, created a navy, and appointed a committee of foreign affairs. Nevertheless the patriots, despite their mounting influence in the provincial assemblies, felt they needed more public support and hesitated to urge a final break with the Crown.

The turning point came in January 1776 with publication in Philadelphia of the pamphlet *Common Sense*, authored anonymously by the recent English immigrant Thomas Paine. Attacking the "myth" of an evil Parliament and a benevolent King, he denounced George III for creating the Colonies' miseries, condemned the British constitution as well as monarchy in general, and exhorted his fellow Americans to declare independence immediately. The pamphlet, widely reprinted, was purchased by many thousands of people and read by thousands more. It created a furor. From Georgia to New Hampshire, independence became the major topic of discussion and debate. The Revolutionaries won thousands of converts.

In May Congress took a bold step toward political freedom by authorizing the Colonies to form permanent governments. Those that had not done so began to oust Crown officials and draft constitutions. Independence, though not yet officially declared, was for all practical purposes a reality.

THE official movement for independence took root in the provincial assemblies. The North Carolina assembly in April 1776 instructed its congressional Delegates to vote for the issue should it be proposed. The next month, on May 4, Rhode Island announced its independence publicly—the first colony to do so. But it was Virginia that prodded Congress to action. On May 15 a Williamsburg convention declared Virginia independent and authorized its delegation at Philadelphia to propose a similar course for the Colonies. On June 7 the delegation's leader, Richard Henry Lee, introduced the following resolution:

> That these United Colonies are, and of right ought to be, free and independent States, that they are absolved from all allegiance to the British Crown, and that all political connection between them and the State of Great Britain is, and ought to be, totally dissolved.

The resolution also incorporated proposals to form foreign alliances; and to devise a plan for confederation, which would be submitted to the Colonies for their approval.

Despite the enthusiastic response of many Delegates, some of them, though they foresaw the inevitability of independence, objected to the timing. They believed the decision should reflect the desires of the people as expressed through the provincial assemblies and pointed out that the Middle Colonies, not yet ripe for freedom, needed more time for deliberation. On June 10 the moderates obtained a postponement of consideration of the Lee resolution until July 1.

On June 11 the Revolutionaries, undaunted by the delay and convinced of their ultimate victory, persuaded Congress to appoint a committee to draft a declaration of independence. Three of its five members, John Adams, Benjamin Franklin, and Thomas Jefferson, were Revolutionaries. Roger Sherman disliked extremism but had recently backed the independence movement. The most unlikely member, Robert R. Livingston, had stood in the front ranks of opposition to Lee's resolution. Possibly he was appointed to exert a moderating effect on its supporters or, conversely, in the hope that his membership would help swing over the conservative New York delegation.

At the time Lee had introduced his resolution, seven of the Colonies—New Hampshire, Rhode Island, Massachusetts, Connecticut, Virginia, North Carolina, and Georgia—favored independence. New York, New Jersey, Pennsylvania, Delaware, South Carolina, and Maryland were either opposed or undecided. Throughout the month, Revolutionaries in those provinces labored to gain control of the assemblies. Delaware and Pennsylvania, unable to reach a decision, instructed their representatives to vote in their colonies' "best interests." New Jersey issued similar directions, but also elected an entirely new and Whig-oriented slate of Delegates. The Maryland assembly, largely through the persuasion of Samuel Chase, Charles Carroll of Carrollton, and William Paca, voted unanimously for independence and so charged its Delegates. The South Carolinians, though they had been authorized months before to cast their lot with the majority, vacillated. The New Yorkers impatiently awaited instructions.

First page of Jefferson's rough draft of the Declaration.

JULY 1 was the day of decision. The Revolutionaries, overconfident from their progress of the preceding month, anticipated an almost unanimous vote for independence. They were disappointed. Following congressional procedure, each colony balloted as a unit, determined by the majority of Delegate opinion. Only nine of the Colonies voted affirmatively; Pennsylvania and South Carolina, negatively; New York abstained; and the two Delegates present from Delaware deadlocked. Technically the resolution had carried, but the solidarity desirable for such a vital decision was missing. Edward Rutledge of South Carolina, hinting his colony might change sides, moved that the vote be retaken the next day.

That day proved to be one of the most dramatic in the history of the Continental Congress. John Adams of Massachusetts exerted an overwhelming influence. South Carolina, its Delegates swayed by Rutledge, reversed its position. Two conservatives among the seven Pennsylvanians, Robert Morris and John Dickinson, though unwilling to make a personal commitment to independence, cooperated by purposely absenting themselves; the remaining Delegates voted three to two in favor. The most exciting moment of the day occurred when Caesar Rodney, Delaware's third Delegate, galloped up to the statehouse after a harrowing 80-mile night ride from Dover through a thunderstorm and broke the Delaware tie. Home on a military assignment, the evening before he had received an urgent plea from Thomas McKean, the Delawarean who had voted for independence, to rush to Philadelphia. In the final vote, 12 Colonies approved Lee's resolution, New York again abstaining. Congress declared the resolution to be in effect.

FOR the remainder of July 2 and continuing until the 4th, Congress weighed and debated the content of the Declaration of Independence, which the drafting committee had submitted on June 28. Its author was young Thomas Jefferson, who had been in Congress about a year. The committee had chosen him for the task because he was from Virginia, the colony responsible for the independence resolution, and because of his reputation as an excellent writer and man of talent and action.

Laboring in his rented rooms on the second floor of a private home at the corner of Seventh and Market Streets, Jefferson had completed a rough draft in about 2 weeks. Apparently Franklin and

In CONGRESS, July 4, 1776.

The unanimous Declaration of the thirteen united States of America.

[Full text of the Declaration of Independence in engraved script, followed by the signatures of the signers.]

Facsimile of the Declaration of Independence, engraved in 1823 while the document was still in relatively good condition.

Adams made some minor changes, and Livingston and Sherman expressed no reservations so far as is known. To Jefferson's irritation, however, Congress altered the final draft considerably. Most of the changes consisted of refinements in phraseology. Two major passages, however, were deleted. The first, a censure of the people of Great Britain, seemed harsh and needless to most of the Delegates. The second, an impassioned condemnation of the slave trade, offended Southern planters as well as New England shippers, many of whom were as culpable as the British in the trade.

THE first official document of the American Republic and one of the most influential in human history, the Declaration expressed the spirit of human freedom and affirmed Man's universal rights. Jefferson's goal in drafting it was not, he said, to invent "new ideas" but to compose "an expression of the American mind" in a tone and spirit suitable for the momentous occasion. Stylistically, the Declaration resembled his own preamble to the Virginia constitution and contained an almost identical list of grievances. Its political philosophy, reflecting the Lockean concepts espoused by many intellectuals of the day, was certainly not new. Jefferson himself had touched on the basic points in previous writings, and in essence he echoed George Mason's "Declaration of Rights," which some of the Philadelphia newpapers had published early in June. In other words, the Declaration assimilated existing concepts into a concise statement of national doctrine.

Jefferson began the preamble with the oft-quoted and stirring words, "When in the course of human events, it becomes necessary for one people to dissolve the political bands which have connected them with another . . . ." He then listed a series of "self-evident" truths—that "all men are created equal" and that they are "endowed by their creator with certain unalienable rights," particularly "life, liberty, and the pursuit of happiness." Governments, "deriving their just powers from the consent of the governed," are instituted by men to insure these rights. When they fail to do so, it is the "right of the people to alter or to abolish" them and to institute new governments. Men should not carelessly change governments, but should only take such action after a long series of abuses and usurpations lead to "absolute despotism." Then it becomes their duty to do so. The longest portion of the Declaration is a list of colonial grievances and

The Pennsylvania GAZETTE.

July 10, 1776.   NUMB. 2481.

Containing the Freſheſt Advices, Foreign and Domeſtic.

In CONGRESS, July 4, 1776.

A DECLARATION

By the REPRESENTATIVES of the UNITED STATES OF AMERICA, in GENERAL CONGRESS assembled.

WHEN, in the Courſe of human Events, it becomes neceſſary for one Pe-ople to diſſolve the political Bands which have connected them with another, and to aſſume among the Powers of the Earth, the ſeparate and equal Station to which the Laws of Nature and of Nature's God entitle them, a decent Reſpect to the Opinions of Mankind requires that they ſhould declare the cauſes which impel them to the Separation.

We hold theſe Truths to be ſelf-evident, that all Men are created equal, that they are endowed by their Creator with certain unalienable Rights, that among theſe are Life, Liberty, and the Purſuit of Happineſs—That to ſecure theſe Rights, Governments are inſtituted among Men, deriving their juſt Powers from the Conſent of the Governed, that whenever any Form of Government becomes deſtructive of theſe Ends, it is the Right of the People to alter or to aboliſh it, and to inſtitute new Government, laying its Foundation on ſuch Principles, and organizing its Powers in ſuch Form, as to them ſhall ſeem moſt likely to effect their Safety and Happineſs. Prudence, indeed, will dictate that Governments long eſtabliſhed ſhould not be changed for light and tranſient Cauſes; and accordingly all Experience hath ſhewn, that Mankind are more diſpoſed to ſuffer, while Evils are ſufferable, than to right themſelves by aboliſhing the Forms to which they are accuſtomed. But when a long Train of Abuſes and Uſurpations, purſuing invariably the ſame Object, evinces a Deſign to reduce them under abſolute Deſpotiſm, it is their Right, it is their Duty, to throw off ſuch Government, and to provide new Guards for their future Security. Such has been the patient Sufferance of theſe Colonies, and ſuch is now the Neceſſity which conſtrains them to alter their former Syſtems of Government. The Hiſtory of the preſent King of Great-Britain is a Hiſtory of repeated Injuries and Uſurpations, all having in direct Object the Eſtabliſhment of an abſolute Tyranny over theſe States. To prove this, let Facts be ſubmitted to a candid World.

He has refuſed his Aſſent to Laws, the moſt wholeſome and neceſſary for the public Good.

He has forbidden his Governors to paſs Laws of immediate and preſſing Importance, unleſs ſuſpended in their Operation till his Aſſent ſhould be obtained; and when ſo ſuſpended, he has utterly neglected to attend to them.

He has refuſed to paſs other Laws for the Accommodation of large Diſtricts of People, unleſs thoſe People would relinquiſh the Right of Repreſentation in the Legiſlature, a Right ineſtimable to them, and formidable to Tyrants only.

He has called together Legiſlative Bodies at Places unuſual, uncomfortable, and diſtant from the Depoſitory of their public Records, for the ſole Purpoſe of fatiguing them into Compliance with his Meaſures.

He has diſſolved Repreſentative Houſes repeatedly, for oppoſing with manly Firmneſs his Invaſions on the Rights of the People.

He has refuſed, for a long Time after ſuch Diſſolutions, to cauſe others to be elected; whereby the Legiſlative Powers, incapable of Annihilation, have returned to the People at large for their Exerciſe; the State remaining in the mean Time expoſed to all the Dangers of Invaſion from without, and Convulſions within.

He has endeavoured to prevent the Population of theſe States; for that Purpoſe obſtructing the Laws for Naturalization of Foreigners; refuſing to paſs others to encourage their Migrations hither, and raiſing the Conditions of new Appropriations of Lands.

He has obſtructed the Adminiſtration of Juſtice, by refuſing his Aſſent to Laws for eſtabliſhing Judiciary Powers.

He has made Judges dependent on his Will alone, for the Tenure of their Offices, and the Amount and Payment of their Salaries.

He has erected a Multitude of new Offices, and ſent hither Swarms of Officers to harraſs our People, and eat out their Subſtance.

He has kept among us, in Times of Peace, Standing Armies, without the Conſent of our Legiſlatures.

He has affected to render the Military independent of and ſuperior to the Civil Power.

He has combined with others to ſubject us to a Juriſdiction foreign to our Conſtitution, and unacknowledged by our Laws; giving his Aſſent to their Acts of pretended Legiſlation:

For quartering large Bodies of Armed Troops among us:

For protecting them, by a mock Trial, from Puniſhment for any Murders which they ſhould commit on the Inhabitants of theſe States:

For cutting off our Trade with all Parts of the World:

For impoſing Taxes on us without our Conſent:

For depriving us, in many Caſes, of the Benefits of Trial by Jury:

For tranſporting us beyond Seas to be tried for pretended Offences:

For aboliſhing the free Syſtem of Engliſh Laws in a neighbouring Province, eſtabliſhing therein an arbitrary Government, and enlarging its Boundaries, ſo as to render it at once an Example and fit Inſtrument for introducing the ſame abſolute Rule into theſe Colonies:

For taking away our Charters, aboliſhing our moſt valuable Laws, and altering fundamentally the Forms of our Governments:

For ſuſpending our own Legiſlatures, and declaring themſelves inveſted with Power to legiſlate for us in all Caſes whatſoever.

He has abdicated Government here, by declaring us out of his Protection and waging War againſt us.

He has plundered our Seas, ravaged our Coaſts, burnt our Towns, and deſtroyed the Lives of our People.

He is, at this Time, tranſporting large Armies of foreign Mercenaries to compleat the Works of Death, Deſolation and Tyranny, already begun with Circumſtances of Cruelty and Perfidy, ſcarcely paralleled in the moſt barbarous Ages, and totally unworthy the Head of a civilized Nation.

He has conſtrained our Fellow-Citizens, taken captive on the high Seas, to bear Arms againſt their Country, to become the Executioners of their Friends and Brethren, or to fall themſelves by their Hands.

He has excited domeſtic Inſurrections amongſt us, and has endeavoured to bring on the Inhabitants of our Frontiers the mercileſs Indian Savages, whoſe known Rule of Warfare is an undiſtinguiſhed Deſtruction of all Ages, Sexes and Conditions.

In every Stage of theſe Oppreſſions we have petitioned for Redreſs in the moſt humble Terms: Our repeated Petitions have been anſwered only by repeated Injury. A Prince, whoſe Character is thus marked by every Act which may define a Tyrant, is unfit to be the Ruler of a free People.

Nor have we been wanting in Attentions to our Britiſh Brethren. We have warned them from Time to Time of Attempts by their Legiſlature to extend an unwarrantable Juriſdiction over us. We have reminded them of the Circumſtances of our Emigration and Settlement here. We have appealed to their native Juſtice and Magnanimity, and we have conjured them by the Ties of our common Kindred to diſavow theſe Uſurpations, which would inevitably interrupt our Connections and Correſpondence. They too have been deaf to the Voice of Juſtice and of Conſanguinity. We muſt, therefore, acquieſce in the Neceſſity, which denounces our Separation, and hold them, as we hold the reſt of Mankind, Enemies in War, in Peace, Friends.

We, therefore, the Repreſentatives of the UNITED STATES OF AMERICA, in GENERAL CONGRESS aſſembled, appealing to the Supreme Judge of the World for the Rectitude of our Intentions, do, in the Name and by Authority of the good People of theſe Colonies, ſolemnly Publiſh and Declare, That theſe United Colonies are, and of Right ought to be, FREE and INDEPENDENT STATES; that they are abſolved from all Allegiance to the Britiſh Crown, and that all political Connection between them and the State of Great-Britain is and ought to be totally diſſolved; and that as FREE and INDEPENDENT STATES, they have full Power to levy War, conclude Peace, contract Alliances, eſtabliſh Commerce, and to do all other Acts and Things which INDEPENDENT STATES may of right do. And for the Support of this Declaration, with a firm Reliance on the Protection of divine Providence, we mutually pledge to each other our Lives, our Fortunes, and our ſacred Honor.

Signed by Order and in Behalf of the Congreſs,
JOHN HANCOCK, Preſident.

Atteſt,
CHARLES THOMSON, Secretary.

JUST PUBLISHED, AND TO BE SOLD BY HALL and SELLERS,
At the New Printing-Office, in Market-ſtreet, Price Two Pounds Seven Shillings.

THE ACTS OF ASSEMBLY
Of the Province of PENNSYLVANIA,
Carefully compared with the Originals.

AND an APPENDIX,
Containing ſuch Acts, and Parts of Acts, relating to Property, as are expired, altered or repealed.

TOGETHER WITH
The Royal, Proprietary, City and Borough CHARTERS;
AND THE
Original Conceſſions of the Hon. WILLIAM PENN to the firſt Settlers of the Province.
Publiſhed by ORDER of ASSEMBLY.

Juſt printed, publiſhed, and now ſelling by ROBERT BELL, in Third-ſtreet,
(Price One Shilling and Threepence)

THE genuine Principles of the ancient SAXON, or ENGLISH CONSTITUTION. Carefully collected from the beſt Authorities; with ſome Obſervations on their peculiar Fitneſs for the United Colonies in general, and Pennſylvania in particular. By DEMOPHILUS.

All human Conſtitutions are ſubject to Corruption, and muſt periſh, unleſs they act timely preſerved by reduing them to their firſt Principles.
SIDNEY.

Where Annual Election ends, Tyranny begins.

HISTORICAL ESSAYS.

N. B. All the New Pamphlets may be had at ſaid Bell's.

July 1, 1776.

WHEREAS an Advertiſement, addreſſed to the Public, appeared in the Gazette ſome time paſt, ſigned Thomas Harvey, regarding the Favour of the Public to embs at the Old Trenton Ferry, where he now lives, and aſſerting that the difference of the diſtance between the Old and New Ferry is more than a mile in favour of the Old, whereas the true difference, on a ſtrict ſurvey, is no more than half a mile and fary foot, and as the ſubſcriber hath lately came to the New Ferry, and prevailed a more commodious Boat than has ever been heretofore at either Ferry, as well as being the ſole cauſe of lowering the Ferriage more than one third of the former price, which is a very great ſaving to the public, he flatters himſelf he will be indulged with their cuſtom, which he will endeavour to merit by his particular care and attention, and is the public's moſt obliged humble ſervant,
THOMAS HARVEY.

Juſt publiſhed, and to be ſold by JOHN DUNLAP, in Market-ſtreet, Philadelphia.

OBSERVATIONS
ON THE
Nature of CIVIL LIBERTY, the Principles of GOVERNMENT, and the Juſtice and Policy of the WAR with AMERICA.

To which is added,
An APPENDIX, containing a State of the National Debt, an eſtimate of the money drawn from the Public by the taxes, and an account of the National Income and Expenditure ſince the laſt War.

How milions overs; non Haſtem, inherienſiqui cedorei.

Pofthac Speti utilis.
By RICHARD PRICE, D.D. F.R.S.

This learned, judicious and liberal author had the thanks of the Common Council, and the Freedom of the City of London preſented to him in a gold box, for this his moſt admired moſt excellent pamphlet on Civil Liberty.—And for which he alſo deſerves the united thanks of America.

July 9, 1776.

SEVEN POUNDS Reward.

RUN away, laſt Sunday night, from the ſubſcriber, living in Cheſter county, the following ſervants, viz.— Edward Gray, about 5 feet 8 inches high, pock-marked, ſtraight black hair, about 26 years or age, ſays he was born in London, and ſerved his time with William Hinkle, in New-Caſtle county; underſtands all ſorts of plantation work, and ſays he worked at the Miller's buſineſs two years with one Reynolds, in Nottingham; had on, when he went away, white country linen ſhirt and trowſers, new coat and jacket, and a leather apron; took with him a ſcythe and hangings; ſaid Gray was baked out of goal by the ſubſcriber, and for my ſecurity indorſed himſelf to me; it is hoped that every honeſt perſon will endeavour to apprehend ſaid Gray, and for the two and baſt in order to bring him to juſtice. The other, named John Dillis, about 25 years of age, born in New-England, a ſtout well built fellow, about 5 feet 10 or 11 inches high, with dirty coloured hair, has fine teeth, white apart; ſays he belongs to the New-gallies, and has been deſcribed about Port-Penn; had on, when he went away, white ſhirt and trowſers, a red under jacket, without ſleeves, no boots or buckles; he is fond of ſtrong drink and company, and a very great ſailor. Whoever takes up the ſaid runaways, and ſecures them, ſo as the ſubſcriber gets them again, ſhall have Five Pounds for Gray, and Forty Shillings for Dillis, and reaſonable charges for Dillis, paid by
WILLIAM KERLIN.

N. B. Dillis run away the 2d of June.

Eaſton, July 3, 1776.

BY virtue of a writ to me directed, will be ſet up at ſale, on the premiſes, on Tueſday, the 30th day of July inſtant, at 2 o'clock in the afternoon, two certain tracts or parcels of land, ſituate in Macoungie townſhip, in the county of Northampton, one of them bounded by the lands of Francis Haines, Henry Probſt and John Fogle, and containing 107 acres; whereon are a ſtone tenement and log tenement, a large log barn, ſtables and other out-houſes, and a conſiderable quantity of good meadow; and the other of the ſaid tracts, ſituated by the lands of Peter Haas and the ſaid Haines, and containing 37 acres unſettled; late the property of Henry Sharp; ſeized and taken in execution by HENRY POLLART, Sheriff.

STOLEN or STRAYED away, from the ſubſcriber, living in Charesford townſhip, York county, Pennſylvania, on the 15th of July, a white Horſe and a black Mare, the horſe about 15 years old, between 13 and 14 hands high, branded on the near ſhoulder I. C. his mane trimmed, a long black tail, and is a natural pacer; had a bell on when he went away; the mare 4 years old, both trots and paces, between 14 and 15 hands high, no brand, ſhe has a ſwitch tail, a ſmall ſtar in her forehead, and wants one of her fore teeth in the upper jaw; both newly ſhod before, when they went away. Whoever takes up the thief, and ſecures ſaid horſe and mare, ſo that the owner may have them again, ſhall have Three Pounds reward, or for the horſe and mare Forty Shillings, or for any of them Twenty Shillings, and reaſonable charges if brought home, paid by
JOHN McNAVY.

STRAYED away, on the 23d of June, from the ſubſcriber, living in Germantown, a freſh milch black COW, with a white head and along her back, alſo on her belly, but what may be remarked is pieces of other horns nailed on the top of her horns. Whoever returns the ſaid cow, and gives a dollar, or makes known ſo that the owner may have her again, ſhall have the reward of Ten Shillings, and reaſonable charges.
GEORGE SHARPLESS.

TEN DOLLARS Reward.

RUN away from the ſubſcriber, living near Talbot Court-houſe, the 25th of laſt April, a dark Mulatto Slave, named HARRY, about 28 years old; he is about 5 feet 8 or 9 inches high, ſtout and ſtrong made; he is of a mild temper, plauſible in ſpeech, and deceptive in converſation. It is ſuppoſed that he will endeavour to paſs for a freeman; he was lately ſeen in Kent county; had on, when ſeen, a country cloth jacket, tow linen ſhirt and trowſers, a beaver hat with one corner turned up. The above reward will be paid if taken out of the province, or ſo miles from home, and ſecured in any goal ſo that I may get him; Forty Shillings, if 30 miles; Thirty Shillings, if 20 miles; with reaſonable travelling expences, if brought home.
ALEXANDER McCALLUM.

Lancaſter Goal, June 20, 1776.

WAS committed to my cuſtody, the following perſon, viz. Francis Morriſon, 23 years of age, black hair and complexion, pitted with the ſmallpox, ſays he lately refuted near Dox-Run, Cheſter county, was for ſome time a private in Captain Reeſe's company, from whom he obtained a diſcharge; Andrew Johnſon, ſays he enliſted with Lieut. Finney, when recruiting for Captain Murray, in Oxford townſhip, Cheſter county, and has a diſcharge, which he ſays he obtained from the Iriſh Hiſtory. Peter Bryan, who ſays he is a deſerter from Fraſer's company, and enliſted with Lieut. Seely, in Hanover townſhip. John William Percy, who ſays he is a ſervant to Capt. Thomas Perry, of Bucks county. And Stephen Archer, who ſays he is a ſervant to Mr. Benjamin Rittenhouſe. The officers and maſters of the ſaid ſervants and ſervants, are deſired to ſend for them, pay charges, and take them away 12 weeks from the date hereof, otherwiſe they will be diſcharged, on paying their fees, by
PETER RIGLEY, Goaler.

examples of the King's tyranny. The final section includes a restatement of Lee's resolution and a pledge by the signers of their lives, their fortunes, and their sacred honor to the cause of independence.

ON July 4 all the Colonies except New York voted to adopt the Declaration. Congress ordered it printed and distributed to colonial officials, military units, and the press. John Hancock and Charles Thomson, President and Secretary of Congress respectively, were the only signers of this broadside copy. On July 8, outside the Pennsylvania State House, the document was first read to the public. During the ensuing celebration, people cheered, bells rang out, and soldiers paraded. At other cities, similar celebrations soon took place. Yet many citizens—the Loyalists, or Tories—could not accept independence now that it had been declared any more than previously when

The New York City Sons of Liberty celebrated independence by pulling down a statue of George III, which they later melted and molded into bullets.

Artist's rendition of the Battle of Germantown (October 1777).

it had been merely a concept. Some of them would continue to dream of reconciliation. Others would flee from or be driven out of the country. In addition, another sizable group of citizens remained noncommittal, neither supporting nor opposing independence.

Four days after obtaining New York's approval of the Declaration on July 15, Congress ordered it engrossed on parchment for signature. At this time, indicative of unanimity, the title was changed from "A Declaration by the Representatives of the United States of America in General Congress Assembled" to "The Unanimous Declaration of the Thirteen United States of America."

CONTRARY to a widespread misconception, the 56 signers did not sign as a group and did not do so on July 4, 1776. The official event occurred on August 2, 1776, when 50 men probably took part. Later that year, five more apparently signed separately and one added his name in a subsequent year. Not until January 18, 1777, in the wake of Washington's victories at Trenton and Princeton, did Congress, which had sought to protect the signers from British retaliation for as long as possible, authorize printing of the Declaration with all their names listed. At this time, Thomas McKean had not yet penned his name.

The most impressive signature is that of John Hancock, President of Congress, centered over the others. According to tradition, Hancock wrote boldly and defiantly so that King George III would not need spectacles to identify him as a "traitor" and double the reward for his head. The other Delegates signed in six columns, which ran from right to left. They utilized the standard congressional voting order, by colony generally from north to south: New Hampshire, Massachusetts, Rhode Island, Connecticut, New York, New Jersey, Pennsylvania, Delaware, Maryland, Virginia, North Carolina, South Carolina, and Georgia.

Those who signed on August 2 undoubtedly did not realize that others would follow them and thus allowed no room to accommodate the signatures of the later six men. Two of them, George Wythe and Richard Henry Lee, found ample room above their fellow Virginians. One, Elbridge Gerry of Massachusetts, crowded his name into the space between the Massachusetts and Rhode Island groups. Two of the others—Thomas McKean and Oliver Wolcott—signed at the bottom of columns following their State delegations. Only Matthew Thornton of New Hampshire needed to add his name separately from his colleagues—at the bottom of the first column on the right at the end of the Connecticut group.

INDEPENDENCE had been declared; it still had to be won on the field of battle. The War for Independence was already underway, but 5 more years of struggle and bloody campaigning lay ahead. In 1781 the Colonies achieved military victory, and 2 years later Britain in the Treaty of Paris officially recognized the independence they had proclaimed in 1776. The building of the Nation could begin.

Part Two

Signers of the Declaration:
Biographical Sketches

ℒIBERALLY ENDOWED as a whole with courage and sense of purpose, the signers consisted of a distinguished group of individuals. Although heterogeneous in background, education, experience, and accomplishments, at the time of the signing they were practically all men of means and represented an elite cross section of 18th-century American leadership. Every one of them had achieved prominence in his colony, but only a few enjoyed a national reputation.

The signers were those individuals who happened to be Delegates to Congress at the time. Such men of stature in the Nation as George Washington and Patrick Henry were not then even serving in the body. On the other hand, Jefferson, the two Adamses, Richard Henry Lee, and Benjamin Rush ranked among the outstanding people in the Colonies; and Franklin had already acquired international fame. Some of the signers had not taken a stand for or against independence in the final vote on July 2. For example, Robert Morris of Pennsylvania had purposely absented himself. Others had not yet been elected to Congress or were away on business or military matters. Some were last-minute replacements for opponents of independence. The only signer who actually voted negatively on July 2 was George Read of Delaware.

THE signers possessed many basic similarities. Most were American-born and of Anglo-Saxon origin. The eight foreign-born—Button

Fervid Revolutionary Patrick Henry numbered among those patriots of national reputation who were not Members of Congress at the time of the signing of the Declaration.

Gwinnett, Francis Lewis, Robert Morris, James Smith, George Taylor, Matthew Thornton, James Wilson, and John Witherspoon— were all natives of the British Isles. Except for Charles Carroll, a Roman Catholic, and a few Deists, every one subscribed to Protestantism. For the most part basically political nonextremists, many at first had hesitated at separation let alone rebellion. A few signed only reluctantly.

The majority were well educated and prosperous. More than half the southerners belonged to the planter class and owned slaves, though Richard Henry Lee, Thomas Jefferson, and others heartily opposed the institution of slavery, as did also several of the signers from the North. On the other hand, William Whipple, as a sea captain early in his career, had likely sometimes carried slaves on his ship.

Although the signers ranged in age at the time from 26 (Edward Rutledge) to 70 (Benjamin Franklin), the bulk of them were in their thirties or forties. Probably as a result of their favored economic

George Washington inspecting his troops at Valley Forge. Busy serving
as commander in chief of the Continental Army, he did not sign
the Declaration.

position, an amazingly large number attained an age that far exceeded
the life expectancy of their time; 38 of the 56 lived into their sixties
or beyond and 14 into the eighties and nineties.

With few exceptions, those who subscribed to the Declaration
continued in public service under the new Federal and State Governments. John Adams and Thomas Jefferson became President; they
and Elbridge Gerry, Vice President. Samuel Chase and James Wilson
won appointment to the Supreme Court. Others served as Congressmen, diplomats, Governors, and judges. Six of the signers—George
Clymer, Benjamin Franklin, Robert Morris, George Read, Roger
Sherman, and James Wilson—also signed the Constitution. Sixteen
of them underwrote the Articles of Confederation. Only two,
Roger Sherman and Robert Morris, affixed their signatures to the
Declaration, Constitution, and Articles.

Caesar Rodney and Joseph Hewes were the only bachelors in the
group. All but five fathered children. Carter Braxton sired no fewer
than 18, but 10 others each had at least 10 offspring. The average

number was about six. Some of the sons of the signers attained national distinction. John Adams' son John Quincy became President; the son of Benjamin Harrison, William Henry, won the same office, as did also Benjamin's great-grandson with the same name. Other male progeny of the signers served as U.S. Congressmen, Governors, and State legislators.

YET the group manifested diversity. Each man tended to reflect the particular attitudes and interests of his own region and colony. Fourteen represented New England; 21, the Middle Colonies; and 21, the South. The largest number, nine, came from Pennsylvania; the least, two, from Rhode Island. All those from three Colonies (Georgia, New Hampshire, and North Carolina) were born elsewhere. About half of the men received their higher education in colonial colleges or abroad; most of the others studied at home, in local schools or private academies, or with tutors. A few were almost entirely self-taught.

Harvard College, about 1725. Indicative of the favored economic circumstances of the signers, about half of them enjoyed a higher education. Eight, including all five from Massachusetts, attended Harvard.

In wealth, the signers ranged from Charles Carroll, one of the wealthiest men in the Colonies, to Samuel Adams, whose friends supplied money and clothes so he could attend Congress. About one-third were born into wealth; most of the others acquired it on their own. Some were self-made men. A few were of humble origin; one, George Taylor, had come to America as an indentured servant.

Many pursued more than one vocation. More than half were trained in the law, but not all of them practiced it. Some won a livelihood as merchants and shippers. Roughly · a quarter of the group earned their living from agriculture, usually as wealthy planters or landed gentry, but just a few could be called farmers. Four—Josiah Bartlett, Benjamin Rush, Lyman Hall, and Matthew Thornton— were doctors. Oliver Wolcott also studied medicine for awhile, but never entered the profession. George Taylor's occupation was ironmaster. Of the four trained as ministers—Lyman Hall, William Hooper, Robert Treat Paine, and John Witherspoon—only the latter made it his lifetime vocation. William Williams received some theological training. Samuel Adams followed no real occupation other than politics.

FOR their dedication to the cause of independence, the signers risked loss of fortune, imprisonment, and death for treason. Although none died directly at the hands of the British, the wife of one, Mrs. Francis Lewis, succumbed as a result of harsh prison treatment. About one-third of the group served as militia officers, most seeing wartime action. Four of these men (Thomas Heyward, Jr., Arthur Middleton, Edward Rutledge, and George Walton), as well as Richard Stockton, were taken captive. The homes of nearly one-third of the signers were destroyed or damaged, and the families of a few were scattered when the British pillaged or confiscated their estates.

Nearly all of the group emerged poorer for their years of public service and neglect of personal affairs. Although a couple of the merchants and shippers among them profited from the war, the businesses of most of them deteriorated as a result of embargoes on trade with Britain and heavy financial losses when their ships were confiscated or destroyed at sea. Several forfeited to the Government precious specie for virtually worthless Continental currency or made donations or loans, usually unrepaid, to their colonies or the Government. Some even sold their personal property to help finance the war.

CERTAINLY most of the signers had little or nothing to gain materially and practically all to lose when they subscribed to the Declaration of Independence. By doing so, they earned a niche of honor in the annals of the United States. Whatever other heights they reached or whatever else they contributed to history, the act of signing insured them immortality.

The following biographical sketches are arranged alphabetically by last name. Readers interested in signers for a certain State should consult the Index under the appropriate State.

John Adams
MASSACHUSETTS

Few men contributed more to U.S. Independence than John Adams, the "Atlas of American Independence" in the eyes of fellow signer Richard Stockton. A giant among the Founding Fathers, Adams was one of the coterie of leaders who generated the American Revolution, for which his prolific writings provided many of the politico-philosophical foundations. Not only did he help draft the Declaration, but he also steered it through the Continental Congress.

The subsequent career of Adams—as a diplomat and first Vice President and second President of the United States—overshadows those of all the other signers except Jefferson. Adams was also the progenitor of a distinguished family. His son John Quincy gained renown as diplomat, Congressman, Secretary of State, and President. John's grandson Charles Francis and great-grandsons John Quincy II, Charles Francis, Jr., Henry, and Brooks excelled in politics, diplomacy, literature, historiography, and public service.

Adams, descended from a long line of yeomen farmers, was born in 1735 at Braintree (later Quincy), Mass. He graduated from Harvard College in 1755, and for a short time taught school at Worcester, Mass. At that time, he considered entering the ministry, but decided instead to follow the law and began its study with a local lawyer. Adams was admitted to the bar at Boston in 1758 and began to practice in his hometown. Six years later, he married Abigail Smith, who was to bear three sons and a daughter. She was also the first mistress of the White House and the only woman in U.S. history to be the wife of one President and the mother of another.

Adams, like many others, was propelled into the Revolutionary camp by the Stamp Act. In 1765 he wrote a protest for Braintree that scores of other Massachusetts towns adopted. Three years later, he temporarily left his family behind and moved to Boston. He advanced in the law, but devoted more and more of his time to the patriot cause. In 1768 he achieved recognition throughout the Colonies for his defense of John Hancock, whom British customs officials had charged with smuggling. Adams later yielded to a stern sense of legal duty but incurred some public hostility by representing the British soldiers charged with murder in the Boston Massacre (1770). Ill health forced him to return to Braintree following a term in the colonial legislature (1770-71), and for the next few years he divided his time between there and Boston.

A 3-year stint in the Continental Congress (1774-77), punctuated by short recuperative leaves and service in the colonial legislature in 1774-75, brought Adams national fame. Because he was sharply attuned to the temper of Congress and aware that many Members resented Massachusetts extremism, he at first acceded to conciliatory efforts with Britain and restrained himself publicly. When Congress opted for independence, he became its foremost advocate, eschewing conciliation and urging a colonial confederation.

Adams was a master of workable compromise and meaningful debate, though he was sometimes impatient. He chaired 25 of the more than 90 committees on which he sat, the most important of which dealt with military and naval affairs. He played an instrumental part in obtaining Washington's appointment as commander in chief of the Continental Army. Adams was a member of the five-man committee charged with drafting the Declaration in June of 1776, though he probably made no major changes in Jefferson's draft. But, more directly involved, he defended it from its congressional detractors, advocated it to the wavering, and guided it to passage.

The independence battle won, exhausted by the incessant toil and strain and worried about his finances and family, Adams in November 1777 retired from Congress—never to return. He headed back to Braintree intending to resume his law practice. But, before the month expired, Congress appointed him to a diplomatic post in Europe—a phase of his career that consumed more than a decade (1777-88).

Adams served in France during the period 1778-85, interrupted only by a visit to the United States in the summer of 1779, during which he attended the Massachusetts constitutional convention. Independent-minded and forthright, as well as somewhat jealous of the fame and accomplishments of others, he frequently found himself at odds with fellow diplomats Benjamin Franklin and Arthur Lee, as well as French officials, whose policies toward the Colonies he mistrusted. He joined Franklin and John Jay, however, in negotiating the Treaty of Paris (1783), by which Britain recognized the independence of the United States.

Meanwhile, during the preceding 3 years, Adams had persuaded the Dutch to recognize the Colonies as an independent Nation, grant a series of loans, and negotiate a treaty of alliance. As the first American Envoy to Great Britain (1785-88), he strove to resolve questions arising from the Treaty of Paris and to calm the harsh feelings between the two countries.

Back in the United States, Adams was soon elected as the first Vice President (1789-97), an office he considered insignificant but in which he emerged as a leader of the Federalist Party. During his stormy but statesmanlike Presidency (1797-1801), he inherited the deep political discord between the Hamiltonians and Jeffersonians that had taken root during Washington's administration. Adams pursued a neutral course without abandoning his principles. He kept the United States out of a declared war with France and achieved an amicable peace. But he proved unable to unite his party, divided by Hamilton's machinations and the ramifications of the French Revolution.

The Jeffersonians drove the Federalists out of office in 1800, and Adams retired to Quincy, where he spent his later years quietly. The death of his wife in 1818 saddened him, but he never lost interest in public affairs and lived to see his son John Quincy become President. John died at the age of 90 just a few hours after Jefferson, on July 4, 1826—dramatically enough the 50th anniversary of the adoption of the Declaration. Except for Charles Carroll, who was to live until 1832, Adams and Jefferson were the last two surviving signers. The remains of John and Abigail Adams are interred in a basement crypt at the United First Parish Church in Quincy.

Samuel Adams
MASSACHUSETTS

"Firebrand of the Revolution," Samuel Adams probably more than almost any other individual instigated and organized colonial resistance to the Crown. A talented polemicist and agitator-propagandist who relied more on his facile pen than the podium in behind-the-scenes manipulation of men and events, he religiously believed in the righteousness of his political causes, to which he persistently tried to convert others. He failed in business, neglected his family, gained a reputation as an eccentric, and demonstrated as much indifference to his own welfare as he did solicitousness for that of the public. His second cousin John Adams, more of a statesman, eclipsed him in the Continental Congress, though Samuel signed both the Declaration and the Articles of Confederation. In his later years, the Commonwealth of Massachusetts bestowed on him many high offices, capped by the governorship.

Adams was one of 12 offspring of a prosperous and politically active brewer and landowner. He was born at Boston in 1722 and enjoyed an excellent education at the Boston Latin School and Harvard College. Upon his graduation in 1740, he first demonstrated his lifelong aversion to normal employment. He studied law for awhile and then skipped from job to job, working for a time in his father's brewery as well as in a counting house and dissipating a paternal loan in an unsuccessful business venture.

When his father died in 1748 and his mother soon afterwards, Adams inherited a sizable estate, including the family home and brewery. By 1764, when the colonial quarrel with Britain began, he had long since lost the latter. And, during the previous 8 years as city tax collector, he had fallen in arrears about £8,000 in his collections. At the age of 42, unable to support a new wife and two children from his first marriage and residing in his rundown birthplace, he was destitute and besieged by creditors. He subsisted mainly on gifts and donations from loyal friends and neighbors.

Adams was a failure by most standards, but he had long before found the only meaningful "occupation" he ever pursued. For almost two decades he had been active in local political clubs, where he earned a reputation as a writer and emerged as leader of the "popular" party that opposed the powerful conservative aristocracy controlling the Massachusetts government. As clerk in the colonial legislature (1765-74), he drafted most of the body's official papers and quickly seized the tools of power. He pounced on the taxation issue raised by the Sugar and Stamp Acts (1764-65), and within a year he and his party fanned popular hatred of the conservatives and gained control of the legislature. He also spurred organization of the militant Boston Sons of Liberty, a secret society. As time went on, the stridency of his anti-British harangues escalated and sometimes became shrill enough to distress John Hancock and John Adams.

The Townshend Acts (1767), imposing a series of taxes on imports, provided Adams with a new cause for dissent. He urged merchants not to purchase goods from Britain, fomented opposition toward customs officials, inflamed the resentment toward British troops stationed in the colony that led to the Boston Massacre (1770), and humiliated the Royal Governor so much that he was recalled. Adams also authored a circular letter protesting British taxation and advocating united opposition. When, in 1768, the Massachusetts legislature sent it to the 12 other colonial assemblies, the Royal Governor dissolved the legislature, soon a common British practice in America. All these activities, coupled with authorship of scores of newspaper articles and extensive correspondence with prominent persons in the Colonies and England, brought Adams fame.

The conservative reaction on the part of merchants, the legislature, and the populace that surfaced after the repeal of practically all the Townshend Acts in 1770 failed to stifle Adams, though his popularity and influence declined. Relentlessly, in perhaps his chief contribution to the Revolution, he kept the controversy alive by filling the columns of the Boston newspapers with reports of British transgressions and warnings of more to come. Furthermore, in 1772 he began constructing the framework of a Revolutionary organization in Massachusetts. Drawing on a similar scheme he had proposed for all the Colonies 2 years earlier but which had come to naught, he convinced Boston and other towns to create committees of correspondence. The next year, he was appointed to the Massachusetts committee, formed in response to a call from the Virginia House of Burgesses.

Passage of the Tea Act (1773) provided the spark Adams was seeking to rekindle the flame of rebellion. He helped to incite and probably participated in the "Boston Tea Party," which engendered a series of rebellious incidents throughout the Colonies and pushed them closer to war. Parliament retaliated the next spring by passing a series of acts designed to punish Massachusetts.

Adams, recognizing that the other Colonies would only adopt non-intercourse measures in concert, urged an intercolonial congress to discuss mutual grievances and plan a united course of action. Subsequently, in June, the Massachusetts house of representatives, meeting behind locked doors to prevent interference by the Royal Governor, resolved to invite the other 12 Colonies to send representatives to Philadelphia in September and also appointed five Delegates, including Adams. That same day, the Royal Governor disbanded the legislature for the last time. Before heading for Philadelphia, outfitted in new clothes supplied by friends, Adams helped organize the convention that adopted the Suffolk Resolves, which in effect declared Massachusetts to be in a state of rebellion.

Adams served in the Continental Congress until 1781, longer than most other Delegates, but his role was less conspicuous than his preceding career augured. In the early sessions, most of the time he shrewdly stayed in the background with his fellow Massachusetts Delegates, whose radicalism offended most of their colleagues. And, throughout the Congress, he walked in the shadow of John Adams, who dominated the proceedings.

But nothing in the latter's career could match the drama of an episode involving Samuel in the interim between the First and Second Continental Congresses. Back at Lexington, Mass., one night in April 1775, he and Hancock had barely escaped the British force seeking to capture the colonial supply depot at Concord. The outbreak of armed conflict the next dawn—a "glorious morning" for Adams—marked the beginning of the War for Independence.

While still in Congress, in 1779-80 Adams participated in the Massachusetts constitutional convention. He returned to Boston for good the next year and entered the State senate (1781-88), over which he presided. He refused to attend the Constitutional Convention of 1787 because of his objection to a stronger National Government, and the following year unenthusiastically took part in the Massachusetts ratifying convention. A lifetime of public service culminated in his election as Lieutenant Governor (1789-93), interim Governor in the latter year upon Hancock's death, and Governor (1794-97). Still living in "honest poverty," he died at Boston in 1803 at the age of 81 and was buried in the Old Granary Burying Ground.

Josiah Bartlett
NEW HAMPSHIRE

Thanks to the voting order in the Continental Congress, Josiah Bartlett of New Hampshire was probably the first Delegate to vote for independence, the second to sign the Declaration (after President John Hancock), and the first to ballot for and pen his name to the Articles of Confederation. He also has the distinction of being one of several physician signers. His State service, more extensive than the National, included the governorship.

Bartlett was born in 1729 at Amesbury, Mass. At the age of 16, equipped with a common school education and some knowledge of Latin and Greek, he began to study medicine in the office of a relative. Five years later, in 1750, he hung out his shingle at nearby Kingston, N.H. He quickly won a name not only as a general practitioner but also as an experimenter and innovator in diagnosis and treatment. Marrying in 1754, he fathered 12 children.

During the decade or so preceding the outbreak of the War for Independence, Bartlett held the offices of justice of the peace, militia colonel, and legislator. In 1774 he cast his lot with the Revolutionaries. He became a member of the New Hampshire committee of correspondence and the first provincial congress, which came into being when the Royal Governor disbanded the colonial assembly. Bartlett was elected that same year to the Continental Congress, but tragedy intervened and kept him at home. Arsonists, possibly Loyalists, burned his house to the ground. Discouraged but undeterred, he immediately constructed a new one on the very same site.

While in Congress (1775-76), Bartlett also served on the New Hampshire council of safety. Although he rarely participated in congressional debates, whose seeming futility vexed him, he sat on various committees. He was reelected in 1777, but was too exhausted to attend. He nevertheless managed in August to lend his medical skills to Gen. John Stark's force of New Hampshire militia and Continental troops. They defeated a predominantly German element of Gen. John Burgoyne's command in the Battle of Bennington, N.Y.—one of the reverses that helped force him to surrender 2 months later at Saratoga, N.Y. Bartlett's last tour in Congress was in 1778-79, after which he refused reelection because of fatigue.

Bartlett spent the remainder of his life on the State scene. Despite his lack of legal training, he sat first as chief justice of the court of common pleas (1779-82), then as associate (1782-88) and chief (1788-90) justice of the Superior Court. Meantime, in 1788, he had taken part in the State convention that ratified the Federal Constitution, which he strongly favored. The next year, probably on account of his age and the weight of his judicial duties, he declined election to the U.S. Senate. The following year, he became chief executive, or president, of the State. He held that title for 2 years, in 1793-94 being named the first Governor, as the newly amended constitution redesignated the position.

Despite all his political activities, Bartlett had never lost interest in the field of medicine. In 1790 Dartmouth College conferred on him an honorary degree of Doctor of Medicine. The next year, he founded the New Hampshire Medical Society and became its first president.

In 1794, the year before he died in Kingston at the age of 65, ill health forced his retirement from public life. His remains lie in the yard of the Universalist Church in Kingston.

Carter Braxton

VIRGINIA

Carter Braxton, an aristocratic planter and probably the most conservative of the seven Virginia signers, originally opposed independence but later changed his mind and signed the Declaration. His tour in the Continental Congress lasted less than a year, but he held State office for most of his life. His two wives bore him 18 children, more than any other signer fathered.

Braxton was born in 1736 at Newington Plantation, on the Mattaponi River, in King and Queen County, Va. His father was a wealthy and politically influential planter. His mother, who died at his birth, was the daughter of Robert "King" Carter, a prominent landowner and politician.

In 1755, the same year Braxton graduated from the College of William and Mary, he married. His bride died in childbirth 2 years later. The following year, he left for an extended visit to England. He returned to Virginia in 1760 and moved into Elsing Green, an estate overlooking the Pamunkey River, in King William County, that his brother George had apparently built for him in 1758 during his absence. At the age of 25, in 1761, Carter remarried and entered the House of Burgesses. He served there, except for a term as county sheriff in 1772-73, until 1775. Meantime, in 1767, he had erected a new home, Chericoke, a couple of miles northwest of Elsing Green.

When the trouble with Great Britain erupted, Braxton, like many other conservatives, sided with the patriots, though he did not condone violence. In 1769 he signed the Virginia Resolves, a document protesting parliamentary regulation of the colony's affairs, and the Virginia Association, a nonimportation agreement. During the period 1774-76, he attended various Revolutionary conventions. In 1775, upon dissolution of the royal government, he accepted a position on the council of safety, the temporary governing body.

In the spring of that year, Braxton was instrumental in preventing the outbreak of war in Virginia. On April 20, the day after the clashes at Lexington and Concord, Royal Governor Lord John M. Dunmore seized the gunpowder in the Williamsburg magazine. Several colonial militia units prepared to retaliate, but moderate leaders such as George Washington and Peyton Randolph restrained them. Patrick Henry, however, refusing to be pacified, led a group of the Hanover County militia into Williamsburg and demanded the return of the gunpowder or payment for it. Before any hostilities occurred, Braxton, as spokesman for Henry, met with crown official Richard Corbin, his father-in-law, and convinced him to pay for the powder.

In the fall of 1775 Braxton was selected to fill a vacancy in Congress caused by the death of Peyton Randolph. Arriving at Philadelphia early in 1776, he at first sharply criticized the independence movement, but eventually yielded to the majority and backed the Declaration. That same year, apparently both in writing and in a speech at a Virginia convention, he urged adoption of a conservative form of State government and expressed such a mistrust of popular government that he lost his congressional appointment. The conservatives, however, elected him to the new State legislature, in which he sat for the rest of his life. For many years, he was also a member of the Governor's executive council.

The War for Independence brought financial hardships to Braxton. At its beginning, he had invested heavily in shipping, but the British captured most of his vessels and ravaged some of his plantations and extensive landholdings. Commercial setbacks in later years ruined him. In 1786, though he retained Chericoke, he moved to Richmond, where he died in 1797 at the age of 61. He was buried in the family cemetery adjacent to Chericoke.

Charles Carroll
MARYLAND

As one of the wealthiest men in America, Charles Carroll III of Carrollton risked his fortune as well as his life when he joined the Revolutionaries. Possessing one of the most cultivated minds of any of the signers, he achieved remarkable success as planter, businessman, and politician. He was the only Roman Catholic signer, the last to survive, and the longest lived.

Of Irish descent, Carroll was born in 1737 at his father's townhouse, Carroll Mansion in Annapolis. Jesuits educated him until he reached about 11 years of age. He then voyaged to Europe and studied the liberal arts and civil law at various schools and universities in Paris, elsewhere in France, and in London.

Carroll sailed home in 1765 at the age of 28, and built a home at Carrollton Manor, a 10,000-acre estate in Frederick County newly deeded to him by his father. At that time, he added "of Carrollton" to his name to distinguish himself from relatives of the same name. For most of his life, however, he preferred for his country residence the family ancestral home, Doughoregan Manor, in Howard County; when in Annapolis, he usually resided at his birthplace. For almost a decade after his return from Europe, barred from public life by his religion, he lived quietly. During that time, in 1768, he married. His offspring numbered seven, three of whom lived to maturity.

In 1773 Carroll became a champion of the patriots through his newspaper attacks on the Proprietary Governor. The latter was opposing reforms in officers' fees and stipends for Anglican clergy that the lower house of the legislature had proposed. From then on, Carroll took a prominent part in provincial affairs. In the years 1774-76 he supported nonimportation measures, attended the first Maryland Revolutionary convention, and served on local and provincial committees of correspondence and the council of safety. In 1776 he and his cousin John, a priest—chosen because of their religion and knowledge of French—traveled to Canada with Benjamin Franklin and Samuel Chase on a congressionally appointed committee that sought but failed to obtain a union of Canada with the Colonies.

Carroll and Chase arrived back in Philadelphia on June 11 that same year, the day after Congress had postponed the vote on Richard Henry Lee's independence resolution (June 7) until July 1. Maryland had refused to commit herself. Carroll and Chase rushed to Annapolis, recruited William Paca's aid, and conducted a whirlwind campaign that persuaded the provincial convention to pass a unanimous independence resolution. It reached Congress just in time to put the colony in the affirmative column on July 1, the day of the first vote. Three days later, Carroll himself became a Delegate and functioned in that capacity until 1778.

Two years before, Carroll had also been elected to the State senate, a seat he retained until just after the turn of the century. Along with fellow signers Chase and Paca, he was a member of the committee that in 1776 drafted Maryland's constitution. Elected to but not attending the Constitutional Convention of 1787, he nevertheless allied himself with the Federalists and helped bring about his State's ratification of the Constitution. In the years 1789-92, while also in the State senate, he served as a U.S. Senator, one of Maryland's first two.

Not reelected to the State senate in 1804, the 67-year-old Carroll retired from public life and concentrated on managing his landholdings, consisting of about 80,000 acres in Maryland, Pennsylvania, and New York, and his business interests. The latter included investments in the Patowmack (Potowmack) Company, which established a canal system in the Potomac and Shenandoah Valleys, and its successor the Chesapeake and Ohio Canal Company. Carroll was also. a member of the first board of directors of the Baltimore and Ohio Railroad.

In his final years, revered by the Nation as the last surviving signer of the Declaration, Carroll spent most of his time at Doughoregan Manor. But he passed the winters in the home of his youngest daughter and her husband in Baltimore. There, in 1832, he died at the age of 95. His body was interred in the family chapel at Doughoregan Manor.

Samuel Chase
MARYLAND

Fervid Revolutionary Samuel Chase led the campaign that crushed conservative opposition and alined his colony with the others in the independence struggle. Labeled the "Demosthenes of Maryland" for his fancy albeit effective oratory, he also demonstrated skill as a writer. But his independent attitude, stormy disposition, and outspokenness diluted his political effectiveness. As an Associate Justice of the U.S. Supreme Court, he became a controversial figure.

Chase was the son of an Anglican clergyman. He was born in 1741 at the farmhouse of his mother's parents on Maryland's Eastern Shore near the city of Princess Anne. His mother had come there from her home at nearby Allen for a visit. She died at or soon after the birth. Likely Chase's grandparents cared for him at least a few years, until about the time his father took over a parish in Baltimore. The latter provided the youth with his initial education, mainly in the classics.

Between the ages of 18 and 20, Chase read law with an Annapolis firm and joined the bar in 1761. The next year, he married; his wife bore at least two sons and two daughters. Two years after his marriage, he entered the colonial/State legislature and retained membership for two decades. From the beginning, he opposed the royal government. Annapolis officials denounced him for his participation in the violent protests of the Sons of Liberty in 1765 against the Stamp Act. In 1774-75 he took part in the Maryland committee of correspondence, council of safety, and the provincial convention.

In the former year, Chase had joined the Continental Congress.

He advocated an embargo on trade with Britain, showed special interest in diplomatic matters, early urged a confederation of the Colonies, defended George Washington from his congressional detractors, and in 1776 journeyed to Montreal with a commission that tried but failed to achieve a union with Canada. When he returned to Philadelphia around the middle of June, Congress had just postponed the vote on the Lee independence resolution. Realizing that Maryland was straddling the fence on the issue, Chase rushed home. Along with Charles Carroll of Carrollton and William Paca, he labored for 2 weeks to overcome opposition and won a committal to independence from the convention. The Maryland Delegates registered it in time for the first congressional vote, on July 1. In 1778 Chase lost his office because of adverse publicity generated by the advantage he had taken of knowledge gained in Congress to engage in a profiteering scheme.

In 1783-84 Chase traveled to London as a State emissary on an unfruitful mission to recover Maryland stock in the Bank of England from two fugitive Loyalists. Upon his return apparently, his first wife having died, he remarried; resumed his law practice; and engaged in various unsuccessful business enterprises that led to bankruptcy in 1789. Meantime, he had reentered politics. In 1785 he had represented Maryland at the Mount Vernon (Va.) Conference, forerunner of the Annapolis Convention. The next year, he moved his family from Annapolis to Baltimore, where he soon became chief judge of the Baltimore County criminal court (1788-95). As a delegate to the Maryland ratifying convention in 1788, he strongly opposed the Constitution, though he later became a staunch Federalist. From 1791 until 1794, while still a county judge, he also held the position of chief justice of the Maryland Superior Court.

Chase achieved his greatest fame as an Associate Justice of the U.S. Supreme Court (1796-1811). He was one of the ablest jurists in the body prior to Chief Justice John Marshall (1801-35), and delivered many influential opinions. His inability to control his political partisanship while on the bench—a trait he shared with some other judges of his time—led to various judicial improprieties and impeachment proceedings against him in 1805. But Congress acquitted him.

Still a Justice, Chase died in Baltimore 2 months after he celebrated his 70th birthday. His grave is in St. Paul's Cemetery.

Abraham Clark

NEW JERSEY

Abraham Clark—farmer, surveyor, self-taught lawyer, and politician— typifies those signers who dedicated most of their lives to public service but never gained national renown.

An only child, Clark was born in 1726 at his father's farm in what is now Roselle, N.J. In his boyhood, he was too frail for farmwork. He received only a minimum of formal education, but in his independent study demonstrated a bent for mathematics. When he reached manhood, besides farming his father's land, he took up surveying and informally read law to aid in mediating land disputes. Although probably never admitted to the bar, he gained a reputation as the "poor man's counselor" for his willingness to dispense free legal advice or accept produce or merchandise in lieu of a fee. He married in 1749, and fathered 10 children.

Clark followed his father's example by taking an active part in civic affairs. For many years, he served the Crown as high sheriff of Essex County and as clerk in the colonial legislature. The exact date of his entry into the patriot ranks is not known, but in the period 1774-76 he became a member and secretary of the New Jersey council of safety, attended several Revolutionary conventions, and won election to the provincial assembly. In June of the latter year, he and four other men replaced the existing congressional Delegates, who were opposing independence.

Despite poor health and deep concern for the welfare of his family and the safety of his home, located not far from an area of British occupation, Clark stayed in Congress throughout the War for Inde-

Thousands of American soldiers, including two of Abraham Clark's sons, endured the agonies of captivity on the British prison ship *Jersey*.

pendence and sometimes sat concurrently in the State legislature. He suffered additional anxiety when the British captured his two soldier sons and incarcerated them for a time on the prison ship *Jersey*, where hundreds of captives perished.

At the end of the war in 1783, Clark resumed his life back in New Jersey. The next year he began a 3-year tour in the State legislature, which he represented at the Annapolis Convention (1786). The following year, ill health prevented his attendance at the Constitutional Convention. He subsequently opposed the Constitution until it incorporated the Bill of Rights. In 1787-89 he returned to the Continental Congress, but in 1789-90 remained in New Jersey as commissioner to settle his State's accounts with the Federal Government. In 1791-94 he climaxed a long career of alternating State-National service as a Representative in the Second and Third Congresses.

Clark was stricken with a sunstroke in 1794 at his birthplace in Roselle, where he had lived all his life except when political duty called him away. He died a few hours later, at the age of 68, in the nearby town of Rahway and was buried there in the Presbyterian Cemetery.

George Clymer
PENNSYLVANIA

George Clymer, a leading Philadelphia merchant, rendered long years of service to his city, State, and Nation. He signed the Constitution as well as the Declaration, and applied his commercial acumen to the financial problems of the Colonies and the Confederation.

Clymer was orphaned in 1740, only a year after his birth in Philadelphia. A wealthy uncle reared and informally educated him and advanced him from clerk to a full-fledged partner in his mercantile firm, which on his death he bequeathed to his ward. Later, Clymer merged operations with the Merediths, prominent businessmen, and cemented the relationship by marrying his senior partner's daughter.

Motivated at least partly by the impact of British economic restrictions on his business, Clymer early adopted the Revolutionary cause and was one of the first to recommend independence. He attended patriotic meetings, served on the Pennsylvania council of safety, and in 1773 headed a committee that forced the resignation of Philadelphia tea consignees appointed by Britain under the Tea Act. Inevitably, in light of his economic background, he channeled his energies into financial matters. In 1775-76 he acted as one of the first two Continental treasurers, even personally underwriting the war by exchanging all his own specie for Continental currency.

In the Continental Congress (1776-77 and 1780-82) the quiet and

George Clymer lived in this Philadelphia townhouse during the Revolutionary period.

unassuming Clymer rarely spoke in debate but made his mark in committee efforts, especially those pertaining to commerce, finance, and military affairs. During and between his two congressional tours, he also served on a series of commissions that conducted important field investigations. In December 1776, when Congress fled from Philadelphia to Baltimore, he and fellow signers George Walton and Robert Morris remained behind to carry on congressional business. Within a year, after their victory at the Battle of Brandywine, Pa. (Sept. 11, 1777), British troops advancing on Philadelphia detoured for the purpose of vandalizing Clymer's home in Chester County, about 25 miles outside the city, while his wife and children hid nearby in the woods.

After a brief retirement following his last tour in the Continental Congress, Clymer was reelected in the years 1784-88 to the Pennsylvania legislature, where he had also served part time in 1780-82 while still in Congress. As a State legislator, he advocated reform of the penal code, opposed capital punishment, and represented Pennsylvania in the Constitutional Convention (1787). The next phase of his career consisted of service as a U.S. Representative in the First Congress (1789-91), followed by appointment as collector of excise taxes on alcoholic beverages in Pennsylvania (1791-94). In 1795-96 he sat on a Presidential commission that negotiated a treaty with the Indians in Georgia.

During his retirement, Clymer advanced various community projects, including the Philadelphia Agricultural Society, the Philadelphia Academy of Fine Arts, and the Philadelphia Bank. At the age of 73, in 1813, he died at Summerseat, an estate a few miles outside Philadelphia at Morrisville that he had purchased and moved to in 1806. His grave is in the Friends Meeting House Cemetery at Trenton, N.J.

William Ellery
RHODE ISLAND

One of a small group of lesser known signers whose achievements were comparatively modest, William Ellery gained little fame beyond his hometown—in sharp contrast to fellow Rhode Island signer Stephen Hopkins. The office of Delegate to the Continental Congress was the only significant position, State or National, to which Ellery ever won election, but he occupied it for a far longer period than most other Members.

The second son in a family of four, Ellery was born in 1727 at Newport, his lifelong residence. He followed in the footsteps of his father, a rich merchant and political leader, by attending Harvard.

On his graduation in 1747, he returned home. During the following two decades or so, he tried his hand at several occupations, eventually taking up the study of law, which he began practicing in 1770. Meantime, he had married twice and was to rear two sons and three daughters. Among his grandchildren were William Ellery Channing, influential theologian and apostle of Unitarianism, and Richard Henry Dana, Sr., noted poet and essayist.

By May 1776, when the colonial legislature sent Ellery to the Continental Congress, he had already earned a reputation for his work on local patriotic committees. Tradition records that, at the formal signing of the Declaration on August 2, he placed himself beside the Secretary and observed "undaunted resolution" on every face as the Delegates subscribed to their "death warrant." The next year, Rhode Island initiated popular election of congressional Delegates, and Ellery's Newport constituency maintained him in office until 1786 except for the years 1780 and 1782. In 1780 he remained in Philadelphia as an ex officio member of the board of admiralty, on which he had been sitting. His other committee assignments included those dealing with commercial and naval affairs. On occasion, to entertain himself and others, he wrote witty epigrams about various speakers. In 1785 he turned down the chief justiceship of the Rhode Island Superior Court to remain in Congress, where he had attained commanding seniority.

The very next year, Ellery terminated his congressional career to accept an appointment as commissioner of the Continental Loan Office for Rhode Island (1786-90). Probably the need to straighten out his finances compelled him to accept. British troops in 1778, during their 3-year occupation of Newport, had destroyed his home and property, and he had been too busy to rebuild his fortune. In 1790 President Washington appointed Ellery as customs collector for the district of Newport, a position he held for three decades. Although he was a Federalist, he managed to retain office during the Democratic-Republican administrations, probably because of his Revolutionary record and competence.

In his later years, Ellery prospered. He kept active in public affairs and spent many hours in scholarly pursuits and correspondence. Living to 92, a more advanced age than all the signers except Charles Carroll, he died in 1820 at Newport. His remains rest there in the Common Ground Cemetery.

William Floyd

NEW YORK

William Floyd, a wealthy landowner-farmer, belongs to the category of signers who played only a peripheral part in the Revolution. Nevertheless, he suffered anguish when British troops and Loyalists ravaged his estate during the war and drove his family into a 7-year exile in Connecticut. He also climbed to the rank of major general in the State militia, and served in the U.S. First Congress.

Floyd was born in 1734 at present Mastic, Long Island, N.Y., in Brookhaven Township. He was the second child and eldest of two sons in a family of nine. His father, a prosperous farmer of Welsh ancestry, kept the youth busy with chores. As a result, his education consisted only of informal instruction at home. When Floyd reached his 20th year, his father and mother died within 2 months of each other, and he inherited a large estate along with the responsibility of caring for his brothers and sisters. Six years later, he married. His bride helped care for the family and assisted in managing the farm, for which slaves supplied most of the labor. A community stalwart, Floyd also devoted considerable time to the affairs of the Brookhaven church, occupied the position of town trustee (1769-71), and moved up in the ranks of the Suffolk County militia to a colonelcy in 1775.

The Revolutionary movement in New York was much less fervent and started later than that in the other Colonies. The spirited Massachusetts opposition to the Tea Act in the later half of 1773 and in

1774 created the first major ferment in New York. One of the scattered focal points was eastern Long Island, where Floyd lived. He and many of his neighbors attended meetings that extended sympathy and aid to Massachusetts and protested the closing of the port of Boston by the British. Despite such local outbursts, by the end of 1774 New York was one of only two Colonies, Georgia being the other, in which the patriots did not control the government. For this reason, the Revolutionaries operated mainly on a county basis.

In 1774 Suffolk County sent Floyd to the Continental Congress. He remained there until 1777, returned in the period 1779-83, and in the interim served in the State senate and on the council of safety. Yielding the floor of Congress to the other New York Delegates, he labored without special distinction on a few committees. But worry about the welfare of his family presented a major distraction. In 1776, when British forces occupied Long Island, his wife, son, and two daughters fled northward across the sound and took refuge in Middletown, Conn. His wife died there in 1781. To make matters worse, the redcoats used his home at Mastic for a barracks, and Loyalists plundered his lands and belongings. When he brought his children back in 1783, he found the fields and timber stripped, the fences destroyed, and the house damaged.

After the war, Floyd sat for several terms in the State senate, attended the constitutional convention of 1801, supported the Federal Constitution, won election in the years 1789-91 as a Representative in the First Congress, served as presidential elector on four occasions, and became a major general in the New York militia. His second wife, whom he had married in 1784, bore him two daughters.

About this time, Floyd acquired an interest in western lands. The year of his marriage, he purchased a tract in central New York at the headwaters of the Mohawk River in the environs of present Rome; he supplemented this 3 years later by obtaining a State grant of more than 10,000 acres in the area. He spent most of his summers visiting and developing the acreage.

In 1803, in his late sixties, at a time when most men possess lesser ambitions, Floyd deeded his Long Island home and farm to his son Nicoll, and set out with the rest of his family to make a new life on the frontier. During the first year, he built a home at present Westernville, N.Y. There he succumbed, at the age of 86 in 1821, and was buried in the Presbyterian Cemetery.

Benjamin Franklin
PENNSYLVANIA

Benjamin Franklin, elder statesman of the Revolution and oldest signer of both the Declaration and the Constitution, sat on the committee that drafted the Declaration, attended the Constitutional Convention, and distinguished himself as a diplomat. But he was a self-made and self-educated intellectual colossus whose interests far transcended politics. He won international renown as a printer-publisher, author, philosopher, scientist, inventor, and philanthropist. On both sides of the Atlantic he mingled with the social elite, whom he impressed with his sagacity, wit, and zest for life.

Franklin was born in 1706 at Boston. He was the tenth son of a soap- and candle-maker. He received some formal education but was principally self-taught. After serving an apprenticeship to his father between the ages of 10 and 12, he went to work for his half-brother James, a printer. In 1721 the latter founded the *New England Courant*, the fourth newspaper in the Colonies. Benjamin secretly contributed to it 14 essays, his first published writings.

In 1723, because of dissension with his half-brother, Franklin moved to Philadelphia. He spent only a year there, and then sailed to London for two more years. Back in Philadelphia, he rose rapidly in the printing industry. He published *The Pennsylvania Gazette* (1730-48), which had been founded by another man in 1728, but his most successful venture was annual *Poor Richard's Almanac*

(1733-58). It won a popularity in the Colonies second only to the Bible, and its fame eventually spread to Europe.

Meantime, in 1730 Franklin had taken a common-law wife, who was to bear him a son and a daughter, as was another woman out of wedlock. By 1748 he had achieved financial independence and gained recognition for his philanthropy and the stimulus he provided to such worthwhile civic causes as libraries, educational institutions, and hospitals. Energetic and tireless, he also found time to pursue his deep interest in science, as well as enter politics.

Franklin served as clerk (1736-51) and member (1751-64) of the colonial legislature, and as deputy postmaster of Philadelphia (1737-53) and deputy postmaster general of the Colonies (1753-74). In addition, he represented Pennsylvania at the Albany Congress (1754), called to unite the Colonies during the French and Indian War. The congress adopted his "Plan of Union," but the colonial assemblies rejected it because it encroached on their powers.

During the years 1757-62 and 1764-75, Franklin resided in England, originally in the capacity of agent for Pennsylvania and later for Georgia, New Jersey, and Massachusetts. During the latter period, which coincided with the growth of colonial unrest, he underwent a political metamorphosis. Until then a contented Englishman in outlook, primarily concerned with Pennsylvania provincial politics, he distrusted popular movements and saw little purpose to be served in carrying principle to extremes. Until the issue of parliamentary taxation undermined the old alliances, he led the conservative Quaker party in its attack on the Anglican proprietary party and its Presbyterian frontier cohorts. His purpose throughout the years at London in fact had been displacement of the Penn family administration by royal authority—the conversion of the province from a proprietary to a royal colony.

It was during the Stamp Act crisis that Franklin evolved from leader of a shattered provincial party's faction to celebrated spokesman at London for American rights. Although as agent for Pennsylvania he opposed by every conceivable persuasive means enactment of the bill in 1765, he did not at first realize the depth of colonial hostility. He regarded passage as unavoidable and preferred to submit to it while actually working for its repeal. His nomination of a friend and political ally as stamp distributor in Pennsylvania, coupled with his apparent acceptance of the legislation, armed his

Benjamin Franklin being arraigned in 1774 by a committee of Lords of Parliament for disloyalty to the Crown. The following day, he was dismissed as deputy postmaster general of the Colonies.

proprietary opponents with explosive issues. Their energetic exploitation of them endangered his reputation at home until reliable information was published demonstrating his unabated opposition. For a time, mob resentment threatened his family and new home in Philadelphia until his tradesmen supporters rallied. Subsequently, Franklin's defense of the American position in the House of Commons during the debates over the Stamp Act's repeal restored his prestige at home.

Franklin returned to Philadelphia in May 1775, and immediately became a Member of the Continental Congress. Thirteen months later, he served on the committee that drafted the Declaration. According to a traditional anecdote, when he finished signing he declared, "Gentlemen, we must now all hang together, or we shall most assuredly all hang separately." He subsequently contributed to the Government in other important ways, and took over the duties of president of the Pennsylvania constitutional convention.

But, within less than a year and a half after his return, the aged statesman set sail once again for Europe, beginning a career as diplomat that would occupy him for most of the rest of his life. In 1776-79, one of three commissioners, he directed the negotiations that led to treaties of commerce and alliance with France, where the people adulated him, but he and the other commissioners squabbled constantly. While he was sole commissioner to France (1779-85), he and John Jay and John Adams negotiated the Treaty of Paris (1783), which ended the War for Independence.

Back in the United States, in 1785-87 Franklin became president of the Supreme Executive Council of Pennsylvania. At the Constitutional Convention (May 1787), though he did not approve of many aspects of the finished document, he lent his prestige, soothed passions, and compromised disputes. In his twilight years, working on his *Autobiography*, he could look back on a fruitful life as the toast of two continents. Active nearly to the last, in 1787 he was elected as first president of the Pennsylvania Society for Promoting the Abolition of Slavery—a cause to which he had committed himself as early as the 1730's. His final public act was signing a memorial to Congress recommending dissolution of the slavery system. Shortly thereafter, in 1790 at the age of 84, Franklin passed away in Philadelphia and was buried in Christ Church Burial Ground.

Elbridge Gerry
MASSACHUSETTS

During an extended and controversial career, Elbridge Gerry experienced many triumphs and disappointments. A prosperous merchant who worked alongside the two Adamses and John Hancock in the cause of independence, he integrated personal interests with public service and translated them into wartime profits. In the course of his long tenure in the Continental Congress, he signed both the Declaration and Articles of Confederation. But throughout his years in office, which crested in the U.S. Vice-Presidency, his inconsistencies, ambivalence, and truculence stirred up animosity among his colleagues— though he usually managed to muster enough party and popular support to win reelection.

Gerry was born in 1744 at Marblehead, Mass., the third of 12 children. His mother was the daughter of a Boston merchant; his father, a wealthy and politically active merchant-shipper who had once been a sea captain. Upon graduating from Harvard in 1762, Gerry joined his father and two brothers in the family business, which consisted of exporting dried codfish to Barbados and Spain. In 1772-74 he entered the colonial legislature, where he came under the influence of Samuel Adams, and took part in the Marblehead and Massachusetts committees of correspondence. In June of the latter year, when Parliament closed Boston Harbor and Marblehead became a major port of entry for supplies donated by patriots throughout the Colonies to relieve the Bostonians, he aided in the transshipment.

Between 1774 and 1776, Gerry attended the first and second

provincial congresses; served with Samuel Adams and John Hancock on the council of safety, which prepared the colony for war; and, as chairman of the committee of supply, a job for which his merchant background ideally suited him, raised troops and dealt with military logistics. During the night of April 18, 1775, he barely eluded capture by the British troops marching on Lexington and Concord. Following the adjournment of a meeting of the council of safety at an inn in Menotomy (Arlington), on the road from Cambridge to Lexington, he had retired for the night but responded to the alarm and fled.

Gerry entered the Continental Congress in 1776 and voted for independence in July, but his absence at the formal ceremonies on August 2 necessitated his signing the Declaration later in the year. His congressional specialties were military and financial matters, in both of which he demonstrated a duality of attitude that was to become his political trademark. He earned the nickname "soldiers' friend" for his advocacy of better pay and equipment, yet he vacillated on the issue of pensions. Despite his disapproval of standing armies, he recommended long-term enlistments. Although mistrustful of military officials, he befriended both George Washington and Thomas Conway, two generals who were implacable enemies.

Until 1779 Gerry sat on and sometimes presided over the congressional treasury board, which regulated Continental finances. An Army procurement agent as well as a merchant-supplier, he utilized information he obtained in Congress to benefit his lucrative business. On the other hand, he denounced profiteering and personally adhered to a fair-price schedule. In 1780, as wartime financial problems mounted, however, the Delegates resolved to revise the schedule. Gerry's vehement objections led to a quarrel, and he stormed out of Congress. Although nominally a Member, he did not reappear for 3 years. During the interim, he engaged in trade and privateering and saw duty in the lower house of the State legislature.

Back in Congress in 1783-85, Gerry numbered among those Representatives who had possessed talent as Revolutionary agitators and wartime leaders but who could not effectually cope with the painstaking task of stabilizing the National Government. He was experienced and conscientious, but created many enemies with his lack of humor, suspicion of the motives of others, and obsessive fear of political and military tyranny. In 1786, the year after leaving Congress, his fortune well established, he retired from business, married, and took a seat in the State legislature. The next year, he moved from Marblehead to Cambridge and purchased a confiscated Loyalist estate, where he was to reside for the rest of his life.

Gerry was one of the most vocal of the delegates at the Constitutional Convention of 1787. He antagonized practically everyone by his inconsistency and, according to a colleague, "objected to everything he did not propose." At first he advocated a strong Central Government, but ultimately rejected and refused to sign the Constitution, especially because it lacked a bill of rights and because he deemed it a threat to republicanism. He led the drive against ratification in Massachusetts. In 1789, when he changed his mind and announced his intention to support the Constitution, he was elected to the First Congress, where to the chagrin of the Antifederalists he championed Federalist policies.

Gerry left Congress for the last time in 1793 and retired for 4 years. During this time, he came to mistrust the aims of the Federalists, particularly their attempts to nurture an alliance with Britain, and sided with the pro-French Democratic-Republicans. In 1797 President John Adams appointed him as the only non-Federalist member of a three-man commission charged with negotiating a reconciliation with France, on the brink of war with the United States. During the ensuing XYZ affair (1797-98), Gerry tarnished his reputation. The French foreign minister duped him into believing that his presence in France would prevent war, and he lingered on long after the departure of the other disgusted commissioners. Finally, the embarrassed Adams recalled him, amid Federalist vituperation.

In 1800-03 Gerry, never very popular among the Massachusetts electorate because of his aristocratic haughtiness, met defeat in four bids for the Massachusetts governorship, but finally triumphed in 1810-12. Near the end of his two terms, scarred by partisan controversy, the Democratic-Republicans passed a devious redistricting measure to insure their domination of the State senate. In response, the Federalists heaped ridicule on Gerry and punningly coined the term "gerrymander" to describe the salamander-like shape of one of the redistricted areas.

Despite his advanced age, frail health, and the threat of poverty brought on by neglect of personal affairs, in 1813 Gerry accepted the Vice-Presidency in James Madison's Democratic-Republican administration. In the fall of 1814, the 70-year-old politician was stricken fatally while on the way to the Senate. He left his wife, who was to live until 1849, the last surviving widow of a signer, as well as three sons and four daughters. Gerry is buried in Congressional Cemetery at Washington, D.C.

Button Gwinnett
GEORGIA

Tempestuousness and ill-fortune marked the destiny of uniquely named Button Gwinnett, whose forename is that of a branch of his mother's family. The second signer to die, he met a tragic end in a duel while only in his forties. The only highlight of his brief tour in the Continental Congress was signing the Declaration. Even in Georgia, where he rose to the acting governorship, controversy and failure usually dogged him. Financial misfortunes were continual distractions, and he found that his paltry rewards as a merchant and planter matched his disappointments in politics.

Gwinnett was likely born in 1735, at the village of Down Hatherly, Gloucestershire, England. The second male in a family numbering at least seven, he was the son of an Anglican vicar of Welsh ancestry and a mother with English ties. He probably learned trade and finance from an uncle, a Bristol merchant, and in 1757 moved to Wolverhampton, Staffordshire. He married a grocer's daughter, who was to bear three girls, and for a time he joined her father in a partnership. In 1759, however, Gwinnett entered the export shipping business and built up an extensive trade with the American Colonies, possibly sometimes visiting them himself.

The date of Gwinnett's emigration to Savannah, Ga., is not known but in 1765 he purchased a store there. Later that same year, for some reason, he sold it and abruptly switched vocation. Apparently dazzled by visions of a planter's life on a great estate but undeterred by his lack of capital, experience, and training, he borrowed £3,000 and purchased large St. Catherine's Island. It was located off the Georgia coast not far from the busy mainland port of Sunbury, a rival of Savannah. At this time, he probably erected a home on the island. Before long, though already deep in debt, he also purchased some coastal lands on credit and received grants of others from the colony; and bought large numbers of slaves to work his holdings. Poachers aggravated his problems by raiding the island's livestock.

Gwinnett's land, slaves, and other possessions were soon gobbled up by creditors. Finally, in 1773, they took over the island, but allowed Gwinnett to maintain his home there. He did so for the rest

Fanciful depiction of Button Gwinnett's duel with Gen. Lachlan McIntosh in 1777 that resulted in the former's death.

of his life. During the war, however, the approach of British vessels, who replenished their food supplies from the livestock on the exposed island, sometimes forced him and his family to scurry over in their boat to Sunbury for temporary refuge.

Meantime, Gwinnett had long since entered politics. In 1768-69 he had been designated as one of His Majesty's justices of the peace and as a local pilotage commissioner. In the years 1769-71 the voters of St. John's Parish elected him to the colonial assembly at Savannah, but he attended only spasmodically because of his financial woes. When they worsened, he left public office for 5 years.

Gwinnett returned on the national level. Unlike the other two Georgia signers, Lyman Hall and George Walton, he belatedly joined the patriot side—apparently held back for some time by his English birth and close family connections in England. His friend Hall, a Sunbury resident and fellow member of the Midway Congregational Church, swung him over, probably beginning in the summer of 1775. The next February, the provincial congress named Gwinnett to the Continental Congress, though he did not arrive in Philadelphia until May. He attended for only about 10 weeks. Right after he signed the Declaration on August 2, he trekked back to Georgia, where he hoped but failed to win at least an Army colonelcy in one of the units the State was forming.

In October Gwinnett was reelected to the Continental Congress, but chose not to attend. Instead, during the next 5 months, he played a key role in drafting the State's first constitution, in the course of which he helped thwart a proposed union of South Carolina and Georgia. Upon the death of the Governor, or president of the Executive Council, in March 1777 the council commissioned Gwinnett as Acting Governor for 2 months, but he failed to achieve reelection. Before leaving office, he had clashed with controversial Gen. Lachlan McIntosh, an old rival. The result was a pistol duel in May just outside Savannah. Both men suffered wounds, but Gwinnett died a few days later of a gangrenous infection in his leg. Colonial Park Cemetery in Savannah contains a grave reputed to be his.

Lyman Hall
GEORGIA

Lyman Hall was one of the four signers originally trained as ministers. He eventually found his pulpit in politics, though he had to preach vigorously to inspire the "congregation" of Georgia. He enthusiastically sparked the slow-developing independence movement there with George Walton and recruited Button Gwinnett, the third Georgia signer. Somehow Hall also managed to pursue careers as doctor, planter, and Governor.

A native of Wallingford, Conn., Hall was born in 1724. He graduated from Yale College in 1747 at the age of 23, returned home, and heeded a family call to the Congregational ministry. An uncle, Rev. Samuel Hall, trained him in theology. In 1749 he began preaching in Bridgeport and adjacent towns. Young and immature, he probably entrapped himself in the middle of a liberal-conservative schism and in some way alienated his congregation, But repentance brought quick reinstatement from dismissal in 1751, and for a couple of years he temporarily filled vacant pulpits.

During this period, in 1752, Hall married, but his wife lived only a year; about 2 years later he remarried, a union that was to bring forth a son. Meantime, Hall had become disillusioned by his ministerial experiences. He studied medicine with a local doctor, partially supporting himself by teaching. When his medical training was completed, he moved back to Wallingford and hung out his shingle.

In 1757 the 33-year-old Hall, seeking brighter fields, emigrated to Dorchester, S.C., a settlement of New England Puritans not far from Charleston. Within a few months, he joined some of the residents in a relocation that had been underway since 1752. They were pushing southward to Georgia's coastal Midway District, in St. John's Parish (present Liberty County). This area provided more land and a healthier climate.

In 1758 the colonists finished their emigration and founded Sunbury. It evolved into the thriving seaport-hub of the surrounding slave-based, rice-indigo economy. Like many other planters, Hall maintained a home there, where it was healthier than inland, as well as at Hall's Knoll, the plantation just north of the present town of Midway that he had purchased shortly after arriving in the area. Because its plantations skirted malarial swamps, Hall kept busy providing medical treatment, as well as managing his estate.

St. John's Parish became the wealthiest in Georgia. This was not its only uniqueness, for the populace was steeped in the New England tradition of independence. When the trouble with Britain erupted in the mid-1760's the parish, guided by Hall, stood apart in its opposition from virtually all the rest of the colony except for another cluster of Revolutionaries at Savannah led by George Walton and others. Georgia, which was to be the last of the Colonies to join the Continental Association, was the youngest, most remote, and most sparsely settled. Also the poorest, it felt less the impact of British economic restrictions. The Loyalist ruling aristocracy of Georgia, regarding the tiny band of Revolutionaries with contempt, resisted their every move.

Hall was appalled by the poor representation of the parishes as a whole and the indecisiveness of Revolutionary conventions he attended at Savannah in the summer of 1774 and the next January, especially by their failure to send Delegates to the Continental Congress. He dejectedly returned to St. John's Parish. It was ready to secede from the colony, and proposed an alliance to South Carolina, which refused. Not to be denied, in March 1775 the parish held its own convention and sent Hall as its own "delegate" to the Continental Congress.

Two months later, Congress admitted Hall as a nonvoting member. In July, Georgia, finally coming into the fold, sanctioned Hall's presence in Congress and appointed four other Delegates. Hall served until 1780. Two years earlier, he had moved his family somewhere to the north just before British troops ravaged and conquered the Georgia coast. In the process, they destroyed Hall's Knoll and Hall's Sunbury residence and confiscated his property.

When the British evacuated Savannah in 1782, Hall settled there and resumed his medical practice to mend his fortune. The next January, St. John's Parish, where he had maintained ties, elected him to the State legislature. That body, in turn, awarded him the governorship (1783-84). His reconstruction-oriented administration, though marred by his purchase of and speculation in lands confiscated from Loyalists, rehabilitated the wartorn State and laid foundations for future growth.

In Hall's final years he acted for a time as a judge of the inferior court of Chatham County and as a trustee of a proposed State university (to be called first Franklin College and later the University of Georgia). But his duties as executor of Button Gwinnett's tangled estate required years of legal wrangling. In 1785 he sold his Hall's Knoll land. Five years later, he moved from Savannah to Burke County and purchased Shell Bluff Plantation, on the Savannah River about 25 miles below Augusta. A few months hence he died and was buried there. His remains are now interred at the Signers' Monument in Augusta.

John Hancock
MASSACHUSETTS

One of the fathers of U.S. independence, John Hancock helped spearhead the pivotal revolt in Massachusetts, presided as President of Congress during the voting for independence and adoption of the Declaration, and boldly penned the first signature on the document. Subsequently he served as the first and longtime Governor of his Commonwealth. Despite all these achievements and the persistent loyalty of his constituents, whom he wooed with lavish expenditures for public projects, his vanity, ostentation, and regal way of life irked many of his professional associates.

Hancock, born in 1737 at Braintree (present Quincy), Mass., lost his father, a Congregational pastor, at the age of 7. He spent the next 6 years with his grandparents at Lexington before joining his guardian, Thomas Hancock, a childless uncle who was one of the richest merchant-shippers in Boston. After studying at Boston Latin School and graduating from Harvard College in 1754, John began working as a clerk in his uncle's business and learned it rapidly. In 1760-61, while visiting London to observe the English side of the business, he attended the funeral of George II and the coronation of George III, who apparently granted him an audience. In 1763 he became a partner of his uncle, who died the next year and willed him the firm, a fortune that was probably the greatest in New England, and a luxurious house on Beacon Street.

Hancock allied with other merchants in protesting the Stamp Act (1765), and the next year inaugurated a long legislative career. But he did not strongly identify with the patriots until 2 years later. At that time, British customs officials, their courage bolstered by the arrival of a warship in Boston Harbor, charged him with smuggling and seized one of his ships. During the ensuing riots, the terrified customs officials fled to an island in the harbor. A few months later, the first major contingent of British troops sailed into port and created a tense situation that resulted in the Boston Massacre (1770). John Adams ably defended Hancock in court until the British dropped the smuggling charge, but the episode made him a hero throughout the Colonies.

Other factors tied Hancock to the patriots. Samuel and John Adams, shrewdly perceiving the advantages of such a rich and well-known affiliate, welcomed him into their ranks, encouraged his idolatry by the populace, and pushed him upward in the Revolutionary hierarchy. When the first provincial congress met at Salem and Concord in 1774, he acted as its president as well as chairman of the vital council of safety. The second provincial congress, convening the next year at Cambridge and Concord, elected him to the Continental Congress.

On April 18, only 3 days after the provincial congress adjourned, British troops marched from Boston to seize rebel stores at Concord. Warned of their approach during the night by Paul Revere, Hancock and Samuel Adams, who were visiting at nearby Lexington, escaped. But the British-American clashes at Lexington and Concord marked the outbreak of war. The two men avoided Boston and hid at various places for 2 weeks before proceeding to Philadelphia. Later that summer, Hancock married, siring a daughter who died in infancy and a son, John George Washington Hancock, who lived but 9 years.

From 1775 until 1777 Hancock presided over the Continental Congress. The very first year, his egotism, which regularly aroused the antipathy of many Members, created personal embitterment as well. Blind to his own limitations, particularly his lack of military experience, he unrealistically entertained the hope that he, instead of Washington, would be appointed as commander in chief of the Continental Army. Hancock also provoked ill will among his fellow New Englanders, especially Samuel Adams, by courting moderates such as John Dickinson and Benjamin Harrison. Hancock believed that Samuel Adams was responsible in 1777 for blocking a congressional vote of thanks for his services and never forgave him.

Only Hancock and Charles Thomson, the President and Secretary of Congress, signed the broadside copy of the Declaration, printed the night of its adoption, July 4, 1776, and disseminated to the public the following day. At the formal signing of the parchment copy on August 2, tradition holds that Hancock wrote his name in large letters so that the King would not need spectacles to recognize him as a "traitor." After resigning as presiding officer in 1777, he remained a Member of Congress until 1780, though he spent much of his time in Boston and for the rest of his life solidified his political position in Massachusetts. In 1778, as a major general in the militia, he commanded an expedition that failed to recapture Newport, R.I., from the British. He made a more tangible contribution to the war by accepting Continental currency from his debtors, even though his fortune had already been dented by wartime-induced reverses.

In 1780, the same year Hancock gave up his seat in Congress and attended his Commonwealth's constitutional convention, he was overwhelmingly elected as first Governor (1780-85). He won re-election in 1787-93. In the interim (1785-86), he once again sat in Congress. In 1788 he chaired the Massachusetts convention that ratified the U.S. Constitution, which he favored.

While still Governor, in 1793 at the age of 56, Hancock died at Boston. His funeral, one of the most impressive ever held in New England, culminated in burial at Old Granary Burying Ground.

Benjamin Harrison
VIRGINIA

Benjamin Harrison, the most conservative of the Virginia signers except for Carter Braxton, was a member of one of the most prominent planter families in the South and was the fifth in a line of active politicians bearing the same name. Because of his rotundity, joviality, love of good foods and wines, and fondness for luxury, he acquired the nickname "Falstaff of Congress." His son, William Henry, and his great-grandson, Benjamin, served as the ninth and 23d Presidents of the United States.

Harrison was born in 1726 at his father's estate, Berkeley, in Charles City County, Va. He matriculated at the College of William and Mary, but left before graduating in 1745 upon the death of his father in order to assume management of the family plantation. Shortly thereafter he married; seven of his children were to survive infancy. In time, his landholdings grew to include eight plantations and other properties, and he also expanded into shipping and shipbuilding. Following the precedent set by his forebears, about 1749 he gained admission to the House of Burgesses. He sat there, frequently as speaker, until 1774, when the Royal Governor disbanded the body.

Harrison's conservatism manifested itself early in the Revolutionary movement. In 1764 the burgesses, learning about the Stamp Act, impending in Parliament, named a committee to draw up a protest. As one of the committeemen, Harrison helped pen the document. The very next year, however, when the act went into effect, he refused to endorse Patrick Henry's resolutions urging civil disobedience as a countermeasure. Forced to take a stand as the rift with the Crown widened, Harrison cast his lot with the patriots. Between 1773 and 1776, he shared in the tasks of the Revolutionary conventions, the committee of correspondence, and the provincial congresses.

Meantime, in 1774, Harrison had been appointed to the First

Continental Congress. Although usually silent on the floor, he made valuable contributions on the foreign affairs, marine, military, and financial committees. As chairman of the committee of the whole (1776-77), he chaired the deliberations leading up to the adoption of the Declaration and the early debates on the proposed Articles of Confederation.

In 1777, the same year Harrison withdrew from Congress, he entered the lower house of the Virginia legislature, where he presided as speaker in the years 1778-81. His three terms as Governor (1781-84) reflected the ascendancy in Virginia of the conservatives, who included in addition to Harrison and Braxton such former extremists as Patrick Henry and Richard Henry Lee. Succeeded by Henry, Harrison rejoined the legislature (1784-91), holding the speakership part of the time. In 1788 at the Virginia ratifying convention he objected to the Federal Constitution because it lacked a bill of rights. Once ratification had occurred, however, he supported the new Government. Three years later, Harrison died in his mid-sixties at Berkeley and was buried there in the family cemetery.

John Hart
NEW JERSEY

Signing the Declaration represented John Hart's one significant act during an ephemeral tour in the Continental Congress, his only role in national politics. Yet, like most of the signers, he was dominant in community and State affairs. And he and his family directly experienced the tragedy of the war. Unfortunately, he died before the attainment of victory.

The year after Hart's birth in 1711 at Stonington, Conn., his parents emigrated to New Jersey and settled on a farm in the Hopewell vicinity. Hart was to live there and till the soil all his life. In 1740 he married and began raising a family of 13. In time, while gaining the sobriquet "Honest John," he acquired considerable property, including grist, saw, and fulling mills, and emerged as a civic leader. From the 1750's until the outbreak of the War for Independence in 1775, despite a paucity of education, he worked his way up the political ladder in Hunterdon County and the State. He held the offices of justice of the peace, county judge, colonial legislator (1761-71), and judge of the New Jersey court of common pleas.

In the legislature's dispute with the Royal Governor, Hart opposed parliamentary taxation and the stationing of British troops in the colony. During the years 1774-76, he attended the New Jersey provincial congresses, where he achieved the vice-presidency, and won appointment to the council of safety and the committee of correspondence. In June 1776 he and four other Delegates were chosen to replace the incumbent conservatives in the Continental Congress. The new delegation arrived at Philadelphia just a few days before the votes for independence on July 1 and 2 and cast affirmative ballots.

In August 1776, just after Hart signed the Declaration, he departed to accept the speakership in the lower house of the New Jersey legislature. That winter, during the British invasion of the province, the redcoats wreaked havoc on his farm and mills and drove him into hiding among the hills surrounding the Sourland Mountains. When he ended his exile in the wake of the American victories at Princeton and Trenton, he discovered that his wife, ill at the time of the attack, had died and his family scattered. In 1777-78 he sat again on the council of safety, but failing health forced his retirement. He died the next year, at the age of 69, on his Hopewell farm. He is buried in the yard of the First Baptist Church at Hopewell.

Joseph Hewes
NORTH CAROLINA

Even in an age and land of such unlimited opportunities as 18th-century America, few men attained such success as merchant Joseph Hewes. He was rarely thwarted in his ambitions and enjoyed wealth and social prestige, reflected in political conservatism.

Born in 1730 at Maybury Hill, an estate on the outskirts of Princeton, N.J., Hewes was the son of a pious and well-to-do Quaker farmer. He received a strict religious upbringing, and studied at a local school. After learning trade from a Philadelphia merchant, he entered business for himself. About 1760, anxious to expand his modest fortune, he moved to the thriving seaport town of Edenton, N.C. There, where he was to reside for the rest of his life, he founded a profitable mercantile and shipping firm and gained prominence. Only one fateful event marred his life. A few days before his intended wedding date, his fiancée suddenly died. Hewes remained a bachelor for the rest of his life.

As a member of the North Carolina assembly (1766-75), the committee of correspondence (1773), and the provincial assemblies (1774-75), Hewes helped the Whigs overthrow the royal government. Elected to the Continental Congress in 1774, he vigorously supported nonimportation measures even though it meant personal financial loss. By the time of the outbreak of the War for Independence, the next year, anathema to the pacifistic Quakers, he had rejected the faith altogether—culminating a trend that had been evolving because of his love of dancing and other social pleasures, as well as his Revolutionary activities.

Joseph Hewes sponsored the American career of his friend John Paul Jones, who became the most famous naval officer of the Revolution.

Hewes was one of those who originally opposed separation from Great Britain. Thus it was a disagreeable task for him, in May 1776, to present the Halifax Resolves to the Continental Congress. Enacted the month before by the provincial assembly, they instructed the North Carolina Delegates to vote for independence should it be proposed. Hewes, who considered the resolves premature, ignored his State's commitment and at first opposed Richard Henry Lee's June 7 independence resolution. According to John Adams, however, at one point during debate a transformation came over Hewes. "He started suddenly upright," reported Adams, "and lifting up both his hands to Heaven, as if he had been in a trance, cried out, 'It is done! and I will abide by it.' "

One episode involving Hewes illustrates the recurring problem of sectional rivalries among the Delegates. As key members of the marine committee, Hewes and John Adams were instrumental in establishing the Continental Navy. When the time came to appoint the Nation's first naval captains, the two men clashed. For one of the positions, Hewes nominated his friend John Paul Jones, an experienced seaman who had recently emigrated to Virginia from Scotland. Adams, maintaining that all the captaincies should be filled by New Englanders, stubbornly protested. New England had yielded to the South in the selection of a commander in chief of the

Continental Army and Adams had fostered the selection of the able Virginian George Washington, so he was not now about to make a concession on the Navy. Hewes, sensing the futility of argument, reluctantly submitted. Jones, who was to become the most honored naval hero of the Revolution, received only a lieutenant's commission.

In 1777 Hewes lost his bid for reelection to Congress, one of the few failures in his life, and in 1778-79 he found solace in the State legislature. In the latter year, despite health problems, he accepted reelection to the Continental Congress. A few months after arriving back in Philadelphia and not long before his 50th birthday, overworked and fatigued, he died. His grave is in Christ Church Burial Ground there.

Thomas Heyward, Jr.
SOUTH CAROLINA

An aristocratic planter, lawyer, and jurist, Thomas Heyward, Jr., sat in the State legislature and the Continental Congress and commanded a militia battalion. He was one of three South Carolina signers captured and imprisoned by the British.

The eldest son of one of the wealthiest planters in South Carolina, Heyward was born in 1746 at Old House Plantation, in St. Helena's Parish (later St. Luke's Parish and present Jasper County) near the

Georgia border about 25 miles northeast of Savannah. In 1771, following 5 years of study in London, he began practicing law. The next year, his parish sent him to the colonial legislature (1772-75), which was feuding with the Royal Governor over parliamentary taxation. During that period, in 1773, he married and settled down at White Hall Plantation, only a couple of miles from the residence of his father.

While a legislator, Heyward apparently joined the Revolutionaries, for in the summer of 1774 he attended a provincial convention that chose Delegates to the Continental Congress. During 1775-76 he was active in the first and second provincial congresses and on the council of safety and the committee that drafted a State constitution. In the Continental Congress (1776-78), he signed the Articles of Confederation as well as the Declaration. At the end of his tour, he journeyed to Charleston and took up residence in the townhouse he had inherited from his father the year before. He became a circuit court judge; represented Charleston in the State legislature, which convened in the city; and held a militia captaincy.

In 1779 Heyward was wounded during Brig. Gen. William Moultrie's repulse of a British attack on Port Royal Island, along the South Carolina coast near Heyward's home. The following year, the British plundered White Hall and carried off all the slaves. When they took Charleston, they captured Heyward, who was helping defend the city. He was imprisoned at St. Augustine, Fla., until July 1781. Shortly before his release, he celebrated Independence Day by setting patriotic verses to the British national anthem. "God save the King" became "God save the thirteen States," a rendition that soon echoed from New Hampshire to Georgia.

From 1782 until 1789 Heyward resumed his position of circuit court judge, concurrently serving two terms in the State legislature (1782-84). In 1785 he helped found and became the first president of the Agricultural Society of South Carolina. The following year, his wife passed away and he remarried; apparently only one child from his two marriages reached maturity. He devoted most of his remaining days, except for attendance in 1790 at the State constitutional convention, to managing his plantation; he sold his Charleston townhouse in 1794. The last to survive among the South Carolina signers, he died in 1809 at the age of 62 and was interred in the family cemetery at Old House Plantation.

William Hooper
NORTH CAROLINA

The ambivalence of William Hooper's convictions prevented him from ever carving a solid niche in the field of politics. His youthful choice of occupation and political affiliation brought estrangement from his family and emigration from Massachusetts to far-off North Carolina. Motivated sometimes by self-interest and sometimes by intense patriotism, he flourished in law and politics. He originally supported the royal government, but became a Whig leader during the Revolution. After the war, his aristocratic leanings caused him to lose favor among the electorate.

Hooper was born in Boston, Mass., in 1742, the first child of William Hooper, a Scotch immigrant and Congregationalist clergyman who 5 years later was to transfer to the Anglican Church. Groomed for the ministry in his youth, Hooper undertook 7 years of preparatory education at Boston Latin School. This qualified him in 1757 to enter Harvard College in the sophomore class. He graduated 3 years later, but much to the chagrin of his father rejected the ministry as a profession. The next year, he further alienated his Loyalist father and isolated himself from his family by taking up the study of law under James Otis, a brilliant but radical lawyer.

Partly to ameliorate family strife and partly to better his legal opportunities, about 1764 Hooper sought his fortune at Wilmington, N.C. Three years later, he married the daughter of an early settler, by whom he was to have two sons and a daughter. He resided either in Wilmington or at his nearby estate, Finian, about 8 miles away on Masonboro Sound, rode the circuit from court to court, and built up a clientele among the wealthy planters of the lower Cape Fear region. Ambitious, he harbored political aspirations and by 1770-71 had obtained the position of deputy attorney general of North Carolina.

In this capacity, protecting his own economic interests and political goals, Hooper sided with Royal Governor William Tryon in a conflict between the government and a group of North Carolina frontiersmen known as the Regulators. They were rebelling against governmental corruption and oppression and high legal and other fees. Hooper urged the use of force to quell the rebellion, and in 1771 accompanied the government forces that defeated the rebels in the Battle of Alamance.

Within a few years, Hooper's allegiance to the royal government waned. At the time of his election to the colonial assembly (1773-75), the act providing for the colony's court system was about to expire. The assembly attempted to attach to the new court act a clause by which the colony could confiscate American property owned by foreign debtors, including inhabitants of Great Britain. When the Royal Governor blocked the bill, a 4-year struggle for control of the colony ensued. Hooper, though deprived of a source of income as a lawyer and dependent upon his wife's small fortune for subsistence, championed the cause of the assembly.

Hooper rose to a position of leadership among the Whigs, though he disapproved of extremism. In a letter dated April 1774 to his friend James Iredell, he prophesized the Colonies' break with Great Britain—the earliest known prediction of independence, which won for Hooper the epithet "Prophet of Independence." In the summer, after the Royal Governor had dissolved the colonial assembly, he helped organize and presided over an extralegal conference at Wilmington. It voted to convene a provincial assembly, which met in August at New Bern and elected Delegates, one of whom was Hooper, to the Continental Congress. Later that same year, he became a member of the committee of correspondence.

During the period 1774-77, Hooper divided his time between Congress, where he gained a reputation as an orator, and the North Carolina provincial assembly, in which he labored to set up a State government. In 1777, however, the financial difficulties with his law practice and a desire to be near his family prompted him to resign from Congress and return to Wilmington. He was immediately elected to the State legislature and served there almost continuously until 1786.

In 1780 the British invaded North Carolina. Hooper moved his family from Finian into Wilmington for safety, but in January 1781, while he was away on business, the city fell to the enemy. Separated from his loved ones for more than 10 months and often destitute, he depended upon friends in Edenton and vicinity for shelter and food.

On one occasion, taken violently ill with malaria, he was nursed back to health by Iredell's wife. Upon the British evacuation of the Wilmington area, in November, Hooper returned to find most of his property, including Finian, in ruins. Shortly thereafter he rejoined his wife and children, who had fled to Hillsborough, which he made his home for the rest of his life.

During the aftermath of the Revolution, Hooper, despite continuing political aspirations, lost favor with the public. Unable to adjust to the rise of republicanism in the State, he adopted a conservative stance. His aristocratic pretensions, forgiving attitude toward Loyalists, and lack of faith in the common people undermined his popularity. In 1788 he strenuously campaigned for State ratification of the Federal Constitution, which occurred early the next year. By this time, he was in ill health and despondent, but lingered on for nearly 2 years. He died in 1790 in his late forties. His remains, moved from the Hillsborough town cemetery in 1894, rest today at Guilford Courthouse National Military Park near Greensboro.

Stephen Hopkins
RHODE ISLAND

This signer, the second oldest next to Benjamin Franklin, is noted for his tremulous signature. Aged 69 and afflicted with palsy, according to tradition he declared, "My hand trembles, but my heart does not!" Before, during, and after a comparatively brief stretch of congressional service, he occupied Rhode Island's highest offices and fostered the cultural and economic growth of Providence.

Hopkins attained success purely by his own efforts. Born in 1707 at Providence and equipped with but a modicum of basic education, he grew up in the adjacent agricultural community of Scituate, earned his living as a farmer and surveyor, and married at the age of 19. Five years later, in 1731, when Scituate Township separated from Providence, he plunged into politics. During the next decade, he held the following elective or appointive offices: moderator of the first town meeting, town clerk, president of the town council, justice of the peace, justice and clerk of the Providence County court of common pleas, legislator, and speaker of the house.

In 1742, about 2 years after he and his brother Esek founded a mercantile-shipping firm, Stephen moved back to Providence. For the next three decades, he built up his business and would probably have acquired a fortune had he not at the same time supported a variety of civic enterprises and broadened his political activities. He continued in the legislature, served as assistant and chief justice of the Superior Court and ten-time Governor, and represented Rhode Island at various intercolonial meetings. At the Albany Congress (1754), he cultivated a friendship with Franklin and assisted him in framing a plan of colonial union that the congress passed but the Colonies rejected. The next year, 2 years after the demise of his first wife, who had given birth to five sons and two daughters, he remarried.

About this time, Hopkins took over leadership of the colony's radical faction, supported by Providence merchants. For more than a decade, it bitterly fought for political supremacy in Rhode Island with a conservative group in Newport, led by Samuel Ward, a political enemy of Hopkins.

Hopkins was a man of broad interests, including humanitarianism, education, and science, and exerted his talents in many fields. About 1754 he helped set up a public subscription library in Providence. He acted as first chancellor of Rhode Island College (later Brown University), founded in 1764 at Warren, and 6 years later was instrumental in relocating it to Providence. He also held membership in the Philosophical Society of Newport. Strongly opposing slavery, in 1774 he authored a bill enacted by the Rhode Island legislature that prohibited the importation of slaves into the colony—one of the earliest antislavery laws in the United States.

Long before, Hopkins had sided with the Revolutionaries. In 1762 he helped found the influential *Providence Gazette and Country Journal*. Two years later, he contributed to it an article entitled "The Rights of the Colonies Examined," which criticized parliamentary taxation and recommended colonial home rule. Issued as a pamphlet the next year, it circulated widely throughout the Colonies and Great Britain and established Hopkins as one of the earliest of the patriot leaders. He also sat on the Rhode Island committee of correspondence and carried on with his duties in the legislature and Superior Court while a Member of the Continental Congress (1774-76). He served on the committees that prepared the Articles of Confederation and that created the Continental Navy and appointed Esek Hopkins as its commander in chief. Ill health compelled Stephen to retire in September 1776, a month after he signed the Declaration.

Hopkins declined subsequent reelections to Congress, but sat in the State legislature for a time and took part in several New England political conventions. He withdrew from public service about 1780 and died 5 years later in Providence at the age of 78. He was interred in the North Burial Ground.

Francis Hopkinson
NEW JERSEY

The literary and artistic talents of this versatile signer brought him more acclaim than his political and legal activities. Although a lawyer and judge by profession, he achieved more eminence as an essayist, poet, artist, and musician. His verse and satirical essays rank among the better literary efforts of the Revolutionary and early Federal periods, and he was one of America's first native composers. His eldest son, Joseph (1770-1842), wrote "Hail Columbia" and won distinction as a lawyer, jurist, U.S. Congressman, and patron of the arts.

Hopkinson was born at Philadelphia in 1737, the eldest of eight children. His father, who died when he was 14, was a prominent lawyer-jurist, politician, and civic leader. Upon graduation from the College of Philadelphia (later part of the University of Pennsylvania) in 1757, young Hopkinson studied law under Benjamin Chew, attorney general of the province, and 4 years later joined the bar. In 1763 he obtained the position of customs collector at Salem, N.J. Three years hence, after failing in business, he sailed to England to seek an appointment as colonial customs collector through the influence of friends and relatives. During his yearlong stay, though unsuccessful in his vocational quest, he visited Benjamin Franklin, Lord North, and other prominent people, and may have studied under artist Benjamin West.

Back in Philadelphia, Hopkinson operated a store and married in 1768. Four years later he became the customs collector at New Castle, Del. About 1774 he took up residence at the home of his father-in-law in Bordentown, N.J., practiced law, and began a 2-year tour in the legislature. As a Member of the Continental Congress for only a few months in 1776, he relieved his ennui by drawing caricatures of his colleagues. His later offices included: chairman (1777-78) of Philadelphia's Continental Navy Board, treasurer of loans (1778-81), judge of the admiralty court of Pennsylvania (1779), and Federal circuit judge for the eastern district of the State (1789-91).

During his busy public career, the ambitious Hopkinson managed to leave his stamp on the fields of music, art, and literature. His "My Days Have Been So Wondrous Free" (1759) probably represents the first American composition of secular music; his "Temple of Minerva" (1781), the first American attempt at opera. In art, he was noted particularly for his crayon portraits and his work on heraldic emblems. But his literary attainments surpassed all his others.

Between 1757 and 1773, Hopkinson contributed numerous poems and essays, many of them in a humorous and satirical vein, to various periodicals. The following year, he began advancing the patriot cause. A profusion of widely read and influential pamphlets, essays, and letters, often presented in an allegorical style, derided and ridiculed the British and the Loyalists, outlined colonial grievances, and encouraged the colonists. *The Prophecy*, written in 1776 before the adoption of the Declaration of Independence, predicted that event.

After the war, Hopkinson continued to treat political and social themes, and became one of the best known writers in the United States.

While a Federal circuit judge, Hopkinson died in Philadelphia at the age of 53. He was laid to rest in Christ Church Burial Ground. Surviving him were his widow and five children.

Samuel Huntington
CONNECTICUT

Several of the signers were self-made men. One of the most successful of them was Samuel Huntington. Reared amid humble surroundings, he educated himself in the law and, despite recurring health problems, climbed to the pinnacles of the State and National Governments.

Born into a large family in 1731 at Windham (present Scotland), Conn., Huntington grew up on a farm, received a limited education, and at the age of 16 began work as a cooper. But his ambition soon pushed him onward. He independently studied borrowed legal tomes, won admittance to the bar about 1758, and set up practice. Two years later, he moved to nearby Norwich. The next year, he married; he and his wife, who were to be childless, later adopted three children. As time went on, he prospered in the law and became a community leader.

In 1764 Huntington began his public career, in the Connecticut legislature. The next year, he was appointed as King's Attorney of the colony and won election as justice of the peace for New London County. He occupied these positions for practically the entire decade or so prior to the outbreak of the War for Independence, in 1775. Meantime, 2 years earlier, the colonial legislature had named him as a judge of the Connecticut Superior Court, an appointment renewed annually for a decade.

In 1774 Huntington, registering his growing sympathy for the Colonies in their struggle against the Crown, resigned as King's Attorney and joined the front ranks of the Revolutionaries. The next year, he became a member of the upper house of the legislature (1775-84), and entered national politics when he became a Delegate to the Continental Congress. His committee assignments included those dealing with Indian affairs, ordnance supply, and marine matters. In the fall of 1776, fatigue and health worries caused him to return to Connecticut. Between then and 1783, plagued with spells of illness, he attended congressional sessions intermittently (1778, 1779-81, 1783), often returning home to recuperate. Despite this burden, he assumed the heavy responsibilities of President of Congress (1779-81), presiding on March 1, 1781, when the Articles of Confederation were adopted.

Huntington's well-earned "retirement" when he returned to Connecticut in 1783, after 8 years of service to the Nation, turned out to involve 12 years of vigorous activity—despite his waning health. Even while he had been in Congress, he had served his State in various other ways, and all his legislative and other positions had been held open for him. A succession of appointive and elective offices followed: chief justice of the Superior Court (1784), Lieutenant Governor (1785), and Governor (1786-96). In the latter capacity, he led the battle for Connecticut's ratification of the Federal Constitution and improved the educational system. As one of Connecticut's seven first presidential electors, in 1789 he won two "favorite son" votes for the Presidency.

Ever interested in education, despite his own lack of a college degree, in the 1780's Huntington received honorary degrees from Princeton, Yale, and Dartmouth; and was appointed one of the original trustees of Plainfield (Conn.) Academy. Before that time, he had acted as adviser to the president of Yale.

In 1796 at the age of 65, still Governor, he died at his home in Norwich and was interred in the Old Burial Ground.

Thomas Jefferson
VIRGINIA

An intellectual and political titan who ranked among the most brilliant men of his time, Thomas Jefferson richly contributed to his State and Nation—as statesman, diplomat, scientist, architect, author, and educator. Graced with a wide-ranging and probing mind, he also delved into linguistics, law, art, geography, ethnology, music, agriculture, paleontology, botany, meteorology, geology, parliamentary practice, and invention.

As author of the Declaration of Independence, influential political theorist, cofounder of the Democratic-Republican Party, Virginia legislator and Governor, first U.S. Secretary of State, second Vice President, and third President, Jefferson has left an indelible impression on our political system and philosophy. Beyond that, he laid the basis for the westward expansion of the Nation; and two of his disciples, Madison and Monroe, followed him into the White House.

Like most successful politicians, however, Jefferson created his share of enemies and felt the sting of failure. Inability to reconcile his contradictory traits of idealism and pragmatism resulted in inconsistencies that rendered him vulnerable. He lacked the aggressiveness and charisma of many leaders. To compensate for his basic shyness and his deficiencies as a speaker, he mastered written expression and learned to exercise administrative power. His governorship ended ignominiously. And his vision of an agricultural America, peopled by well-educated and politically astute yeomen farmers was never to be realized. Yet none of these factors diminishes his stature or undermines his achievements.

The eldest of two sons in a family of ten, Jefferson was born in 1743 at Shadwell, a frontier plantation in Goochland (present Albemarle) County, Va. But 2 years later his father, Peter, a self-made surveyor-magistrate-planter who had married into the distinguished Randolphs, moved his family eastward to Tuckahoe Plantation, near Richmond. His reason for doing so was a promise he had made to his wife's newly deceased first cousin, William Randolph, to act as guardian of his son, Thomas Mann Randolph. Young Jefferson passed most of his boyhood in the Randolph home, beginning his elementary education with private tutors. In 1752, when he was about 9 years old, the family returned to Shadwell. His father died 5 years later and bequeathed him almost 3,000 acres.

In 1760, at the age of 17, Jefferson matriculated at the College of William and Mary, in Williamsburg. An incidental benefit was the chance to observe the operation of practical politics in the colonial capital. Jefferson graduated in 1762, studied law locally under the noted teacher George Wythe, and in 1767 was admitted to the bar.

At Shadwell, Jefferson assumed the civic responsibilities and prominence his father had enjoyed. In 1770, when fire consumed the structure, he moved to his nearby estate Monticello, where he had already begun building a home. In 1772 he married Martha Wayles Skelton, a widow. During their decade of life together, she was to bear six children, but only two daughters reached maturity.

Meanwhile, in 1769 at the age of 26, Jefferson had been elected to the House of Burgesses in Williamsburg. He was a member continuously until 1775, and alined himself with the anti-British group. Unlike his smooth-tongued confreres Patrick Henry and Richard Henry Lee, Jefferson concentrated his efforts in committee work rather than in debate. A literary stylist, he drafted many of the Revolutionary documents adopted by the House of Burgesses. His *A Summary View of the Rights of British America* (1774), one of the most influential essays of the era, disavowed parliamentary control of the Colonies and contended that they were tied to the King only by their own volition and recognition of mutual benefits.

Jefferson utilized the same working methods in the Continental Congress (1775-76), where his decisiveness in committee contrasted

A

SUMMARY VIEW

OF THE

RIGHTS

OF

BRITISH AMERICA.

SET FORTH IN SOME

RESOLUTIONS

INTENDED FOR THE

INSPECTION

OF THE PRESENT

DELEGATES

· OF THE

PEOPLE OF VIRGINIA.

NOW IN

CONVENTION.

BY A NATIVE, AND MEMBER OF THE HOUSE OF BURGESSES.

by Thomas Jefferson.

WILLIAMSBURG:
PRINTED BY CLEMENTINA RIND.

Title page of Thomas Jefferson's pamphlet *A Summary View* (1774), one of the earliest and most influential Revolutionary tracts.

markedly with his silence on the floor. His colleagues, however, rejected several of the documents he drafted his first year because of
their extreme anti-British tone. But, by the time he returned the
following May, after spending the winter in Virginia, the temper of
Congress had changed drastically. The very next month, though
only 33 years old, he was assigned to the five-man committee chosen
to draft the Declaration of Independence, a task his colleagues
assigned to him. In September, not long after Congress had adopted
the draft with modifications and most of the Delegates signed it,
Jefferson returned to Virginia—anxious to be nearer home and
feeling he could make a deeper political mark there.

A notable career in the House of Delegates (1776-79), the lower
house of the legislature, followed. There Jefferson took over leadership of the "progressive" party from Patrick Henry, who relinquished
it to become Governor. Highlights of this service included revision
of the State laws (1776-79), in which Jefferson collaborated with
George Wythe and Edmund Pendleton; and authorship of a bill for
the establishment of religious freedom in Virginia, introduced in
1779 but not passed until 7 years later.

Although hampered as Governor (1779-81) by wartime conditions
and constitutional limitations, Jefferson proved to be a weak executive, even in emergencies hesitating to wield his authority. When
the British invaded the State in the spring of 1781, the situation
became chaotic. On June 3, while the legislature was meeting in
Charlottesville because the redcoats held Richmond, Jefferson
recommended the combining of civil and military agencies under
Gen. Thomas Nelson, Jr., and virtually abdicated office. The next
day, British raiders almost captured him and a group of legislators
he was entertaining at Monticello. Although later formally vindicated
for his abandonment of the governorship, the action fostered a conservative takeover of the government and his reputation remained
clouded for some time.

Jefferson stayed out of the limelight for 2 years, during which
time his wife died. In 1783 he reentered Congress, which the next
year sent him to Paris to aid Benjamin Franklin and John Adams
in their attempts to negotiate commercial treaties with European
nations. During his 5-year stay, Jefferson succeeded Franklin as
Minister to France (1785-89), gained various commercial conces-
sions from and strengthened relations with the French, visited

The University of Virginia in 1826, the year of the death of founder Jefferson.

England and Italy, absorbed European culture, and observed the beginnings of the French Revolution.

In the years that followed, interspersed with pleasant interludes at Monticello, Jefferson filled the highest offices in the land: Secretary of State (1790-93), Vice President (1797-1801), and two-term President (1801-9). Ever averse to political strife, he occupied these positions as much out of a sense of civic and party duty as personal ambition. Aggravating normal burdens and pressures were his bitter feuds with Alexander Hamilton on most aspects of national policy, and the vindictiveness of Federalist attacks. Jefferson took considerable satisfaction, however, from his many accomplishments. Among these was the cofounding with James Madison of the Democratic-Republican Party, which in time drove the Federalists out of power.

Physically and mentally exhausted, in 1809 Jefferson retired for the final time to Monticello. He retained his health and varied interests and corresponded with and entertained statesmen, politicians, scientists, explorers, scholars, and Indian chiefs. When the pace of life grew too hectic, he found haven at Poplar Forest, a retreat near Lynchburg he had designed and built in 1806-19. His pet project during most of his last decade was founding the University of Virginia (1819), in Charlottesville.

Painfully distressing to Jefferson, however, was the woeful state of his finances. His small salary in public office, the attendant neglect of his fortune and estate, general economic conditions, and debts he inherited from his wife had taken a heavy toll. He lived more frugally than was his custom in an attempt to stave off disaster and sold off as many of his lands and slaves as he could. But when a friend defaulted on a note for a large sum, Jefferson fell hopelessly into debt and was forced to sell his library to the Government. It became the nucleus of the Library of Congress.

Jefferson died only a few hours before John Adams at the age of 83 on July 4, 1826, the fiftieth anniversary of the adoption of the Declaration of Independence. For his tombstone at Monticello, ignoring his many high offices and multitudes of other achievements, he chose three accomplishments that he wanted to be remembered for: authorship of the Declaration of Independence and the Virginia Statute for Religious Freedom and the founding of the University of Virginia.

Francis Lightfoot Lee
VIRGINIA

No less a patriot than his dynamic elder brother Richard Henry and his gifted younger brothers Arthur and William, Francis Lightfoot Lee preferred the uneventful life of a country squire to the public spotlight and chose to follow rather than to lead. Despite his shyness and weakness as a speaker, he exercised extensive political influence, took an active part in the Revolution, and signed both the Declaration and the Articles of Confederation.

Lee, a member of one of the most famous families in Virginia and U.S. history and the sixth son and eighth child of planter Thomas Lee, was born in 1734 at the family estate, Stratford Hall, in Westmoreland County, Va. He was educated by a private tutor and never attended college. In 1750, upon the death of his father, he inherited Coton, an estate in Fairfax County. Seven years later, newly created Loudoun County absorbed Coton. At that time, the colonial legislature nominated him as Loudoun lieutenant. The next year, he moved to Coton and became trustee of the newly incorporated village of Leesburg, named after him or his brother Philip Ludwell, both local landowners. For the next decade, Francis Lightfoot represented the county in the House of Burgesses.

In 1769 Lee married socialite Rebecca Tayloe of Richmond County. The newlyweds resided at Mount Airy estate with Rebecca's parents for a few months until Menokin, a new home that Colonel Tayloe was building nearby for them, was completed. From then until 1774, Lee sat again with the burgesses.

Lee had joined the Revolutionary movement at an early date. From the time of the Stamp Act (1765) until the outbreak of war a decade later, he participated in most of the Virginia protests and assemblies. He rarely debated on the floor in Congress (1775-79), but often opposed the position of his brother Richard Henry, and served on the military and marine committees as well as that charged with drafting the Articles of Confederation.

In 1779, weary of office and longing for the peace and quiet of Menokin, Lee left Congress. Except for a few years in the State legislature, he abandoned public service altogether and lived quietly. In 1797, only a few months after the death of his childless wife, at the age of 62 he succumbed. Burial took place in the Tayloe family graveyard at Mount Airy.

Richard Henry Lee
VIRGINIA

Richard Henry Lee, brilliant orator and fiery Revolutionary leader, introduced the independence resolution in the Continental Congress, served for awhile as its President, and later became a U.S. Senator. Fearing undue centralization of power, he fought against the Constitution and led the campaign that brought inclusion of the Bill of Rights. Throughout his life, he strenuously opposed the institution of slavery. He and Francis Lightfoot Lee were the only brothers among the signers.

Fifth son and seventh of 11 children, Lee was born in 1732 along the Potomac shore at Stratford Hall. His initial tutorial education was supplemented by extensive study at Wakefield Academy, in Yorkshire, England, and a tour of northern Europe. He sailed home about 1751 at the age of 19, the year after his father's death, and resided with his eldest brother Philip Ludwell at Stratford Hall. In 1757 Richard Henry married. About this time, he began building and soon occupied Chantilly, about 3 miles to the east on land leased from his brother. In 1768 Richard Henry's wife died, leaving four children; the next year, he remarried, a union that yielded five more offspring.

Lee meantime, following family tradition, had committed himself to politics. In 1757, at the age of 25, he became justice of the peace for Westmoreland County. The following year, he moved up to the House of Burgesses and sat there until 1775. One of the first to oppose Britain, he early allied with Patrick Henry. As a protest against the Stamp Act (1765), Lee drew up the Westmoreland Association (1766), a nonimportation agreement signed by some of the citizens of his county. The next year, he denounced the Townshend Acts. And a year later he proposed in a letter to John Dickinson of Pennsylvania that the individual colonies set up committees to correspond with each other—an idea that did not come to fruition for 5 years.

In 1769, when Lee and Henry penned an address to the King protesting several actions of Parliament, the Royal Governor disbanded the House of Burgesses. Lee thereupon met with other patriots at Raleigh's Tavern and helped frame the Virginia Association, a nonimportation agreement. Many other colonies formed similar associations, but in 1770 Parliament repealed most of the duties and the protest spirit subsided.

In March 1773, when anti-British feeling flared once again, Lee, Henry, and Jefferson, who had entered the House of Burgesses in 1769, organized a Virginia committee of correspondence and invited the other colonies to do likewise. Learning of the British closing of Boston Harbor in May 1774, they persuaded their colleagues to declare, as a protest, a day of fasting and prayer. The Royal Governor again dissolved the burgesses. The Revolutionaries reconvened at Raleigh's Tavern, drew up a new nonimportation agreement, and resolved to appeal to the other colonies for an intercolonial congress. But, before such action could be taken, Virginia received an invitation from Massachusetts to send representatives to a congress to be held in September at Philadelphia—the First Continental Congress. Virginia's first provincial assembly met in August and designated seven Delegates, including Lee and Henry.

Lee's outstanding congressional act was the introduction on June 7, 1776, of the resolution for independence from Britain, seconded by John Adams. This document, Lee's condensed redraft of one forwarded him by a convention that had met in Williamsburg on May 15, proposed severing relations with Britain, the forming of foreign alliances, and preparation of a plan for confederation. On June 13, or 2 days after a committee was appointed to draft the Declaration, Lee journeyed back to Virginia, apparently because of illness in the family. He did not return and sign the Declaration until sometime subsequent to the formal ceremony on August 2. Like his brother Francis Lightfoot, in 1777 he also subscribed to the

Articles of Confederation. After 1776, however, his influence in Congress waned, and 3 years later ill health forced his resignation.

As a State legislator (1780-84) Lee joined the conservative faction, which represented the interests of the large planters. A Member of Congress again in the period 1784-89, he served in 1784-85 as its President. In 1787, though elected to the Constitutional Convention, he refused to attend and led congressional opposition to the Constitution, especially because of the absence of a bill of rights. Although he was well aware of the deficiencies of the Articles of Confederation, he and others feared a stronger Central Government. Lee's "Letters of the Federal Farmer to the Republican," the collective title for two pamphlets outlining his objections to the Constitution, epitomized antifederalist sentiment.

In 1789 Lee entered the U.S. Senate, but because of failing health resigned in 1792, the year after the Bill of Rights was incorporated into the Constitution. He died in 1794, aged 62, at Chantilly. His grave is in the Lee family cemetery near Hague, Virginia.

Francis Lewis
NEW YORK

Few other signers felt the tragedy of the War for Independence more directly than Francis Lewis, whose wife died as a result of British imprisonment. To further the cause, he also expended a considerable portion of the fortune he had acquired as a merchant.

Lewis was the only child of a minister. He was born in 1713 at Llandaff, Glamorganshire, Wales. Orphaned at an early age and raised by relatives, he studied at Westminster School in London and then took employment with a local firm. In 1738, deciding to go into business for himself, he set up branches in New York and Philadelphia and for a few years shuttled between those cities and northern European ports. In 1745 he married a New York girl, his partner's sister.

During the French and Indian War, in 1756, while functioning as a clothing contractor for British troops at Fort Oswego, in present New York, Lewis was taken captive and sent to France for imprisonment. Upon his release, apparently in 1763, as a recompense the British Government awarded him a large land grant in America. He returned to New York City, reentered business, and quickly earned a fortune. In 1765 he retired to the village of Whitestone (now part of Flushing), on Long Island, but in 1771 he temporarily returned to New York City to help his son enter the business world, even probably making a voyage to England with him.

Back home, Lewis devoted most of his energies to the Revolutionary movement, which he had joined in 1765 by attending the Stamp Act Congress. He was also likely one of the leaders of the New York Sons of Liberty. In 1774 he became a member of the New York Revolutionary committees of fifty-one and sixty, the next year attended the provincial convention, and subsequently helped set up the State government.

In the Continental Congress (1775-79), Lewis rarely took the floor but served on the marine, foreign affairs, and commerce committees, as well as sitting on the Board of Admiralty and engaging in troop supply matters. He defended Gen. George Washington from the attacks of the Conway Cabal. Because of Tory dominance in New York, Lewis and the other Delegates were instructed not to vote for independence on July 1 and 2, 1776, but Lewis signed the Declaration on August 2.

That same year, when the British invaded Long Island, they destroyed Lewis' home in Whitestone and took his wife into custody. She was eventually released in an exchange for wives of British officials, but the hardships she had endured ruined her health and brought about her death in 1779. The grief-stricken Lewis immediately left Congress, but remained on the Board of Admiralty until

1781, at which time he abandoned politics altogether. He lived in retirement with his sons, and died in 1802 at the age of 89 in New York City. He was buried there in an unmarked grave in the yard of Trinity Church.

Philip Livingston
NEW YORK

A member of the landed gentry, merchant Philip Livingston lived a princely life and devoted much energy to civic affairs and philanthropic enterprises. He was a conservative in politics, and at first opposed independence. On the other hand, despite wartime business reverses, he contributed generously to the Revolutionary effort and continued in public service until the day he died.

Livingston was the fifth son of Philip Livingston, second lord of Livingston Manor, of Scotch descent, and Catherine Van Brugh, of Dutch lineage. Young Livingston was born in 1716 at his father's townhouse in Albany and spent most of his childhood there or at the family manor at Linlithgo, about 30 miles to the south.

Upon receiving a degree from Yale in 1737, Livingston entered the import business in New York City. Three years later, he mar-

The Brooklyn home of Philip Livingston from 1764 until his death in 1778. When the British occupied New York, they used it as a hospital. In 1811 fire destroyed it.

ried and moved into a townhouse on Duke Street in Manhattan; he was to sire five sons and four daughters. As time went on, he built up a fortune, particularly as a trader-privateer during the French and Indian War (1754-63). In 1764, though retaining his Duke Street home, he acquired a 40-acre estate on Brooklyn Heights overlooking the East River and New York Harbor.

While prospering as a merchant, Livingston devoted many of his energies to humanitarian and philanthropic endeavors. Among the organizations he fostered, financially aided, or helped administer were King's College (later Columbia University), the New York Society Library, St. Andrew's Society, the New York Chamber of Commerce, and New York Hospital.

Livingston was also a proponent of political and religious freedom. As a New York City alderman (1754-63), he identified with the popular party that opposed the aristocratic ruling class of the colony. In a decade of service (1759-69) in the colonial legislature, he stood behind the Whigs in their quarrel with the Royal Governor and attended the Stamp Act Congress in 1765. But, a believer in the sort of dignified protests mounted by lawyers and merchants, he resented the riotous behavior of such groups as the Sons of Liberty.

In the 1769 elections the Tories gained control of the legislature. In his bid for reelection, Livingston, fearful of the rise of extremism among the populace, attempted to unite the moderate factions. Defeated in New York City, which from then on was Tory-dominated, he managed to obtain reelection from the Livingston Manor district. The new assembly, claiming he could not represent an area in which he did not reside, unseated him.

In 1774 Livingston became a member of the committee of fifty-one, an extralegal group that selected New York City Delegates to the Continental Congress, one of whom was Livingston. He also served on the committee of sixty, formed to enforce congressional enactments. The next year, he won election to the committee of one hundred, which governed New York City temporarily until the first provincial congress of the colony met later that year.

Between 1774 and 1778 Livingston divided his time between the Continental Congress and the New York provincial assembly/legislature. In Congress he sat on committees dealing with marine, commerce, finance, military, and Indian matters. He was absent on July 1-2, 1776, perhaps on purpose even though the New York Delegates abstained from voting on the independence issue, but on August 2 he signed the Declaration.

After their defeat in the Battle of Long Island (August 27, 1776), Washington and his officers met at Livingston's residence in Brooklyn Heights and decided to evacuate the island. Subsequent to the ill-fated peace negotiations at Staten Island in September between Admiral Lord Richard Howe and three representatives of the Continental Congress, the British occupied New York City. They utilized Livingston's Duke Street home as a barracks and his Brooklyn Heights residence as a Royal Navy hospital, as well as confiscating his business interests. He later sold some of his remaining property to sustain public credit. With the advance of the British, Livingston and his family had fled to Esopus (later Kingston), N.Y., where the State capital was temporarily located before moving to nearby Poughkeepsie.

Livingston passed away at the age of 62 in 1778, the third earliest signer to die (after John Morton and Button Gwinnett). At the time, though in poor health, he was still in Congress, then meeting at York, Pa. He is buried in Prospect Hill Cemetery in that city.

Thomas Lynch, Jr.
SOUTH CAROLINA

Like two of the three other South Carolina signers, Heyward and Middleton, Thomas Lynch, Jr., was an aristocratic planter. But, despite his wealth and social position, he experienced one of the most tragic lives of all the signers. He was stricken by illness in the midst of his political and military labors for his State, never fully recovered his health, and perished at sea in his 30th year. He died at a younger age than any other signer, though a couple succumbed at an earlier date. He was also the second youngest in the group, next to fellow South Carolinian Edward Rutledge.

The only son of Thomas Lynch, Sr., a rich rice planter, Lynch was born in 1749 at Hopsewee Plantation, located at Winyaw on the North Santee River in Prince George's Parish (present Georgetown County), S.C. After attending the Indigo Society School at nearby Georgetown, from 1764 until 1772 he studied abroad at Eton and Cambridge and read law in London. Upon his return home, deciding not to engage in the law, he married and settled at Peach Tree Plantation. A gift from his father, it was situated in St. James Parish (present Charleston County) on the South Santee River about 4 miles south of Hopsewee.

As the heir of one of the most fervent Revolutionaries and influential men in the colony, Lynch naturally took a deep interest in politics and enjoyed strong support from the electorate. During the years 1774-76, while his father served in the Continental Congress, he labored on the home front, attending the first and second provincial congresses as well as the first State legislature and sitting on the State constitutional committee.

In 1775, however, fate dealt Lynch a cruel blow. He accepted a captaincy in the First South Carolina Regiment of Continentals—to the dismay of his father who had hoped to use his position to obtain a higher rank for him. On a recruiting trip to North Carolina, young

Lynch contracted bilious fever. This ended his military days and rendered him a partial invalid for his few remaining years.

Early in 1776 at Philadelphia the elder Lynch suffered a stroke that virtually incapacitated him for further public service. In the spring, his concerned colleagues in South Carolina elected his son to the Continental Congress, probably so that he could care for his father and act officially on his behalf. Although ill himself, Lynch made the onerous trip to Philadelphia. He stayed there throughout the summer, long enough to vote for and sign, at the age of 27, the Declaration of Independence. His father was unable to take part in the ceremony. The two were the only father-son team that served concurrently in the Continental Congress.

By the end of the year, the failing health of both men compelled them to start homeward. En route, at Annapolis, Md., a second stroke took the life of the senior Lynch. His son, broken in spirit and physically unable to continue in politics, retired to Peach Tree. Late in 1779 he and his wife, heading for southern France in an attempt to regain his health, boarded a ship bound for the West Indies that foundered. The couple died childless.

Thomas McKean
DELAWARE

Lawyer-jurist Thomas McKean stands out from the other signers in a variety of ways. He was the last to pen his signature to the Declaration, sometime after January 18, 1777. Although many Delegates simultaneously took part in State affairs, none did so as extensively as McKean—and he figured prominently in not one but two States, Delaware and Pennsylvania. He was also the only signer to be the chief executive of and concurrent officeholder in two States. Furthermore, he numbered among those who also subscribed to the Articles of Confederation, and he served a long tour in Congress.

Of Scotch-Irish ancestry, McKean was born in 1734. He was the second son of a farmer-tavernkeeper who lived in New London Township, in Chester County, Pa., near the New Jersey and Delaware boundaries. After studying for 7 years at Rev. Francis Alison's academy at nearby New London, McKean read law with a cousin at New Castle, Del. In 1754, at the age of 20, he was admitted to the Delaware bar and soon expanded his practice into Pennsylvania and New Jersey.

During the next two and a half decades, McKean occupied an array of appointive and elective offices in Delaware, some simultaneously: high sheriff of Kent County; militia captain; trustee of the loan office of New Castle County; customs collector and judge at New Castle; deputy attorney general of Sussex County; chief notary officer for the province; and clerk (1757-59) and member (1762-79) of the legislature, including the speakership of the lower house (1772-73). In 1762, he had also helped compile the colony's laws.

McKean's Revolutionary tendencies had first revealed themselves during the Stamp Act (1765) controversy. He was one of the most vociferous of the delegates at the Stamp Act Congress. In 1774, a year after the death of his wife, whom he had wed in 1763, he remarried and established his home in Philadelphia. He nevertheless retained membership in the Delaware legislature, which that same year elected him to the Continental Congress. Except for the period December 1776-January 1778, when conservative opposition unseated him, he stayed there until 1783 and served as President for a few months in 1781. He played a key role in the Revolutionary program, at the same time fostering the establishment of governments in Delaware and Pennsylvania.

Furthermore, it was McKean who was responsible for breaking the Delaware tie in the congressional vote for independence. On July 1, 1776, date of the first vote, the two Delaware representatives present, McKean and George Read, deadlocked. McKean, who had balloted affirmatively, dispatched an urgent message to the third Delegate, Caesar Rodney, who was at his home near Dover, Del., on military matters, to rush to Philadelphia. Rodney, making an 80-mile horseback ride through a storm, arrived just in time to swing Delaware over to independence on July 2.

During the hiatus in his congressional career, from late 1776 until early in 1778, McKean had remained in the lower house of the

Delaware legislature, of which he became speaker once again. In that capacity, in September-November 1777, he temporarily replaced the president of Delaware, whom the British had captured. In vain they also pursued McKean, who was forced to move his family several times. Meantime, in July, he had been appointed chief justice of the Pennsylvania Superior Court, a position he was to hold for 22 years.

After 1783, when his congressional service ended, McKean focused his political activities in Pennsylvania. As a Federalist, in 1787 he was instrumental in that State's ratification of the U.S. Constitution. In the State constitutional convention of 1789-90 he demonstrated mistrust of popular government. During the 1790's, disenchanted with Federalist foreign policy, he switched to the Democratic-Republicans.

While Governor for three terms (1799-1808), McKean was the storm center of violent partisan warfare. Although he exercised strong leadership and advanced education and internal improvements, his imperiousness infuriated the Federalists, alienated many members of his own party, and resulted in an attempt to impeach him. Especially controversial were his rigid employment of the spoils system, including the appointment of friends and relatives, and his refusal to call a convention to revise the constitution. As a result, he won reelection only with the support of members of both parties who opposed the revision.

McKean lived out his life quietly in Philadelphia. He died in 1817 at the age of 83, survived by his second wife and four of the 11 children from his two marriages. He was buried in Laurel Hill Cemetery. His substantial estate consisted of stocks, bonds, and huge tracts of land in Pennsylvania.

Arthur Middleton
SOUTH CAROLINA

Despite long years of study in England, exceptional wealth, and social eminence, Arthur Middleton evolved into an avid Revolutionary. Because of preoccupation with State matters, particularly military defense, his attendance in Congress was spasmodic. The British captured him during their attack on Charleston and ravished his estate.

Middleton was born in 1742 at Middleton Place, the family estate on the Ashley River near Charleston. His father, who owned a score of plantations comprising 50,000 acres and employing some 800 slaves, ranked among the wealthiest and most politically active men in the province. While still a young boy, Arthur sailed to England for an education. He attended Hackney School, graduated from Cambridge University, and studied law in London. In 1764, the year after his return, he wed the woman who was to bear him nine children, and embarked on a career as justice of the peace and colonial legislator. In the years 1768-71, however, he and his wife made an extended tour of Europe.

Reelected the next year to the legislature, Middleton joined the Revolutionaries in their campaign against the Royal Governor. While sitting in the first and second provincial assemblies (1775-76), Middleton aided in organizing a night raid on public arms stores at Charleston before the Governor could seize them, raised money for armed resistance, recommended defense measures for Charleston Harbor, served on the council of safety, and urged tight enforcement of the Continental Association. An extremist, he advocated the tarring and feathering of Loyalists and confiscation of the estates of those who had fled the country.

In 1776, while engaged in helping draft a State constitution, Middleton was chosen to replace his more conservative father in the Continental Congress. Two years later, when young Middleton declined reelection, he also rejected an offer of the governorship of South Carolina by the legislature, which had enacted a new constitution that he opposed. In 1779 and 1780, though reelected to the Continental Congress, Middleton failed to attend, probably because of concern over the British threat to his State. While serving in the militia during the siege of Charleston in 1780, along with fellow signers Heyward and Rutledge he was captured by the British and imprisoned at St. Augustine, Fla., until July 1781.

Two months later, Middleton returned to Congress and served throughout 1782. He then retired to Middleton Place, which had been ravaged by the British. He rehabilitated it, resumed his life as a planter, sat intermittently in the State legislature, and accepted assignment as one of the original trustees of the College of Charleston. He died in 1787 at the age of 44. His remains rest at Middleton Place.

Lewis Morris
NEW YORK

Although Lewis Morris was a wealthy landowner who enjoyed the prestige of the social elite, he represented the patriot element in Tory-dominated New York. The British sacked his estate during the war, and his three eldest sons fought under Washington.

Born in 1726, Morris was the eldest son of the second lord of the vast manor of Morrisania, in Westchester (present Bronx) County, N.Y. Upon graduating from Yale College in 1746, he helped manage the estate. Three years later, he married, siring 10 children. In 1762, when his father died, he inherited Morrisania and became its third lord. About this time, he gained an interest in local politics, and in 1769 served a term in the colonial legislature.

As time went on, though residing in a pro-Loyalist county, Morris became increasingly critical of British policy. In 1775 he helped organize a meeting at White Plains that overcame strong opposition and chose county delegates, including Morris as chairman, to New York's first provincial convention. It elected him to the Continental Congress (1775-77), where he specialized in military and Indian affairs. For most of 1776, he was absent from Philadelphia, serving as a brigadier general in the Westchester County militia. During the British invasion of New York that year, the redcoats ravaged Morrisania, and forced Morris' family to flee.

When his career in Congress ended, Morris rose to the rank of major general in the militia and became a county judge (1777-78) and State senator (1777-81 and 1784-88). After war's end in 1783, when he was able to return to Morrisania, he devoted much of his time to rehabilitating it. In 1784 he sat on the first board of regents of the University of New York. And 4 years later, at the State ratifying convention in Poughkeepsie, he strongly supported Alexander Hamilton's successful drive for approval of the U.S. Constitution.

Morris died in 1798 at Morrisania at the age of 71. His grave is in the family vault in the yard of St. Ann's Church in the Bronx.

Robert Morris
PENNSYLVANIA

Merchant Robert Morris was a man of many distinctions. One of the wealthiest individuals in the Colonies and an economic wizard, he won the accolade "Financier of the Revolution," yet died penniless and forgotten. He and Roger Sherman were the only signers of all three of the Nation's basic documents: the Declaration of Independence, Articles of Confederation, and Constitution. Morris, who turned down appointment as the first Secretary of the Treasury, also served as a Senator in the First Congress.

Morris was born in or near Liverpool, England, in 1734. At the age of 13, he emigrated to Maryland to join his father, a tobacco exporter at Oxford, Md. After brief schooling at Philadelphia, the youth obtained employment with Thomas and Charles Willing's well-known shipping firm. In 1754 he became a partner, and for almost four decades was one of the company's directors as well as one of Philadelphia's most influential citizens. Marrying in 1769 at the age of 35, he fathered five sons and two daughters.

During the Stamp Act turmoil in 1765, Morris had joined other merchants in protest, but not until the outbreak of hostilities a decade hence did he fully commit himself to the Revolution. In 1775 the Continental Congress contracted with his firm to import arms and ammunition; and he was elected to the Pennsylvania council of safety (1775-76), the committee of correspondence, the provincial assembly (1775-76), the State legislature (1776-78), and the Continental Congress (1775-78). In the latter body, on July 1, 1776, he voted against independence, which he personally considered premature, but the next day purposely absented himself to facilitate an affirmative ballot by his State.

Morris, a key Member of Congress, specialized in financial affairs and military procurement. Although he and his firm profited hand-

In 1794 Robert Morris began building this palatial townhouse in Philadelphia. After his imprisonment for debt in 1798, the unfinished house came to be known as "Morris' Folly." It stood until 1800.

somely, had it not been for his assiduous labors the Continental Army would probably have needed to demobilize. He worked closely with General Washington, wheedled money and supplies from the States, borrowed money in the face of overwhelming difficulties, and on occasion even obtained personal loans to further the war cause. Immediately following his congressional service, Morris sat for two more terms in the Pennsylvania legislature in the period 1778-81. During this time, Thomas Paine and others attacked him for profiteering in Congress, which investigated his accounts and vindicated him. Nevertheless, his reputation slipped.

Morris embarked on the most dramatic phase of his career by accepting the office of Superintendent of Finance (1781-84) under the Articles of Confederation. Congress, recognizing the perilous state of the Nation's finances and its impotence to remedy it, granted him dictatorial powers and acquiesced to his condition that he be allowed to continue his private commercial enterprises. He slashed all governmental and military expenditures, personally purchased Army and Navy supplies, tightened accounting procedures, prodded the States to fulfill quotas of money and supplies, and when necessary strained his personal credit by issuing notes over his own signature or borrowing from friends.

To finance Washington's Yorktown campaign in 1781, in addition to the above techniques Morris obtained a sizable loan from France. He used part of it, along with some of his own fortune, to organize the Bank of North America, chartered that December. The first Government-incorporated bank in the United States, it aided war financing.

Although Morris was reelected to the Pennsylvania legislature in 1785-86, his private commercial ventures consumed most of his time. In the latter year, he attended the Annapolis Convention, and the following year the Constitutional Convention, where he sympathized with the Federalists. In 1789, declining Washington's offer of appointment as the first Secretary of the Treasury, he took instead a senatorial seat in Congress (1789-95).

During the later years of his public life, Morris speculated wildly, often on overextended credit, in lands in the West and at the site of Washington, D.C. To compound his difficulties, in 1794 he began constructing on Philadelphia's Chestnut Street a palatial townhouse designed by Maj. Pierre Charles L'Enfant. Not long thereafter, Morris attempted to escape creditors by retreating to The Hills, the country estate along the Schuylkill River on the edge of Philadelphia that he had acquired in 1770.

Arrested at the behest of creditors in 1798 and forced to abandon completion of the townhouse, henceforth known in its unfinished state as "Morris' Folly," Morris was thrown into the Philadelphia debtors' prison, where he was well treated. Nevertheless, by the time he was released in 1801, under a Federal bankruptcy law, his property and fortune had vanished, his health deteriorated, and his spirit been broken. He lingered on amid poverty and obscurity, living in a simple Philadelphia home on an annuity Gouverneur Morris had obtained for his wife. He died in 1806 in his 72d year. He was buried in the yard of Christ Church.

John Morton
PENNSYLVANIA

John Morton, one of the nine signers from Pennsylvania, is better known there than in the Nation, but he rendered meritorious service to both. He cast the decisive ballot that swung his State over to an affirmative vote for independence in the Continental Congress. He was the first signer to die.

Morton was born of Finnish-Swedish descent in 1725, shortly after the death of his father, on a farm in Ridley Township, Chester (present Delaware) County. John Sketchley, an Englishman who subsequently married the widowed mother of the youth, reared and educated him. Their relationship was apparently close, for Morton later named his eldest son Sketchley. The stepfather, learned in mathematics, taught the boy the three R's as well as surveying. He practiced that profession on and off all his life, as well as farming, politics, and jurisprudence. He married in his early 20's, in 1748 or 1749, and fathered five daughters and four sons.

At the age of 30, Morton entered politics, which from then on absorbed most of his energies. From 1756 until a few months before he died in 1777, he served 18 terms in the colonial/State legislature (1756-66 and 1769-76), which he presided over during the last year and a half. In 1774 he won appointment as an associate justice of the Pennsylvania Supreme Court.

Meantime, despite his rise in State circles, Morton had always maintained strong ties with his own county. He resided there all his life, remained active in civic and church affairs, and stayed close to the people. Between terms of office as county justice of the peace (1757-64 and 1770-74), he worked in a tour as sheriff (1766-69).

Morton's service to the Nation began in 1765, while he was a member of the Pennsylvania legislature. He and two colleagues represented the colony at the Stamp Act Congress in New York. His most dramatic act as Delegate to the Continental Congress (1774-77), in which he numbered among the moderates, was his sudden and crucial switch on July 1, 1776, to the side of his friend Benjamin Franklin and James Wilson in the vote for national independence. On the final vote the next day, these three ballots outweighed those of Thomas Willing and Charles Humphreys. Robert Morris and John Dickinson being purposely absent, Pennsylvania registered a "yea." Less glamorously, Morton was a member of many committees, in 1777 chairing the committee of the whole on the adoption of the Articles of Confederation, finally ratified after his death.

Within a year of signing the Declaration, in the spring of 1777, Morton fell ill and died on his farm at the age of 51. A few months earlier, he had bequeathed his land and property, including a few slaves, to his wife and five daughters and three surviving sons. But he could not will them security; shortly after his demise they had to flee from their home in the face of an imminent British attack. Morton's grave is located in Old St. Paul's Cemetery in Chester, Pa.

Thomas Nelson, Jr.
VIRGINIA

Thomas Nelson, Jr., a rich planter-merchant who at one time owned more than 400 slaves, was one of the most active of the Virginia patriots. Mainly because of health problems, however, his career in Congress was brief and undistinguished, though he made great financial sacrifices during the war and won fame as a militia commander and State politician.

The eldest of five sons, Nelson was born at Yorktown, Va., in 1738. At the age of 14, he sailed to England to supplement his initial tutorial education. In 1761, after graduating from Hackney School and Cambridge University, he returned to Virginia to help his father manage his plantation and mercantile business. The next year, young Nelson married; he and his wife were to have 11 children.

In 1764 Nelson became a justice of the peace for York County and entered the House of Burgesses. He served in the house until May 1774, when Royal Governor Lord Dunmore, provoked at its protests over the Boston Port Act, dissolved it. That year and the next, Nelson attended three of the Virginia provincial assemblies, where he worked closely with Patrick Henry. The last assembly elected Nelson to the Continental Congress, at which time he resigned his colonelcy in the Virginia militia.

In Congress, Nelson was outspoken in his desire to sever the bonds with England. He journeyed to Virginia in the spring of 1776. At a convention held in Williamsburg in May, he introduced and won approval for a resolution recommending national independence, drafted by Edmund Pendleton. Nelson carried it to Philadelphia and presented it to Richard Henry Lee, who redrafted and condensed it into his June 7 resolution. Not long afterward, Nelson's health began to decline. Subsequently, he divided his time between Philadelphia and Virginia, and in the spring of 1777 resigned from Congress.

Back in Virginia, Nelson was awarded the rank of brigadier general in the militia and was elected to the lower house of the legislature. In the spring of 1778 Congress appealed to men of means in the Colonies to form troops of light cavalry. Nelson, partially at his own expense, raised, outfitted, and trained such a unit. In July he marched it northward to Philadelphia. The next month, Congress decided it was not needed and it returned home.

Nelson served in Congress again for a short time in 1779, but poor health forced him to retire once more. Nevertheless, the next year he obtained munitions and supplies for the militia, commanded troops, attended the legislature, and raised money to help subsidize the war. He was particularly effective in soliciting funds from wealthy plantation owners, to whom he pledged to repay the loans personally if the State should fail to do so.

When the British invaded Virginia in 1780-81, civilian control seriously hampered Nelson's effectiveness as a militia commander.

This painting commemorates one of the highlights of the siege of Yorktown (1781). Thomas Nelson, Jr., commander in chief of Virginia troops, took an active part.

Consequently, in the latter year the legislature elected him as Governor and granted him powers approaching those of a military dictator. Although still bothered by bad health, he kept the government intact and strengthened defenses. In September-October 1781, while taking part in the Yorktown siege, according to family tradition he ordered troops to shell his own mansion when he learned it was a British headquarters. Soon after the victory at Yorktown, overwhelmed by the burdens of office and still in poor physical condition, he resigned the governorship.

That same year, Nelson partially retired to Offley Hoo, a modest estate in Hanover County that his father had willed to him on his death in 1772. In financial distress from his wartime sacrifices, the younger Nelson lacked money to renovate his Yorktown home, where he had lived since 1767. Except for occasional tours in the legislature and visits to Yorktown, he devoted the rest of his life to his business affairs. He died at Offley Hoo in 1789 at the age of 50. His grave is at Yorktown in the yard of Grace Episcopal Church.

William Paca
MARYLAND

William Paca was one of the earliest Revolutionaries in a conservative colony. A wealthy planter and eminent lawyer and judge, he held numerous State offices, including the governorship, but his role in national affairs was limited.

The second son of a prominent planter-landowner, Paca was born, probably of Italian descent, in 1740 at Chilbury Hall, near Abingdon in Harford County, Md. He received his early education from private tutors and at the age of 15 matriculated at the College of Philadelphia (later part of the University of Pennsylvania). Upon graduating, he studied with an attorney in Annapolis and read law in London. In 1763, the year before initiating his practice in the former city, he married a local girl from a wealthy family and began building a home, completed 2 years later. When in the country, he resided at Wye Plantation, in Queen Annes County, which he had purchased about 1760.

In 1768 Paca won a seat in the colonial legislature, where he soon alined himself with Samuel Chase and other Whigs in protesting the powers of the Proprietary Governor. In the early 1770's Paca joined other Maryland patriots in urging governmental regulation of fees paid to civil officers and in opposing the poll tax, used to pay the salaries of Anglican clergy, representing the established church. In 1773 he became a member of the Maryland committee of correspondence. The following year, along with Samuel Chase and Thomas Johnson, he acted as counsel for fellow legislator Joseph H. Harrison, who had been jailed for refusing to pay the poll tax. All three men also attended the first provincial convention that same year and received appointments to the First Continental Congress. About this time, Paca's wife died.

Although he sat in Congress until 1779, Paca's most noteworthy efforts were on the State level. In the spring and early summer of 1776, the provincial convention, a relatively conservative body, refused to authorize its congressional Delegates to vote for independence. Paca, aiding Chase and Carroll, drummed up enough support on the home front to persuade the convention to change its mind and bring Maryland into the affirmative column in the congressional voting on July 1-2, 1776. A few months later, he helped draft a State constitution. The next year, he began a 2-year term in the Maryland senate and saw militia duty. In addition, he sat on the council of safety and spent large amounts of his own money outfitting troops.

Between the years 1778 and 1782, Paca distinguished himself first as chief justice of the State Superior Court and then as chief judge of the circuit court of appeals in admiralty and prize cases. During that time, in 1780, a few months after the demise of his second wife, whom he had married 3 years earlier, he sold his home in Annapolis and moved permanently to Wye Plantation. In 1782 he raised funds for Washington College, founded that same year in Chestertown as the first institution of higher learning in Maryland, and served on its board of visitors. As Governor of Maryland (1782-85), he concerned himself with the welfare of war veterans and other postwar problems.

A delegate to the State convention to ratify the Federal Constitution in 1788, Paca urged its adoption if amended and helped draw up a list of proposed amendments. In 1789 President Washington appointed him as Federal district judge. He held this position until 1799, the year of his death at the age of 58, at Wye Hall, on Wye Island across the narrows from his own home, Wye Plantation. The former was the home of his son John, probably the only one of his five children from his two or possibly three marriages who reached maturity. At first interred at Wye Hall, Paca's remains now rest in the family burial ground near Wye Plantation.

Robert Treat Paine
MASSACHUSETTS

A clergyman turned lawyer-jurist, Robert Treat Paine spent only a short time in Congress but enjoyed considerable political prestige in Massachusetts. His second son (1773-1811) and great-grandson (1835-1910), both bearing exactly the same names as he, gained fame respectively as poet and businessman-philanthropist.

Among the ancestors of Paine, who was born at Boston in 1731, were many New England religious and political leaders. His father was a merchant who had once been a clergyman. Young Paine led his class at Boston Latin School and graduated from Harvard in 1749. He then taught school for a time before yielding to family tradition and entering the ministry.

In 1755, during the French and Indian War, he served as chaplain on a military expedition to Crown Point, N.Y. To improve his health, he made a voyage to the Carolinas, England, Spain, and Greenland. About this time, he decided to forsake the ministry for the law, in which he had become interested during his theological studies. Admitted to the Massachusetts bar in 1757, he opened an office in Portland but in 1761 moved to Taunton.

Paine, a friend of John Adams and John Hancock, early became involved in the patriot movement. As a result, he was chosen in 1770 as one of the prosecuting attorneys in the Boston Massacre trial and thus gained recognition throughout the Colonies. That same year, he married, siring eight children. Between 1773 and 1778, except in 1776, he served in the Massachusetts legislature, in 1777 being speaker of the lower house. He was one of the first five Delegates sent by Massachusetts to the Continental Congress (1774-76), where he specialized in military and Indian affairs. He gained the nickname "Objection Maker" because he argued against so many proposals.

Although reelected to Congress in 1777, Paine chose to stay in Massachusetts. In addition to his legislative speakership, he was elected as the first attorney general, a position he held until 1790. Between 1778 and 1780 he played a prominent role in drafting the Massachusetts constitution. From 1790 until 1804, appointed by his old friend Hancock, he sat as an associate justice of the Superior Court.

Meantime, in 1780, Paine had moved from Taunton to Boston and become active in civic affairs. Indicative of his lifelong interest in science, that same year he was one of the founders of the American Academy of Arts and Sciences. In religion, he broke away from Calvinism and embraced Unitarianism. Politically, he alined himself with the Federalists. In 1804 increasing deafness brought about his retirement from the Superior Court, and he died a decade later at the age of 83 in Boston. He was buried in the Old Granary Burying Ground.

John Penn
NORTH CAROLINA

Like fellow signers Joseph Hewes and William Hooper, John Penn adopted North Carolina as his home. Except for a 5-year stint in the Continental Congress and a brief career in State service, he passed the years peacefully as a country lawyer far from the clamor of the public forum.

Penn was born in 1740 or 1741 in Caroline County, Va. His father was a well-to-do farmer, and his mother the daughter of a prominent county judge. Despite the family's social position, Penn received only a few years of formal schooling. At the age of 18, when his father died, he inherited a sizable estate. But he was dissatisfied with the prospects it offered, and decided to continue his education. Encouraged by a relative, Edmund Pendleton, a well-known lawyer who made available his personal library, Penn studied law on his own and within 3 years gained admittance to the bar. Soon thereafter he married; he and his wife reared three children.

In 1774, at the end of more than a decade of successful law practice in Virginia, Penn journeyed to Granville County, N.C., and made his home near Stovall. The next year, he was elected to the provincial assembly and only a few weeks later to the Continental Congress (1775-80). In 1777, upon the retirement of Hewes and Hooper, he inherited the leadership of his State's delegation. He was one of the 16 signers of the Declaration who also signed the Articles of Confederation.

Unobtrusive and unassuming but remarkably efficient, likeable, and discreet, Penn quickly won the respect of his congressional colleagues. He rarely disputed with others, but when he did his good humor and peaceful manner saved the day. On one occasion, he feuded with President of Congress Henry Laurens of South Carolina over a personal matter. He accepted Laurens' challenge to a duel, but en route to the proposed site convinced Laurens that they should bury their differences and drop the matter.

Late in 1780 the Governor of North Carolina recalled Penn from Congress to sit on the emergency Board of War, created by the legislature in September to share with the Governor responsibility for military affairs. The three-man board, of which Penn became the leading member, in effect soon assumed control of all military matters. The Governor and military officials, resenting the infringement upon their prerogatives and their loss of authority, persuaded the legislature to abolish the board in January 1781.

His health declining, the following July Penn declined an appointment to the Governor's Council. With the exception of a short tour in 1784 as State tax receiver for the Confederation, he apparently devoted his last years to his law practice. In 1788, only in his late forties, he died at his home near Stovall. Originally buried in the family graveyard adjacent to his home, his remains now rest in Guilford Courthouse National Military Park near Greensboro.

George Read
DELAWARE

Conservative lawyer George Read was the only signer who voted against independence in the final congressional vote on July 2, 1776. In addition to attaining many prominent State offices, he attended the Constitutional Convention, where he defended the rights of the smaller States, and subsequently served as a Senator in the First Congress.

Read's mother was the daughter of a Welsh planter, and his Dublin-born father a landholder of means. Soon after George's birth in 1733 near North East in Cecil County, Md., his family moved to New Castle, Del., where the youth grew up. He attended school at Chester, Pa., and Rev. Francis Alison's academy at New London, Pa., and about the age of 15 began reading law with a Philadelphia lawyer. In 1753 he was admitted to the bar and began to practice. The next year, he journeyed back to New Castle, hung out his shingle, and before long enlisted a clientele that extended into Maryland. In 1763 he wed the widowed sister of future fellow signer George Ross, and she bore him four sons and a daughter.

While crown attorney general (1763-74) for the Three Lower

Counties (present Delaware), Read protested against the Stamp Act. In 1765 he began a career in the colonial legislature that extended for more than a decade. A moderate Whig, he supported nonimportation measures and dignified protests. His attendance in Congress (1774-77) was irregular. Like his friend John Dickinson, he was willing to protect colonial rights but was wary of extremism. He balloted against independence on July 2, 1776, apparently either bowing to the strong Tory sentiment in Delaware or believing reconciliation with Britain was still possible.

That same year, Read gave priority to State responsibilities. He presided over the Delaware constitutional convention, in which he chaired the drafting committee, and began a term as speaker of the legislative council, which in effect made him vice president of the State. When the British captured Wilmington the next fall, they captured the president, a resident of the city. At first, because Read was away in Congress, Thomas McKean, speaker of the lower house, took over as acting president. But in November, after almost being captured himself while he and his family were en route to Dover from Philadelphia, newly captured by the British, Read assumed the office and held it until the spring of 1778.

During 1779, in poor health, Read resigned from the legislative council, refused reelection to Congress, and began a period of inactivity. In the years 1782-88, he again sat on the council, and concurrently held the position of judge of the court of appeals in admiralty cases. Meantime, in 1784, he had served on a commission that adjusted New York-Massachusetts land claims. In 1786 he attended the Annapolis Convention. The next year, he participated in the Constitutional Convention. He later led the ratification movement in Delaware, the first State to ratify.

In the U.S. Senate (1789-93), Read's attendance was again spasmodic, but when present he allied with the Federalists. He resigned to accept the post of chief justice of Delaware. He held this office until his death at New Castle 5 years later, just 3 days after he celebrated his 65th birthday. His grave is located there in the Immanuel Episcopal Churchyard.

Caesar Rodney
DELAWARE

Self-educated Caesar Rodney climbed to high State and National offices, but his military-political duties in Delaware spared him little time for the affairs of Congress. He is noted mainly for his emergency ride to Philadelphia that broke his State's deadlock in the vote for independence, but he was also one of two bachelor signers and the only native of the three from Delaware.

Rodney was born in 1728 on his father's 800-acre plantation, Byfield, near Dover in Kent County. In 1745, as the eldest child, he inherited the plantation. Despite a lack of formal and legal education, a decade later he accepted the first of a series of county offices: high sheriff, register of wills, recorder of deeds, clerk of the orphans' court, justice of the peace, militia captain, and cotrustee of the loan office.

On the provincial level, for most of the period 1758-76 Rodney functioned as a justice of the Superior Court for the Three Lower Counties (present Delaware) and as a legislator in the lower house, including many tours as speaker. Between 1765 and 1774, he owned and occupied a townhouse that he used while in Dover. He and Thomas McKean compiled the colony's laws, and they both attended the Stamp Act Congress (1765). Three years later, the two of them and George Read, all three later to sign the Declaration, drafted a protest to the King concerning the Townshend Acts. In 1774, after Parliament closed Boston Harbor, Rodney usurped the prerogative

of the Proprietary Governor by calling a special meeting of the legis-
lature at New Castle, the first Revolutionary convention in the State.
Rodney, McKean, and Read were sent to the First Continental
Congress.

Although a congressional Member for 2 years, Rodney was often
absent in Delaware, sometimes presiding over the legislature and
sometimes meeting military responsibilities. In May 1775 he was
elected a colonel in the militia, and in September moved up to
brigadier general. Late the next June, while the independence resolution was pending in Congress, he was investigating Loyalist agitations
in Sussex County. On the evening of July 1, after his return to
Byfield, he received McKean's dispatch pointing out that Read had
voted against independence that day and pleading with Rodney to
hurry to Philadelphia to break the tie. Riding all night through a
thunderstorm and stopping only to change horses, he completed the
80-mile trip just in time to make possible an affirmative vote for
Delaware.

This brought down the wrath of the Kent County conservatives on
Rodney, who was not reelected to Congress nor to the legislature and
not appointed to the State constitutional convention. Out of office,
that fall and the next year he turned to military affairs, recruiting
troops and taking part in minor actions in Delaware and New Jersey.
In September 1777 acting State president McKean commissioned
him as a major general.

That spring, the legislature had designated Rodney as an admiralty
judge. In December it reelected him to the Continental Congress.
The next year, it nominated him as State president (1778-81), in
which capacity he stimulated the Delaware war effort. When he left
office, he belatedly sought medical treatment in Philadelphia for a
cancerous growth on his face, which had been bothering him for a
decade and which he had covered with a green silk veil. In 1783,
though a dying man, he entered the State senate and accepted the
speakership, but passed away the next year at the age of 55. Interred
originally at Byfield Plantation, his remains are now buried in the
yard of Christ Episcopal Church in Dover.

George Ross
PENNSYLVANIA

A few of the signers, such as George Ross, were latecomers to the Revolutionary cause. Like many others, he exerted more influence in State than national affairs.

The oldest son of an Anglican clergyman who had immigrated from Scotland, Ross was born in 1730 at New Castle, Del. After a preliminary classical education, he read law with his stepbrother John at Philadelphia and in 1750 entered the bar. Settling the next year at Lancaster, Pa., where he married and fathered two sons and a daughter, he built up a successful law practice and served as crown prosecutor for Cumberland County (1751-63). A member of the colonial legislature from 1768 until 1775, he sometimes joined in its disputes with the Proprietary Governor and demonstrated an interest in Indian affairs.

Meantime, in 1774, despite his Loyalist leanings, a provincial convention to which Ross had been elected sent him to the Continental Congress. The next year, by which time he had for some reason decided to affiliate with the Revolutionaries, he also served on the Pennsylvania council of safety and held a militia colonelcy. In 1776 he assisted in negotiating a peace treaty with the Indians in northwestern Pennsylvania, and acted as vice president of the State constitutional convention, for which he helped draft a declaration of rights. Not a Member of Congress during the voting for independence on July 1-2, 1776, he received his appointment soon enough to sign the Declaration on August 2. He won a reputation among his colleagues for his eloquence, wit, and conviviality, but made no noteworthy contributions to congressional proceedings. Illness brought about his resignation in January 1777.

In 1778, while Ross was acting as admiralty judge in Pennsylvania, a congressional court of appeals overruled his decision in a case involving a dispute between a citizen of Connecticut and the State of Pennsylvania. Ross, refusing to acknowledge the authority of the higher court to counter State decisions, initiated a dispute between Pennsylvania and the Central Government that represented an early manifestation of the States rights controversy and did not subside until 1809. But Ross did not live to see the outcome, for he died in Philadelphia in 1779 at the age of 49. He was buried in Christ Church Burial Ground.

Benjamin Rush
PENNSYLVANIA

Doctor, medical educator, chemist, humanitarian, politician, author, reformer-moralist, soldier, temperance advocate, abolitionist—Benjamin Rush was all of these. One of the younger signers, only 30 years of age at the time, he was already a physician of note.

Rush, the fourth of seven children, was born in 1745 at Byberry ("The Homestead"), near Philadelphia. At the age of 5, his farmer-gunsmith father died. The youth obtained a sound education at West Nottingham Academy, in Rising Sun, Md., operated by an uncle, and graduated from the College of New Jersey (later Princeton University). Returning to Philadelphia in 1760, he apparently first considered studying law but chose medicine. In 1766, at the end of a 5-year apprenticeship to a local physician, he sailed to Scotland, where 2 years later the University of Edinburgh awarded him a medical degree.

While there, assisted by a fellow college alumnus and one-day fellow signer, Richard Stockton, Rush helped overcome the objections of John Witherspoon's wife and persuaded Witherspoon to accept the presidency of the College of New Jersey. In 1769, after further training in London, where Rush made the acquaintance of Benjamin Franklin, and a short visit to Paris, he came back to Philadelphia and set up practice. Before the year was out, he obtained the first professorship of chemistry in the country at the College of Philadelphia, and wrote the first American textbook on the subject.

While prospering as a physician, Rush cultivated the friendship of such men as Thomas Jefferson, John Adams, and Thomas Paine. In fact, Rush suggested to the latter that he write his famous tract *Common Sense* (1776), supplied the title, and aided in its publication. He also contributed political articles to the press. That same year, he married Stockton's eldest daughter, Julia.

Rush's tour in the Continental Congress was brief. In June 1776 he attended a Pennsylvania conference of patriots and helped draft a declaration of the colony's support for national independence. In recognition of these services, the following month the provincial convention sent him to Congress—after the adoption of the Declaration. In December, Philadelphia threatened by British invasion, the Government fled to Baltimore. Rush apparently, however, did not spend much time there. That same month, he relocated his wife at the home of a relative in Cecil County, Md., and took part in General Washington's New Jersey campaign as a surgeon in the Philadelphia militia.

In April 1777, not reelected to Congress because of his opposition to the Pennsylvania constitution of the previous year, Rush accepted

Benjamin Rush long served on the staff of Philadelphia's Pennsylvania Hospital, shown here in 1799. Founded in 1751 and still in use today, it is the oldest hospital in the United States.

the position of surgeon general in the Middle Department of the Continental Army. Abhorring the deplorable conditions prevailing in the medical service, in a complaint to Washington he accused his superior, Dr. William Shippen, of maladministration. Washington referred the matter to Congress, which vindicated Shippen. In January 1778 Rush angrily resigned. His subsequent criticisms of Washington and his participation in the Conway Cabal, a movement to replace General Washington, ended his military and, for a time, his political career. He resumed his medical practice in Philadelphia.

In 1787 Rush wrote tracts in the newspapers endorsing the U.S. Constitution. In the Commonwealth ratifying convention that same year, he aided James Wilson in the struggle for its adoption. In 1789-90 Rush attended the Pennsylvania constitutional convention. From 1797 until 1813 he served as Treasurer of the U.S. Mint.

Meantime Rush, through his writings and lectures, had become probably the best known physician and medical teacher in the land, and he fostered Philadelphia's ascendancy as the early medical center of the Nation. His students, who idolized him, came from as far away as Europe to attend his classes at the College of Philadelphia, and its successors the University of the State of Pennsylvania and the University of Pennsylvania (1791). He also served on the staff of the Pennsylvania Hospital from 1783 until the end of his life, helped found the Philadelphia College of Physicians (1787), and held office as first president of the Philadelphia Medical Society. In 1786 he founded the Philadelphia Dispensary, the first free medical clinic in the country. His work among the insane at the Pennsylvania Hospital resulted in *Medical Inquiries and Observations Upon the Diseases of the Mind* (1812), which to some degree foreshadowed modern psychiatric techniques.

Rush won much less favor from his professional peers than he did from his students. His critics particularly attacked his theory of bleeding and purging for the treatment of disease. Although he was one of the few doctors who remained in Philadelphia during the devastating yellow fever epidemics of 1793 and 1798, his opponents criticized his methods of treatment.

Aroused by the idealism of the Revolution as well as the plight of the poor and sick he encountered in his medical practice, Rush helped pioneer various humanitarian and social movements that were to restructure U.S. life in the 19th century. These included abolition of slavery and educational and prison reform. Rush also condemned public and capital punishment and advocated temperance. Many of his reform articles appeared in *Essays: Literary, Moral, and Philosophical* (1798).

Finally, Rush helped organize and sat as a trustee of Dickinson College (1783); aided in founding the Pennsylvania Society for Promoting the Abolition of Slavery (1787) and later served as its president; enjoyed membership in the American Philosophical Society; and was a cofounder and vice president of the Philadelphia Bible Society, which advocated the use of scripture in the public schools.

A typhus epidemic claimed Rush's life at the age of 67 in 1813. Surviving him were six sons and three daughters of the 13 children he had fathered. His grave is in Christ Church Burial Ground at Philadelphia.

Edward Rutledge
SOUTH CAROLINA

Edward Rutledge, at the age of 26, was the youngest of the signers. Despite his youth, he had already made a name for himself in South Carolina as a lawyer-politician and had assumed leadership of his congressional delegation. A moderate, he at first fought against the independence resolution but finally submitted to the majority and voted for it. His later State career, which included combat action in the militia, culminated in the governorship.

The fifth son and youngest child of an Irish immigrant and physician, Rutledge was born in 1749 at or near Charleston, S.C. Like Middleton, Lynch, and Heyward, the other South Carolina signers, as a young man he studied law in England. In 1773, during his first year of practice on his return to Charleston, he won Whig acclaim by obtaining the release of newspaper publisher Thomas Powell, who had been imprisoned by the Crown for printing an article critical of the Loyalist upper house of the colonial legislature. The next year, the grateful Whigs named Rutledge as one of five Delegates to the First Continental Congress; and he married Henrietta Middleton, his colleague's sister. The Rutledges were to have three children.

Rutledge spent his first congressional term in the shadow of the more experienced South Carolina Delegates, among them his older brother, John, and his father-in-law, Henry Middleton. During 1775-76, however, both in Congress and in two South Carolina provincial assemblies, his increasing self-confidence and maturation of judgment brought him the esteem of his associates. In the latter year, two of the senior South Carolina Delegates, Christopher Gadsden and Henry Middleton, retired from Congress and Thomas Lynch, Sr., suffered an incapacitating stroke. Rutledge, his brother absent on State business, found himself the delegation leader.

On June 7, 1776, when Richard Henry Lee of Virginia proposed national independence, Rutledge led the moderates in securing a delay in the voting. He knew that independence was inevitable. In March his colony, preceded only by New Hampshire, had adopted a constitution. Moreover, that same month the provincial assembly had empowered its Delegates to vote for independence if they so desired. Yet Rutledge firmly believed that the Colonies should first confederate and nurture foreign alliances to strengthen themselves for the perilous step they were about to take. When the vote on independence came up on July 1, he refused to yield and South Carolina balloted negatively. But nine of the Colonies voted affirmatively. Rutledge, realizing that the resolution would probably carry anyway, proposed that the vote be recast the following day. He persuaded the other South Carolina Delegates to submit to the will of the majority for the sake of unanimity, and South Carolina reversed its position.

Rutledge's last important assignment occurred in September, when he accompanied John Adams and Benjamin Franklin on a vain peace mission to Staten Island to negotiate with British Admiral Lord Richard Howe, who in union with his brother, Gen. William Howe, was belatedly and idealistically trying to resolve the differences between the Colonies and the mother country. Two months later, Rutledge departed from Congress in order to resume his law practice in Charleston.

In 1778 Rutledge accepted a seat in the State legislature and the next year won reelection to Congress, though military duties prevented his attendance. As a militia captain, in February 1779 he took part in Gen. William Moultrie's defeat of the British at Port Royal Island, S.C. But in May, 1780, during the siege of Charleston, the redcoats captured Rutledge, as well as Heyward and Middleton, and imprisoned them at St. Augustine, Fla., until July 1781.

From 1782 until 1798 Rutledge sat in the State legislature, which on three occasions designated him as a presidential elector. During this period, his mistrust of unbridled republicanism reinforced his conservatism and brought him into the Federalist Party. In private life he flourished, his wealth increasing through his law practice and investments in plantations. In 1792 his first wife died and he remarried. To crown his achievements, 6 years later the people of South Carolina chose him as Governor. But, his health poor, he died at Charleston early in 1800 at the age of 50, nearly a year before the end of his term. The yard of St. Philip's Episcopal Church is the site of his grave.

Roger Sherman
CONNECTICUT

By dint of self-education, hard work, and business acumen, Roger Sherman soared above his humble origins to prominence in local, State, and National political affairs. He was a member of the committee that drafted the Declaration of Independence. He and Robert Morris were the only men to sign the three bulwark documents of the Republic: the Declaration of Independence, Articles of Confederation, and Constitution. Twice married, Sherman fathered 15 children.

In 1723, when Sherman was 2 years of age, his family relocated from his Newton, Mass., birthplace to Dorchester (present Stoughton). As a boy, he was spurred by a desire to learn, and read widely in his spare time to supplement his minimal education at a common school. But he spent most of his waking hours helping his father with farming chores and learning the cobbler's trade from him. In 1743, or 2 years after his father's death, Sherman joined an elder brother who had settled at New Milford, Conn.

Residence of Roger Sherman, in New Haven, Conn., from 1768 until his death in 1793.

Purchasing a store, becoming county surveyor, and winning a variety of town offices, Sherman prospered and assumed leadership in the community. Without benefit of a legal education, he was admitted to the bar in 1754 and embarked upon a distinguished judicial and political career. In the period 1755-61, except for a brief interval, he served as a representative in the colonial legislature and held the offices of justice of the peace and county judge. Somehow he also eked out time to publish an essay on monetary theory and a series of almanacs incorporating his own astronomical observations and verse.

In 1761, abandoning his law practice, Sherman moved to New Haven, Conn. There he managed a store that catered to Yale students and another one in nearby Wallingford. He also became a friend and benefactor of Yale College, functioning for many years as its treasurer.

Meanwhile, Sherman's political career had blossomed. He rose from justice of the peace and county judge to an associate judge of the Connecticut Superior Court and to representative in both houses of the colonial assembly. Although opposed to extremism, he early joined the fight against Britain. He supported nonimportation measures and headed the New Haven committee of correspondence.

Sherman was a longtime and influential Member of the Continental Congress (1774-81 and 1783-84). He won membership on the committees that drafted the Declaration of Independence and the Articles of Confederation, as well as those concerned with Indian affairs, national finance, and military matters. To solve economic problems, at both the National and State levels, he advocated high taxes rather than excessive borrowing or the issuance of paper currency. While in Congress, Sherman remained active in State and local politics, continuing to hold the office of judge of the Connecticut Superior Court, as well as membership on the council of safety. In 1783 he helped codify Connecticut's statutory laws. The next year, he was elected mayor of New Haven (1784-86).

Sherman could not resist the lure of national service. In 1787 he represented his State at the Constitutional Convention, in which he played a major role. He conceived and introduced the Connecticut, or so-called Great, Compromise, which broke a deadlock between the large and small States by providing for a dual legislative system—representation by proportion of population in the lower house and equal representation in the upper house. He was also instrumental in Connecticut's ratification of the Constitution.

Sherman capped his career by serving as U.S. Representative (1789-91) and Senator (1791-93), espousing the Federalist cause. He died at New Haven in 1793 at the age of 72 and is buried in the Grove Street Cemetery.

James Smith
PENNSYLVANIA

James Smith, a lawyer who had emigrated from Ireland to the Colonies, represented the Pennsylvania back-country in Revolutionary conventions and the Continental Congress. He also helped draft the Pennsylvania constitution.

Smith, the second son in a large family, was born in northern Ireland about 1719. When he was around 10 years old, his father emigrated to America and settled on acreage west of the Susquehanna River in York County, Pa. James studied surveying and classical languages at Rev. Francis Alison's academy in New London, Pa., and then read law in the office of his elder brother at Lancaster. He was admitted to the bar in 1745 and moved westward to the Shippensburg vicinity in Cumberland County. A lack of clients and surveying work caused him about 1750 to relocate eastward to York, where he married a decade later. Although he was the only lawyer in town until 1769, he experienced difficulty in recruiting clients. Probably for this reason, during the years 1771-78 he undertook iron manufacturing, but the venture failed and he lost £5,000.

Smith early emerged as a local Whig leader. In 1774, at a provincial convention in Philadelphia, he supported nonimportation measures and advocated an intercolonial congress. That same year, at York he raised a militia company, in which he served as captain and later honorary colonel. At two provincial meetings in 1775-76, he championed the interests of the western counties and helped formulate resolutions calling for independence, the strengthening of defenses, and establishment of a new provincial government. During the latter year, he sat on the drafting committee in the State constitutional convention. Elected to Congress (1776-78) on July 20, 1776, after the vote on independence had been taken, he arrived in Philadelphia in time to sign the Declaration. Among his colleagues he gained a reputation as a wit, conversationalist, and eccentric.

During the period 1779-82 Smith held various State offices: one-term legislator, judge of the Pennsylvania high court of errors and appeals, brigadier general in the militia, and State counselor during the Wyoming Valley land dispute between Pennsylvania and Connecticut. In 1785 he turned down reelection to Congress because of his age. His major activity prior to his retirement in 1801 was the practice of law. Smith died at about the age of 87 in 1806 at York, survived by two of his five children. His grave is in the First Presbyterian Church Cemetery.

Richard Stockton
NEW JERSEY

Circumstances of the times draw some men into public life who otherwise might avoid its burdens—and sorrows. One of these was Richard Stockton, whose wartime detention by the British contributed to his untimely death.

Stockton, son of a wealthy landowner and judge, was born in 1730 at Morven, the family estate and his lifelong home, at Princeton, N.J. After a preparatory education at West Nottingham Academy, in Rising Sun, Md., he graduated in 1748 from the College of New Jersey (later Princeton University), then in Newark but relocated 8 years hence at Princeton. In 1754 he completed an apprenticeship with a Newark lawyer and joined the bar. The next year, he wed poetess Annis Boudinot, by whom he had two sons and four daughters. By the mid-1760's he was recognized as one of the ablest lawyers in the Middle Colonies.

Like his father a patron of the College of New Jersey, in 1766 Stockton sailed on its behalf to Scotland to recruit Rev. John Witherspoon for the presidency. Aiding in this endeavor, complicated by the opposition of Witherspoon's wife, was Benjamin Rush, a fellow alumnus then enrolled at the University of Edinburgh. In 1768, the year after Stockton's departure, Witherspoon finally accepted.

Stockton resumed his law practice, spending his spare hours at Morven breeding choice cattle and horses, collecting art objects, and expanding his library. Yet, though he had some time before expressed disinterest in public life, in 1768 he began a 6-year term on the executive council of New Jersey and then sat on the provincial Supreme Court (1774-76).

Stockton became associated with the Revolutionary movement during its initial stages. In 1764 he advocated American representation in Parliament, but during the Stamp Act crisis the next year questioned its right to control the Colonies at all. By 1774, though dreading the possibility of war, he was espousing colonial self-rule under the Crown. Elected to Congress 2 years later, he voted for independence and signed the Declaration. That same year, he met defeat in a bid for the New Jersey governorship, but rejected the chance to become first chief justice of the State Supreme Court to remain in Congress.

Late in 1776 fate turned against Stockton. In November, while inspecting the northern Continental Army in upper New York State with fellow Congressman George Clymer, Stockton hurried home when he learned of the British invasion of New Jersey and removed his family to a friend's home in Monmouth County. While he was there, Loyalists informed the British, who captured and imprisoned him under harsh conditions at Perth Amboy, N.J., and later in New

York. A formal remonstrance from Congress and other efforts to obtain his exchange resulted in his release, in poor physical condition, sometime in 1777. To add to his woes, he found that the British had pillaged and partially burned Morven. Still an invalid, he died at Princeton in 1781 at the age of 50. He is buried at the Stony Brook Quaker Meeting House Cemetery.

Thomas Stone
MARYLAND

By the time the Continental Congress voted for independence from Great Britain on July 2, 1776, only a handful of conservatives remained in the body. Included in this group were Thomas Stone of Maryland, Carter Braxton of Virginia, George Read of Delaware, and Edward Rutledge of South Carolina—erstwhile opponents of independence who, except for Read, submitted to the will of the majority and balloted for it. Stone, a rich planter-lawyer of retiring disposition, preferred to stay in the background during his long but limited political career.

Stone was born in 1743 at Poynton Manor, his father's plantation near the village of Welcome in Charles County, Md. He enjoyed all the advantages that accrued to the eldest son. Following tutorial instruction in the classics as a youth, he apprenticed himself to an Annapolis lawyer and in 1764 joined the bar. For the first 2 years he practiced at Frederick, Md., and then settled in his home county. He married 2 years later. Apparently with part of his wife's dowry, he purchased land a few miles to the northeast of his birthplace.

There, near Port Tobacco, in 1771 he built Habre-de-Venture, his home and principal residence for the rest of his life.

Stone entered politics in 1773 as a member of the Charles County committee of correspondence. The next year, on behalf of the Proprietary Governor, he helped prosecute Joseph H. Harrison, a Maryland legislator who had refused to pay the poll tax for the support of the Anglican clergy. This action, despite its legal ethicality, did not endear Stone to the patriots. His opponents, counsel for the defense, consisted of Thomas Johnson, Samuel Chase, and William Paca—all three of whom later became his congressional colleagues.

That same year, 1774, Stone won appointment to the provincial convention, which the following year sent him to Congress. A far less enthusiastic Revolutionary than most Congressmen, he heartily favored reconciliation almost up to the time of the vote on independence and was one of the few Delegates who favored peace negotiations with Britisher Lord Richard Howe in September 1776, some 2 months after the adoption of the Declaration. A poor speaker, Stone rarely participated in debates but sat on the committee that drafted the Articles of Confederation, though he did not sign the document. He remained in Congress until 1778.

Meantime, a couple of years earlier, Stone had begun a tour in the State senate that was to last for practically the remainder of his life. In 1784 he also returned to the Continental Congress, where he served for a few days as acting President but resigned before the year expired to resume his law practice. His last act of public service occurred the following year, when he and two others represented Maryland at the Mount Vernon Conference.

In 1787 Stone's wife, whose health had been failing for more than a decade, passed away at the age of 34. The grief-stricken Stone abandoned his work, declined to attend the Constitutional Convention to which he had been elected, and decided to visit England. A few months later, though only in his mid-forties, he died suddenly while awaiting a vessel at Alexandria, Va. Three of his children survived him. Stone is buried in the family graveyard adjacent to Habre-de-Venture.

George Taylor
PENNSYLVANIA

Surmounting the poverty that forced him to come to the American Colonies from Ireland as an indentured servant to an ironmaster, George Taylor climbed to the top of the industry. In the process, merging politics with commerce, he gained enough distinction in county and State affairs to win election to the Continental Congress—his only service on the national level. Even then, he attended only a few months, just long enough to sign the Declaration. He contributed more directly to the cause of liberty as an ironmaster, producing ordnance for the Continental Army.

When Taylor was about 20 years of age, he indentured himself and emigrated from northern Ireland, where he had been born in 1716, to Pennsylvania. He began as a laborer and then became a clerk at Warwick Furnace, in Chester County, and within 3 years rose to bookkeeper-manager of nearby Coventry Forge, another enterprise of his employer. In 1742, the year after the latter died, Taylor acquired his business when he married his widow; she bore him a son and daughter.

In the mid-1750's Taylor moved northeastward to Bucks County, where he and a partner leased Durham Furnace, about 2 miles south of the Northampton County line and 10 miles south of Easton. Apparently after 1763 Taylor lived much of the time at or near Easton and acquired property there. In 1768 his wife died; he subsequently sired five children by his housekeeper out of wedlock. The year of his wife's death, he built a home about 15 miles west of the city on a 331-acre tract he had purchased the year before. In 1771 he leased most of the land out as a farm, and 5 years later sold the house and land.

Taylor had begun his public life in 1747, when he took a commission as a captain in the Chester County militia. In 1761 he was appointed as justice of the peace for Bucks County, but devoted most of his energies to Northampton County, which he served as justice of the peace (1764-75) and representative in the colonial legislature (1764-70). In 1774 Taylor, a political moderate, became a member of the Northampton County committee of correspondence. The next year, he attended a provincial Revolutionary convention, was elected to the provincial assembly, served on the council of safety, and became a colonel in the Bucks and Northampton County militias.

In July 1776 the Pennsylvania assembly selected Taylor as one of its new Delegates to the Continental Congress. His only noteworthy action there was signing the Declaration. The next January, however, he and fellow signer George Walton of Georgia negotiated a peace treaty with the Six Indian Nations (Iroquois) at Easton, Pa., but Congress did not ratify it. In March the voters of Northampton County elected Taylor to the new Supreme Executive Assembly of Pennsylvania, but illness and financial difficulties restricted his participation to only 6 weeks, at the end of which he retired from public life.

By this time, Taylor's Durham Furnace was turning out grapeshot, cannonballs, bar shot, and cannon for the Revolutionary army—for which Taylor was ill-compensated. In 1778 the State dispossessed him of his lease on the Durham Furnace, owned by the Philadelphia Loyalist John Galloway and confiscated by the State. Taylor then moved to Greenwich Township, N.J., and leased Greenwich Forge, which he operated until his death at the age of 65 in 1781. The year before, his health failing, Taylor had returned to Easton and leased a home. Originally buried in the yard of the German Evangelical Lutheran Church at Easton, his body was later moved to the Easton Cemetery.

Matthew Thornton
NEW HAMPSHIRE

Probably six of the 56 signers belatedly penned their signatures, eight of them were foreign-born, and four were physicians. Matthew Thornton belongs in all three categories. Less exclusively, he ranks among the substantial number of signers whose national service was brief or relatively insignificant.

Thornton was born in Ireland about 1714. Approximately 4 years later, his Scotch-Irish parents emigrated with their family to America, settling first at Wiscasset, in present Maine, and then near Worcester, Mass. Young Thornton, after attending common schools, undertook the study of medicine with a local doctor. In 1740 he began what proved to be a thriving practice in the Scotch-Irish town of Londonderry (present Derry Village), N.H. Five years later, as a surgeon in the New Hampshire militia during King George's War (1740-48), he participated in the British expedition from New England that captured Louisbourg, the French fortress in Nova Scotia.

By 1758 Thornton was representing Londonderry in the colonial legislature and stayed there until 1775. During the long interim, about 1760 he married and began a family of five; and throughout the period he figured prominently in New Hampshire politics and Revolutionary activities. In 1775-76 he held the offices of president of the provincial assembly and constitutional convention, chairman of the council of safety, and member of the upper and lower houses of the legislature, as well as speaker of the former. Although he did not enter Congress until November 1776, or 3 months after the formal signing of the Declaration, he was granted permission to affix his signature.

About a year later, Thornton left Congress to devote his time to his duties as associate justice of the State Superior Court. Despite a lack of legal education, he had acquired this position in 1776. He held it until 1782, some 2 years after he retired from his medical practice in Londonderry and settled on a farm he purchased near Merrimack, N.H. Later, in 1784-86, he completed a tour in the State senate. He spent his last years farming and operating a ferry— Lutwyche's (later Thornton's) Ferry—across the Merrimack River.

Thornton died in 1803 at about the age of 89 while visiting his daughter in Newburyport, Mass. His grave is in Thornton's Ferry Cemetery, near the site of his Merrimack home.

George Walton
GEORGIA

Like signers Button Gwinnett and Lyman Hall a nonnative of Georgia, George Walton fought hard to win independence for his adopted State and his Nation—both in the political arena and on the battlefield. He was wounded in the British siege of Savannah late in 1778 and endured captivity for almost a year. He evinced the same kind of tenacity in all his other endeavors and conquered a string of adversities in his ascent from humble origins to the highest National and State offices.

Born sometime in the 1740's near Farmville, Va., Walton was orphaned early and reared by an uncle, who apprenticed him to a carpenter. Walton supplemented extensive independent study with some formal schooling. In 1769 he moved to Savannah, Ga., read law under a local attorney, and 5 years later joined the bar.

That same year, Walton plunged into politics. Rallying Revolutionaries at Savannah as did Lyman Hall in St. John's Parish—the two Whig hotbeds in a lukewarm colony—Walton helped organize and played a key part in meetings at Savannah in July and August 1774 and the first provincial congress the next January. But these meetings, to which only a few parishes sent representatives, hardly set the dissent in motion. The divided delegates, aware of their limited constituency, failed to send Delegates to the Continental Congress, as had all the other Colonies, and thus alienated St. John's Parish. Except for creation of a committee of correspondence, to which Walton was appointed, the conferees for the most part substituted patriotic talk for action. During this period, Walton, blending political activism with romance, took a bride. She later gave birth to two sons.

By July 1775, when the second provincial congress convened and designated Walton as secretary, apathy in the Revolutionary ranks had given way to aggressiveness. The congress dispatched four Delegates to the Continental Congress to join Hall, already an unofficial "delegate" from St. John's Parish. The next year, the third provincial congress elected Walton, by this time chairman of the council of safety, as a Delegate (1776-81). In this capacity, he sat on committees dealing with western lands, national finance, and Indian affairs. His only lapse in attendance occurred in 1778-79, when the military defense of his own State took precedence over his congressional obligations. As a colonel in the Georgia militia, he was wounded and captured during the siege of Savannah in November-December 1778—the beginning of the British invasion of the South. He was imprisoned until the following September, when he was exchanged for a navy captain.

Right after his release, at Augusta Walton became involved in a factional dispute between two groups of Revolutionaries. Walton's group, irritated because their conservative opponents had taken advantage of the confusion generated by the British occupation of Savannah by putting their own "governor" into office without benefit of a general election, countered by selecting Walton as its "governor" (November 1779-January 1780). In January the new legally elected legislature picked a Governor, another anti-conservative. Walton returned to the Continental Congress in 1780-81, after which he headed back to Georgia.

Walton's subsequent career suffered no diminution. His offices included those of chief justice (1783-89) and justice (1790-95 and 1799-1804) of the State Superior Court; delegate to the State constitutional convention (1788); presidential elector (1789); Governor (1789-90); and U.S. Senator (1795-96), filling out an unexpired term. Meantime, he had been elected as a delegate to the U.S. Constitutional Convention (1787), but did not attend. An advocate of higher education, he was also a trustee and founder of Richmond Academy, in Augusta, and Franklin College (later the University of Georgia), in Athens.

About 1790 while Governor, changing his residence from Savannah to the capital of Augusta, Walton built "Meadow Garden" cottage on the northern edge of the city on confiscated Loyalist lands he had acquired. He lived in the cottage for 5 years, when he moved to College Hill, a country estate he erected on the western outskirts. He died there in 1804. Assigned first to the Rosney Cemetery in Augusta, his remains now rest at the Signers' Monument in that city.

William Whipple
NEW HAMPSHIRE

William Whipple, a sea captain turned merchant, retired from business to further the Revolution. In addition to sitting in Congress, he commanded New Hampshire militia in two major campaigns and held various State offices.

Whipple, the eldest of five children, was born in 1730, at Kittery, in present Maine. He attended local schools and went to sea while still a boy. In his early twenties he became a shipmaster, and later probably sometimes engaged in the slave trade. About 1760 he gave up the sea and founded a mercantile firm at Portsmouth, N.H., with his brother Joseph. In 1767 he married the daughter of a wealthy merchant-sea captain; their only child died in infancy.

By the outbreak of the Revolution, Whipple had become one of the leading citizens of Portsmouth. In 1775, his fortune well established, he left business to devote his time to public affairs. That year, he represented Portsmouth in the provincial assembly at Exeter, and served on the New Hampshire council of safety. The following year, he won seats in the upper house of the State legislature and in the Continental Congress. His congressional tour, interrupted intermittently by militia duty, lasted until 1779. He concerned himself mainly with military, marine, and financial matters. A tough-minded, independent individual, he recommended military aggressiveness in the war instead of diplomacy and favored severe punishment of Loyalists and speculators.

In the fall of 1777 Whipple, a brigadier general in the New Hampshire militia, led four regiments to upper New York State and helped encircle and besiege the British army at Saratoga. He was present on October 17 at the surrender of Gen. John Burgoyne; signed the Convention of Saratoga, ending the New York campaign; and helped escort the British troops to a winter encampment near Boston to await embarkation for England. In 1778 he led another contingent of New Hampshire militia into Rhode Island on a campaign that sought but failed to recapture Newport from the British.

During his last years, Whipple held the offices of State legislator (1780-84), associate justice of the New Hampshire Superior Court (1782-85), receiver of finances for Congress in New Hampshire (1782-84), and in 1782 president of a commission that arbitrated the Wyoming Valley land dispute between Connecticut and Pennsylvania. Ill the remaining few years of his life, he passed away in 1785 at the age of 55 at Portsmouth, where he was buried in Union Cemetery. His wife survived him.

William Williams
CONNECTICUT

Merchant William Williams was prominent in Connecticut politics, but never won national fame except for signing the Declaration.

A Congregational pastor's son, Williams was born in 1731 at Lebanon, Conn., his lifelong home. After graduating from Harvard in 1751, he began studying for the ministry under his father. Four years later, during the French and Indian War (1754-63), he accompanied a British expedition to Lake George, in northeastern New York, that won a victory. Back home, he became a merchant. In 1771 he married a daughter of Jonathan Trumbull, Royal Governor of Connecticut; they had three children.

During his long political career, Williams held a myriad of local, provincial, and State offices: town clerk (1752-96) and selectman (1760-85); member, clerk, and speaker of the lower house of the colonial legislature (1755-76); State legislator (1781-84); member of the Governor's council (1784-1803); judge of the Windham County court (1776-1805); and probate judge for the Windham district (1775-1809). He also represented Connecticut at various New England meetings, and attended the 1788 convention that ratified the Federal Constitution, of which he approved.

Upon the outbreak of the Revolution, Williams threw his weight behind the cause. Besides writing tracts for the press expressing the colonial viewpoint, he prepared Revolutionary state papers for Governor Trumbull. Williams also raised money for and personally contributed to the war effort. Between 1773 and 1776 he held a colonelcy in the Connecticut militia and served on the provincial council of safety. In Congress (1776-78 and 1783-84), he sat on the Board of War and helped frame the Articles of Confederation, though he did not sign them. During the winter of 1780-81, while a French regiment was stationed in Lebanon, he moved out of his home and turned it over to the officers.

Williams died at the age of 80 in 1811. His grave is in the Trumbull Cemetery, about a mile northeast of town.

James Wilson
PENNSYLVANIA

Brilliant yet enigmatic James Wilson possessed one of the most complex and contradictory personalities of all the signers. Never able to reconcile his strong personal drive for wealth and power with his political goals nor to find a middle road between conservatism and republicanism, he alternately experienced either popularity or public scorn, fame or obscurity, wealth or poverty. Yet his mastery of the law and political theory enabled him to play a leading role in framing the U.S. Constitution and to rise from frontier lawyer to Justice of the Supreme Court.

Wilson was born in 1741 or 1742 at Carskerdo, near St. Andrews, Scotland, and educated at the universities of St. Andrews, Glasgow, and Edinburgh. He then emigrated to America, arriving in the midst

From 1778 until 1790 James Wilson resided in this Philadelphia residence, which became known as "Fort Wilson" in 1779, when a mob of citizens and militiamen attacked it.

of the Stamp Act agitations in 1765. Early the next year, he accepted a position as Latin tutor at the College of Philadelphia, but almost immediately abandoned it to study law under John Dickinson.

In 1768, the year after his admission to the bar, Wilson set up practice at Reading, Pa. Two years later, he moved westward to the Scotch-Irish settlement of Carlisle, and the following year took a bride. He specialized in land law and built up a broad clientele. On borrowed capital, he also began to speculate in land. In some way he managed, too, to lecture for many years on English literature at the College of Philadelphia.

Wilson also became involved in Revolutionary politics. In 1774 he took over chairmanship of the Carlisle committee of correspondence, attended the first provincial assembly, and completed preparation of *Considerations on the Nature and Extent of the Legislative Authority of the British Parliament*. This tract circulated widely in England and America and established Wilson as a Whig leader. It denied Parliament's authority over the Colonies, though it did not question their allegiance to the Crown, and recommended a reorganization of the imperial structure similar to the later British Commonwealth of Nations.

The next year, Wilson was elected to both the provincial assembly and the Continental Congress, where he sat mainly on military and Indian affairs committees. In 1776, reflecting the wishes of his constituents, he joined the moderates in voting for a 3-week delay in considering Richard Henry Lee's resolution of June 7. On July 1, however, Wilson dissented from the majority of the Pennsylvania delegation and balloted with John Morton and Benjamin Franklin for independence. On July 2 the three men, representing a majority of the Commonwealth's Delegates present, voted the same. Wilson's strenuous opposition to the republican Pennsylvania constitution of 1776, besides indicating a switch to conservatism on his part, led to his removal from Congress the following year. To avoid the clamor among his frontier constituents, he repaired to Annapolis during the winter of 1777-78, and then took up residence in Philadelphia.

Wilson affirmed his newly assumed political stance by closely identifying with the aristocratic and conservative republican groups, multiplying his business interests, and accelerating his land speculation. He also took a position as Advocate-General for France in America (1779-83), dealing with commercial and maritime matters, and legally defended Loyalists and their sympathizers.

In the fall of 1779, during a period of inflation and food shortages, a mob, including many militiamen and led by radical-constitutionalists, set out to attack the republican leadership. Wilson was a prime target. He and some 35 of his colleagues barricaded themselves in his home at Third and Walnut Streets, henceforth known as "Fort Wilson." During a brief skirmish, several people on both sides were killed or wounded. The shock cooled sentiments and pardons were issued all around, though major political battles over the Commonwealth constitution still lay ahead.

During 1781 Congress appointed Wilson as one of the directors of the Bank of North America, newly founded by Robert Morris with the legal advice of Wilson. In 1782-83, by which time the conservatives had regained some of their power, he was reelected to Congress, as well as in the period 1785-87.

Wilson reached the apex of his career in the U.S. Constitutional Convention (1787), in which he was one of the leaders, both in the floor debates and the drafting committee. That same year, overcoming powerful opposition, he led the drive for ratification in

Pennsylvania, the second State to ratify. The new Commonwealth constitution, drafted in 1789-90 along the lines of the U.S. Constitution, was also primarily Wilson's work and represented the climax of his 14-year fight against the constitution of 1776.

For his services in the formation of the Federal Government, though Wilson expected to be appointed Chief Justice, in 1789 President Washington named him as an Associate Justice of the Supreme Court. He was chosen that same year as the first law professor at the College of Philadelphia. Two years hence, he began an official digest of the laws of Pennsylvania, a project he never completed, though he carried on for awhile after funds ran out.

Wilson, who wrote only a few opinions, did not achieve the success on the Supreme Court that his capabilities and experience promised. Indeed, during those years he was the object of much criticism and barely escaped impeachment. For one thing, he tried to influence the enactment of legislation in Pennsylvania favorable to land speculators. Between 1792 and 1795 he also made huge but unwise land investments in western New York and Pennsylvania, as well as in Georgia. This did not stop him from conceiving a grandiose but ill-fated scheme, involving vast sums of European capital, for the recruitment of European colonists and their settlement on western lands. Meantime, in 1793, a widower with six children, he had remarried; the one son from this union died in infancy.

Four years later, to avoid arrest for debt, the distraught Wilson moved from Philadelphia to Burlington, N.J. The next year, apparently while on Federal circuit court business, he arrived at Edenton, N.C., in a state of acute mental stress and was taken into the home of James Iredell, a fellow Supreme Court Justice. He died there within a few months. Although first buried at Hayes Plantation near Edenton, his remains were later reinterred in the yard of Christ Church at Philadelphia.

John Witherspoon
NEW JERSEY

Rev. John Witherspoon, the only active clergyman among the signers, achieved a greater reputation as a religious leader and educator than as a politician. Emigrating from Scotland to America in the midst of the controversy between the Colonies and the Crown, he took part in the Revolution, lost a son during the war, and signed the Articles of Confederation as well as the Declaration. He is better known, however, for his role in the growth of the Presbyterian Church and for his distinguished presidency of the College of New Jersey (later Princeton University).

The son of a Calvinist minister, Witherspoon was born in 1723 at the village of Gifford, near Edinburgh. He attended grammar school at the neighboring town of Haddington and won master of arts (1739) and divinity (1743) degrees from the University of Edinburgh. In 1743 the Haddington Presbytery licensed him to preach. He was ordained 2 years later at Beith, where he occupied a pulpit until 1757. He then transferred to Paisley, not far from Glasgow. Meantime, in 1748, he had married; only five of his ten children survived childhood.

Over the years, Witherspoon attained leadership of a group of conservative clergymen who were engaged in a prolonged struggle with a group of their colleagues to maintain the "purity" of orthodox Church doctrine. Witherspoon penned a stream of sermons and tracts attacking the opposition and denouncing moral decay in Scotland. He also defended the traditional prerogative of the people to choose their own ministers, a right ecclesiastical authorities had taken from them.

In 1768 Witherspoon channeled his energies in a new direction. He gave up his post at Paisley and accepted the presidency of the College of New Jersey, after two representatives of the college had visited him and finally at the end of 2 years of effort overcome the objections of his wife. He sailed to America with his family. The college bloomed under his direction. He increased the endowment, instituted new methods of instruction, and broadened and revitalized the curriculum. Continuing also as a minister and church leader, he patched up a major schism in the Presbyterian Church; stimulated its expansion, especially in the Middle Colonies; and worked closely with the Congregationalists.

The Revolution fanned Witherspoon's hatred of the English, which had originated in Scotland. By 1770 his students were openly demonstrating in favor of the patriot cause. In a commencement oration he advocated resistance to the Crown, which became his favorite theme in sermons and essays. In 1774-76 he represented his county in the New Jersey provincial assemblies, and sat on local committees of correspondence. In the latter year he figured prominently in the agitations that led to the removal from office and imprisonment of

The College of New Jersey (later Princeton University) in 1764. Rev. John Witherspoon served as its president from 1768 until 1794. The main building, Nassau Hall, is on the left; the President's House, on the right.

the Royal Governor, and then received an appointment to the Continental Congress.

On July 2, 1776, in a congressional speech urging independence, Witherspoon declared that the Colonies were "not only ripe for the measure but in danger of rotting for the want of it." In November, when the British invaded New Jersey, he closed the College of New Jersey. The redcoats occupied its major building, Nassau Hall, burned the library, and committed other acts of destruction. The next year, Witherspoon's son James lost his life at the Battle of Germantown, Pa.

Witherspoon stayed in Congress until 1782. His main committee assignments dealt with military and foreign affairs. He also participated in the debates on the Articles of Confederation, aided in setting up the executive departments, and argued for financial stability. Meantime, in 1779, he had moved from the President's House at Princeton to Tusculum, a country home he had earlier built nearby. He left the Rev. Samuel S. Smith, his son-in-law and the college vice president, in charge of the nearly defunct institution.

Witherspoon devoted most of his effort during the postwar years to rebuilding the college, which never fully recovered its prewar prosperity during his lifetime. In addition, during the years 1783-89 he sat for two terms in the State legislature, attended the New Jersey (1787) convention that ratified the Federal Constitution, participated in the reorganization of the Presbyterian Church, and moderated its first general assembly (1789). In 1791, at the age of 68, Witherspoon took a second wife, a 24-year-old widow, who bore him two daughters. Blind his last 2 years, he died in 1794, aged 71, at Tusculum. His remains rest in the Presidents' Lot at Princeton Cemetery.

Oliver Wolcott
CONNECTICUT

Oliver Wolcott, as much a soldier as a politician, helped convert the concept of independence into reality on the battlefield. He also occupied many local, provincial, and State offices, including the governorship. One of his five children, Oliver, also held that position and became U.S. Secretary of the Treasury.

Wolcott was the youngest son in a family of 15. Sired by Roger Wolcott, a leading Connecticut politician, he was born in 1726 at Windsor (present South Windsor), Conn. In 1747, just graduated from Yale College at the top of his class, he began his military career. As a militia captain during King George's War (1740-48), he accompanied an unsuccessful British expedition against the French in New France. Back home, he studied medicine for a time with his brother before deciding to turn to law.

In 1751, when Litchfield County was organized, Wolcott moved about 30 miles westward to the town of Litchfield and immediately took over the first of a long string of county and State offices: county sheriff (1751-71); member of the lower house (1764, 1767-68, and 1770) and upper house (1771-86) of the colonial and State legislatures; and probate (1772-81) and county (1774-78) judge. By 1774 he had risen to the rank of colonel in the militia.

The next spring, the legislature named him as a commissary for Connecticut troops and in the summer the Continental Congress designated him as a commissioner of Indian affairs for the northern department. In that capacity he attended a conference that year with the Iroquois (Six Nations) at Albany, N.Y., that temporarily gained their neutrality in the war. Before the year was out, he also aided in arbitrating land disputes between Pennsylvania and Connecticut and New York and Vermont.

Wolcott sat in Congress from 1775 until 1783 except for the year 1779. In June 1776 illness caused him to return to Connecticut. Absent at the time of the voting for independence the next month and at the formal signing of the Declaration in August, he added his signature sometime after his return to Congress in October. Throughout his tour, Wolcott devoted portions of each year to militia duty, highlighted by participation as a brigadier general in the New York campaigns of 1776-77 that culminated in the surrender of Gen. John Burgoyne in October of the latter year at Saratoga (Schuylerville). During 1779, as a major general, Wolcott defended the Connecticut seacoast against the raids of William Tryon, Royal Governor of New York.

Wolcott's postwar career was varied. On the national level, he helped negotiate two Indian treaties: the Second Treaty of Fort Stanwix, N.Y. (1784), in which the Iroquois ceded to the United States some of their lands in New York and Pennsylvania; and another (1789) with the Wyandottes, who gave up their tract in the Western Reserve, in present Ohio. On the State level, Wolcott continued his long period of service in the upper house of the legislature (ended 1786); enjoyed a lengthy stint as Lieutenant Governor (1787-96); attended the convention (1788) that ratified the U.S. Constitution; and, like his father before him and his son after him, held the office of Governor (1796-97).

While occupying the latter position, Wolcott died, aged 71, at East Windsor. His remains rest in the East Cemetery at Litchfield.

George Wythe
VIRGINIA

Virginia's George Wythe spent only about a year in the Continental Congress, never aspired to any other national office, and played a minor part in the Constitutional Convention. But he made a deep impress on legal education in the Nation and strongly influenced the government and jurisprudence of his State. A brilliant classical scholar and the first professor of law in an American college, he instructed scores of young lawyers. Included among them were Thomas Jefferson, James Monroe, John Marshall, and Henry Clay.

Wythe was born in 1726, the second of three children, on his father's plantation on the Back River in Elizabeth City County, Va., within the confines of present Hampton. He lost his parents at an early age and grew up under the guardianship of his older brother, Thomas. George acquired a knowledge of the classics from his well-educated mother before her death, and he probably attended for a time a grammar school operated by the College of William and Mary.

Wythe's brother later sent him to Prince George County to read law under an uncle. In 1746, at the age of 20, he joined the bar, moved to Spotsylvania County, and became associated with a lawyer there. In December 1747, he married his partner's sister, but she succumbed the next year. In 1754 Lt. Gov. Robert Dinwiddie appointed him as acting colonial attorney general, a position he held for a few months and which likely required that he spend some time in Williamsburg. The next year, Wythe's brother died and he inherited his birthplace. He chose, however, to live in Williamsburg in the house that his new father-in-law, an architect, designed and built for him and his betrothed, whom he married about 1755. Their only child died in infancy.

At Williamsburg, Wythe immersed himself in further study of the classics and the law and achieved accreditation by the colonial Supreme Court. Like his father, he served in the House of Burgesses (mid-1750's until 1775), first as delegate and after 1769 as clerk. During this period, in 1768 he held the mayorship of Williamsburg, and the next year sat on the board of visitors of the College of William and Mary. He also had found time during the years 1762-67 to train youthful Thomas Jefferson in the law. The two men, at first as mentor and pupil and later as political allies, maintained a lifetime friendship.

Wythe first exhibited Revolutionary leanings in 1764 when Parliament hinted to the Colonies that it might impose a Stamp Tax. By then an experienced legislator, he drafted for the House of Burgesses a remonstrance to Parliament so strident that his fellow legislators modified it before adoption. Wythe was one of the first to express the concept of separate nationhood for the Colonies within the British Empire.

Although elected to Congress in 1775-76, Wythe exerted little influence in that body. He spent considerable time helping draft a State constitution and design a State seal, and was not present at the time of the formal signing of the Declaration in August 1776. Furthermore, within a few months, Wythe, Jefferson, and Edmund Pendleton undertook a 3-year project to revise Virginia's legal code. In 1777 Wythe also presided as speaker of the lower house of the legislature.

An appointment as one of the three judges of the newly created Virginia high court of chancery followed the next year. Sitting on it for 28 years, during 13 of which he was the only chancellor, Wythe charted the course of Virginia jurisprudence. In conjunction with these duties, he was an ex officio member of the State Superior Court.

Wythe's real love was teaching. In 1779 Jefferson and other officials of the College of William and Mary created the first chair of law in a U.S. institution of higher learning and appointed Wythe to fill it. In that position, he educated America's earliest college-trained lawyers, among them John Marshall and James Monroe. To supplement his lectures, Wythe introduced the use of moot courts and legislatures, in which students could put their knowledge into actual practice. In 1787 he also demonstrated his love of the classics and literature by offering free to anyone interested a class in Latin, Greek, and English literature. That same year, he attended the U.S. Constitutional Convention, but played an insignificant role and did not sign the Constitution. The following year, however, he was one of the Federalist leaders at the Virginia ratifying convention.

In 1791, the year after Wythe resigned his professorship, his chancery duties caused him to move his home to Richmond, the State capital. But he was reluctant to give up his teaching and opened a private law school. One of his last and most promising pupils was a teenager named Henry Clay.

In 1806, in his eighth decade, Wythe died at Richmond under mysterious circumstances—probably of poison administered by his heir, a favorite grandnephew. Reflecting a lifelong aversion to slavery, Wythe emancipated his slaves in his will. His grave is in the yard of St. John's Episcopal Church at Richmond.

Part Three

Signers of the Declaration:
Survey of Historic Sites and Buildings

$\mathcal{O}$VER the decades that separate present-day America from the early periods of its history, a large number of the structures commemorating those periods have been marred or obliterated. Those relating to the signers of the Declaration of Independence have not been spared. The ravages of war, urbanization, fire, aging, weathering, neglect, and vandalism have destroyed all the residences of 21 of these 56 men and seriously impaired some of those that have survived.

Beyond those factors detrimental to all historic buildings are two special ones that have hampered the marking and preserving of signers' homes and other sites. For decades following adoption of the Declaration, these individuals were not accorded the reverence bestowed on them in modern times. Secondly, many of them have received only slight historical recognition because they lacked national reputations other than as signers.

Yet among the residences and buildings that remain are many of major significance. As a whole, they reveal much about the way of life of the signers and illuminate the events involved in the creation of the Declaration. Of outstanding significance is Independence National Historical Park, Pa. Within its boundaries the document was written, debated, approved, and signed. The National

Park Service administers the park in cooperation with the city of Philadelphia and various private agencies. Three residences of signers are also units of the National Park System: Adams National Historic Site, Mass.; the Floyd House, in Fire Island National Seashore, N.Y.; and the Nelson House, part of Colonial National Historical Park, Va.

Almost half the extant homes of the signers are owned by private individuals, many of whom personally reside in them and a few of whom are descendants of the signers. The rest of the residences are owned and maintained by States, cities, and a wide variety of nongovernmental institutions, such as patriotic-civic organizations, memorial associations, local historical societies, foundations, universities, churches, and corporations and business firms.

Reflecting the dedicated efforts of many of the above individuals and agencies, a considerable number of the buildings and residences provide fine examples of historic preservation and restoration. Unfortunately, some structures have badly deteriorated. But the increased recent interest in the signers has enhanced the identification, renovation, and preservation of pertinent sites and buildings.

In addition to the preservation of sites and buildings, the subject of this book, the signers have been honored in many other ways. Commemoration varies widely, however, from State to State and from signer to signer. Some have been recognized in a major way; others hardly at all.

In the forefront of the groups that have marked extant homes and buildings, as well as the sites of former structures and graves, or otherwise memorialized the signers are: Daughters of the American Revolution; Daughters of the Revolution; Colonial Dames of America; National Society of Colonial Dames of America; Sons of the American Revolution; Sons of the Revolution; and the Descendants of the Signers of the Declaration of Independence, Inc., chartered by Congress in 1907.

A major share of the sites of residences with no physical remains has been marked. The 20 signers for whom no existing homes have been located are: Samuel Adams, Abraham Clark, William Ellery, Benjamin Franklin, Lyman Hall, John Hart, Francis Lewis, Philip Livingston, Thomas McKean, Lewis Morris, Robert Morris, John Morton, Robert Treat Paine, John Penn, George Read, Caesar Rodney, George Ross, Benjamin Rush, Roger Sherman, and James

Smith. Another signer, Samuel Chase, is represented in this volume only by a structure (Chase-Lloyd House) that he began building but never resided in.

Monuments and memorials range from simple plaques to the Thomas Jefferson Memorial, D.C., in the National Park System. Statues of several signers are located in the U.S. Capitol. Special monuments have been erected to those from two States. The Founders' Monument, in Augusta, Ga., is dedicated to the three signers from that State (Gwinnett, Hall, and Walton) and contains the burial places of the latter two. A monument to the three North Carolina signers (Hewes, Hooper, and Penn) at Guilford Courthouse National Military Park, in Greensboro, N.C., includes the tombs of Hooper and Penn.

DESCRIBED in the following pages are the principal buildings associated with the signers of the Declaration. They are comprised of three categories: National Park Service Areas, National Historic Landmarks, and Other Sites Considered.

The principal aim of the National Survey of Historic Sites and Buildings is to identify nationally important sites that are not *National Park Service Areas*, but no survey of historic places would be complete without including them. This is particularly true because many of them were designated as National Historic Landmarks before they became part of the National Park System. Further information about a particular area may be obtained by writing directly to the park superintendent at the address listed immediately following the location.

National Historic Landmarks are those sites judged by the Advisory Board on National Parks, Historic Sites, Buildings, and Monuments to meet the criteria of national significance in commemorating the history of the United States (pp. 270-271). They have been declared by the Secretary of the Interior to be eligible for designation as National Historic Landmarks. Final designation occurs when the owners apply for such status. They receive certificates and bronze plaques attesting to the distinction.

Other Sites Considered consist of those sites deemed by the Advisory Board to possess noteworthy historical value but not national significance. The list of sites included in this category does not purport to be exhaustive; it is merely a representative sampling, all that is possible because of space limitations.

Many sites in the Other Sites Considered category in all phases of history are listed on the National Register of Historic Places, maintained by the National Park Service's Office of Archeology and Historic Preservation. The register consists not only of sites in the National Park System and National Historic Landmarks but also those of State and local significance, nominated through appropriate channels by the various States. It is published biennially and distributed by the Superintendent of Documents, U.S. Government Printing Office, Washington, D.C., 20402. The latest volume is *The National Register of Historic Places, 1972,* price $7.80.

SIGNERS OF THE DECLARATION

HISTORIC SITES OF NATIONAL SIGNIFICANCE

★ Sites in the National Park System

⚠ National Historic Landmarks

—·—·— Present State boundaries

0   100   200   300

SCALE OF MILES

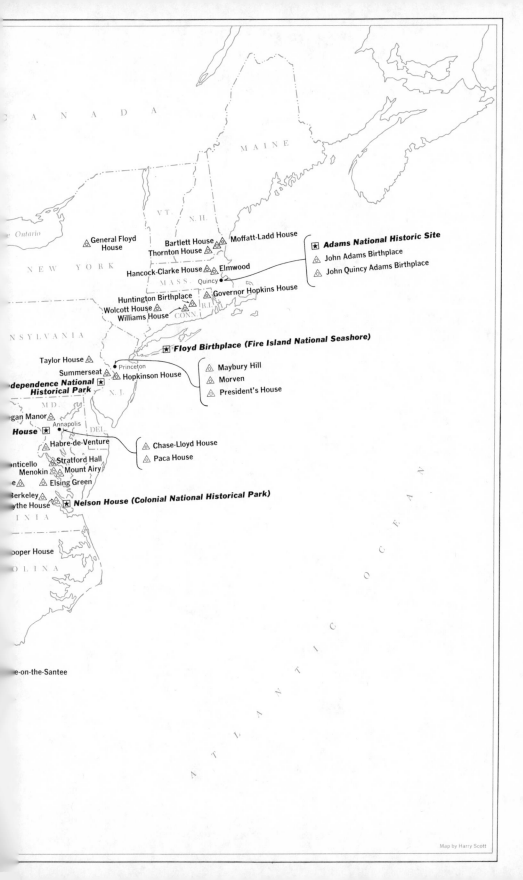

△ General Floyd House

△△ Bartlett House △ Moffatt-Ladd House
△ Thornton House

★ **Adams National Historic Site**
△ John Adams Birthplace
△ John Quincy Adams Birthplace

Hancock-Clarke House △△ Elmwood
Quincy ●

Huntington Birthplace △ Governor Hopkins House
Wolcott House △ △△
Williams House

★ **Floyd Birthplace (Fire Island National Seashore)**

Taylor House △
Summerseat △ ● Princeton
△△ Hopkinson House

△ Maybury Hill
△ Morven
△ President's House

ependence National ★
Historical Park

gan Manor △
House ★ ● Annapolis

△ Chase-Lloyd House
△ Paca House

△ Habre-de-Venture

nticello △ △ Stratford Hall
Menokin △△ Mount Airy
e △ △ Elsing Green

Berkeley △△
ythe House △ ★ **Nelson House (Colonial National Historical Park)**

ooper House

e-on-the-Santee

Map by Harry Scott

For the convenience of users of this volume, sites and buildings are listed alphabetically by State. The following code indicates site categories:

Site Categories

⊞ NATIONAL PARK SERVICE AREAS

⚠ NATIONAL HISTORIC LANDMARKS

⊗ OTHER SITES CONSIDERED

NOTE: *The following descriptions indicate sites that are open to the public. Before visiting any of them, inquiry should be made to the owners or custodians concerning dates and hours of access and admission costs, usually nominal. Special permission should be obtained to visit privately owned sites.*

Huntington Birthplace, Connecticut ⚠

Location: Windham County, on the north side of Conn. 14, about 2 blocks west of its junction with Conn. 97, Scotland.

This plain but charming farmhouse on the bank of Merrick's Brook was the birthplace and home of Samuel Huntington through his boyhood and early manhood. He lived in it from 1731 probably unitl 1760, the year he moved to Norwich.

The house, built in the period 1700-22, is shaded by huge trees and fronted by a spacious lawn. It is a large, two-story, clapboarded-frame structure of saltbox design. The gable roof slopes steeply at the rear. Exterior windows are topped by projecting cornices; the center door, by a rectangular transom. A one-story kitchen wing with front porch at the northeast end of the house along the main axis was added early in the 19th century.

The floor plan is typical of a central chimney New England dwelling. Behind a short central entrance hall, which contains an L-shaped stairway, is a large stone central chimney with three fireplaces. Two of these heat the parlor and dining room, entered from the hall; a huge third one serves the large original kitchen, which ranges across the rear two-thirds of the house behind the dining room and chimney.

Huntington Birthplace.

A small bedroom is situated back of the parlor alongside the original kitchen, between it and the one-story new kitchen addition. Three additional bedrooms, one of which has a fully paneled fireplace wall, are located upstairs. Wallpaper has been added to some of the rooms, but the fireplaces, wainscoting, and wide-board floors are original.

The privately owned house, which is in good condition and little altered, has never been restored, though some modern conveniences have been installed. It is not open to the public.

Huntington House, Connecticut   ⊗

Location: New London County, 34 East Town Street, Norwich.

Samuel Huntington erected this house in the years 1783-85 and lived in it until his death in 1796. Since that time, the frame dwelling has been extensively modified on both the exterior and interior and a major addition made at the rear.

Originally the residence was a large, two-story, rectangular structure with a gable roof, two interior chimneys, tall corner pilasters, and triangular pediments above the first-story windows. By the

Huntington House.

middle of the 19th century, however, the structure had been re-modeled in Greek Revival style, including the construction of a two-story portico across the entire front, or north, side, and in the center of this facade a central two-tiered porch. Later in the century, the portico and the two interior chimneys were removed. Sometime during the century, a large two-story section was added to the rear of the house, and a projecting two-story bay on the west side.

The present two-tiered porch at the entrance is a modern replacement whose design differs considerably from the earlier one. Four large Doric columns support it, and a railing runs around the second-story level. The east entranceway consists of a one-story portico with an elliptical plan and Doric columns. Other modern features include clapboarding and window sash.

The central hall, extending from the entranceway through the rest of the house and rear addition, has always dominated the floor plan, which otherwise has been completely obliterated. Interior partitions have either been removed to create larger rooms or added to make smaller ones. Stairs are located in the front and rear of the hall. Little, if any, of the original interior finish remains.

The house, also known as the Governor Huntington House, in excellent condition, is owned and occupied by a charitable organization and is not open to the general public. Huntington's remains rest in the adjacent Old Burial Ground.

Williams Birthplace, Connecticut ⊗

Location: New London County, on the west side of Conn. 87 at the south end of the commons, Lebanon.

William Williams was born in this house in 1731 and lived in it until 1755, when his father gave him a residence elsewhere in Lebanon. Constructed about 1712 by Rev. Samuel Welles, a Congregational minister, it later came into the possession of Rev. Solomon Williams, the signer's father, and is also known as the Welles-Williams House. Over the years, considerable alteration has occurred.

The rectangular frame structure is two stories high with a gable roof. Exterior louvered shutters flank the windows on both stories. The Greek Revival architrave of the central door was added about 1830. A one-story ell, containing a kitchen and part of the dining

Williams Birthplace.

room, is located at the rear southwest corner of the house. A barn has been built on the end of the ell. A more recent one-story frame wing extends from the southeast rear corner. The residence was recently covered with clapboard.

In modern times the original large central stone chimney has been replaced by a much smaller brick one, which provides a fireplace for the present living room. This has resulted in a major revamping of the typical central chimney floor plan. It once consisted of two tiers of four rooms but today is divided into large living room, dining room, and parlor, plus a bath, and three bedrooms upstairs. Two of the latter originally had fully paneled walls. Only one is paneled today.

The house, a private residence not accessible to the public, is in good condition.

Williams House, Connecticut ⚠

Location: New London County, southeast corner of the junction of Conn. 207 and Conn. 87, Lebanon.

Of the two extant residences of William Williams, this house, where he lived the greater part of his life, is less altered. His father, Rev. Solomon Williams, acquired it in 1748 and 7 years later presented it to William, who resided there until his death in 1811.

The dwelling is a two-story, rectangular frame building. A long, 1½-story service wing extends from the center of the rear of the house. The original clapboard siding, covered with asbestos shingles in the 1930's, has recently been reexposed. The front entranceway, in the Greek Revival style, was probably constructed about 1830. Other exterior changes to the main house are limited to the lowering of the two original interior chimneys on the back side of the ridge of the gabled roof, the addition of a brick chimney at the north end, and the insertion of a one-story bay window in the living room at the south end.

The central hall divides each floor into two large rooms. Downstairs, to the north of the hall, which incorporates the original stairway, is a parlor, whose entire fireplace wall is still covered with the

Williams House.

old paneling; to the south of the hall is the living room. Its entrance-way from the hall has been widened and two columns inserted. Upstairs are two bedrooms with fully paneled fireplace walls. The six original fireplaces, except for the one in the kitchen, have been closed up, but their mantels have been left in place. All the original wide floorboards remain. The rear service wing contains a dining room and kitchen on the first floor and four small bedrooms above.

The well-preserved house is today a private home and is not open to the public.

Wolcott House, Connecticut ⚠

Location: Litchfield County, on the east side of South Street nearly opposite its intersection with Wolcott Avenue, Litchfield.

Oliver Wolcott erected and occupied this residence in 1753, some 2 years after he moved from Windsor to Litchfield, and lived in it until he died in 1797. Except for a major rear addition, it has been only slightly altered.

The two-story, frame structure has a gable roof, a large central chimney, and slight overhangs at the gable ends. Attached to the

Wolcott House.

south end of the house on the main axis is a small, 1½-story frame wing with gambrel roof. A one-story porch, added by Wolcott about 1783, extends across this wing. The roof of the porch is of the coved, or "barrow," type. The walls of the main house and wing are covered with clapboards, and the windows have louvered shutters. Triangular pediments cap the first-story windows. The center door, topped by a round arch fanlight, is sheltered by a Federal period broken-pediment portico supported by two fluted columns.

Later additions include small bay windows on each side of the chimney in the south end wall of the south wing; a wide dormer in the west, or front, upper story of the wing; and a two-story, frame, clapboard-covered service wing, added in the 1880's at the northeast corner on the rear of the main house, which gave the structure its present L-shape. The service wing, which cannot be seen from the street, contains the present kitchen and servants' workrooms and bedrooms.

The floor plan of the main house is the central chimney type. To the rear of the short central hall, which is equipped with the original L-shaped stairway and divides this portion of the house into two tiers of rooms, is the central chimney. On the first floor, to the north of the hall, is the dining room; to the south, the parlor. The fireplace walls in both rooms are fully paneled, and the floors have wide boards. Back of the parlor, a hall leads on the south to the morning room, or bedroom, in the south wing; and on the north, to the original kitchen, which contains a large fireplace. Four bedrooms occupy the second story of the main house, two of them featuring paneled overmantels, and one bedroom is located on the second floor of the south wing.

One of Wolcott's descendants, who acquired and restored the house about 1920, resides in it today. In excellent condition, it is the oldest extant structure in Litchfield Historic District, a National Historic Landmark relating primarily to colonial architecture. The house is not accessible to the public.

The White House, District of Columbia △

Location: 1600 Pennsylvania Avenue NW., Washington.

Signers John Adams and Thomas Jefferson were the first two occupants of the White House, official residence of our Nation's

South facade of the White House.

Presidents since 1800. It is a national shrine that symbolizes the honor and dignity of the highest office in the land, and has been the scene of many historic events and brilliant social affairs. Like the Nation itself, it bears the influences of successive Chief Executives. Although rebuilt and modernized, it retains the simplicity and charm of its original appearance.

President George Washington approved the plans for the White House, drawn by Irish-born James Hoban, winner of the prize competition. Maj. Pierre Charles L'Enfant, the French artist-engineer, located the mansion in his plan of the Federal City, in which it and the Capitol were the first public buildings erected. The cornerstone was laid on October 13, 1792. Workmen used light gray sandstone from the Aquia Creek Quarries, in Virginia, for the exterior walls. During the course of construction or soon thereafter, they apparently

North facade of the White House in 1807.

were painted white. The building was thus unofficially termed the "White House" from an early date, but for many years it was usually referred to as the "President's House" or the "President's Palace."

In the Palladian style of architecture, the main facade resembles the Duke of Leinster's mansion in Dublin. Hoban probably derived the details of other faces and the interior arrangement from other contemporary European mansions. He supervised the original construction; the rebuilding after the burning by British forces, in 1814; and the erection of the north and south porticoes, some years later. Over the course of time, however, various architects modified Hoban's original plans, notably Benjamin H. Latrobe during and after the Jefferson administration.

President and Mrs. John Adams were the first occupants, in November 1800 when the Government moved from Philadelphia to Washington. The interior had not yet been completed, and Mrs. Adams used the unfinished East Room to dry the family wash. During Jefferson's administration the east and west terraces, or pavilions, were built. Jefferson, who practiced democratic simplicity in his social life, opened the mansion each morning to all arrivals.

During the War of 1812, British forces captured the city and set the torch to the White House, the Capitol, and other Government buildings in retaliation for the destruction by U.S. troops of some public buildings in Canada. Only the partially damaged exterior walls and interior brickwork of the White House remained in the spring of 1815 when reconstruction began. In 1817 the recently elected President, James Monroe, was able to occupy the structure. In 1824 builders erected the south portico; and in 1829, the large north portico over the entrance and driveway. The west wing, including the President's oval office, was added during the first decade of the 20th century. The east wing was built in 1942.

Over the years, the White House proper has been extensively renovated and modernized on various occasions. The old sandstone walls have been retained, however. The aim has been to keep the historical atmosphere while providing a more livable home for the President and his family.

Located on the first floor of the main building are the East Room, Green Room, Blue Room, Red Room, State Dining Room, and Family Dining Room. These richly furnished rooms are open to the public on a special schedule. The ground and second floors are restricted to the use of the presidential family and guests. On the ground floor are the Diplomatic Reception Room, Curator's Office, Vermeil Room, China Room, and Library. The second floor contains the Lincoln Bedroom, Lincoln Sitting Room, Queens' Bedroom (Rose Guest Room), Treaty Room, Yellow Oval Room, and Empire Guest Room. Neither of the wings, reserved for the President and his staff, are ordinarily accessible to the public.

The simple dignity of the White House is enhanced by the natural beauty of its informal but carefully landscaped grounds.

College Hill, Georgia ⚠

Location: Richmond County, 2216 Wrightsboro Road, Augusta.

In 1795 George Walton built this house on the western outskirts of Augusta on land that had been granted him by the State of Georgia in 1787. He lived in it until his death in 1804.

College Hill.

The handsome, two-story, frame structure features weather-boarded and clapboarded walls, a gable roof, and a brick chimney at each end. Of special interest is the two-tiered veranda extending across the entire main facade. At its front and sides on both levels are a series of segmental arches supported by delicate square columns on high pedestals. The fine balustrade is composed of delicate, sheaf-like balusters. Central double doors are located on the front of both stories. The doors are framed by pilasters and sidelights and topped by segmental fanlights. The windows have exterior louvered shutters. A one-story kitchen, added in 1898, extends from the southwest rear corner of the house.

The central hall, which contains a U-shaped stairway, divides the main section of the structure into two pairs of rooms. The larger front two are equipped with fireplaces and have original mantels decorated in the Adam style. Behind the main hall is a smaller rear hall. The hall walls are plastered, and the board walls of the principal rooms are covered with paper and wainscoting. Five bedrooms occupy the second floor. The original kitchen was situated in a separate building that is no longer extant.

Known today as the Walton-Harper House, since 1885 College

Hill has been owned by the Harper family, descendants of Walton. Little altered but never restored, it is a private residence and is not shown publicly.

Meadow Garden, Georgia

Location: Richmond County, 1320 Nelson Street, Augusta.

About 1790 Gov. George Walton moved from Savannah to Augusta, then the capital. At that time, he built Meadow Garden cottage at the northern edge of the city, on confiscated Loyalist lands in his possession. He resided in it until 1795, the year he constructed and occupied a larger home, College Hill, just west of Augusta. He deeded Meadow Garden under trusteeship to Thomas Watkins, who later conveyed it to George Walton, Jr. Over the years, it has been doubled in size and otherwise altered.

Meadow Garden was originally a modest 1½-story cottage of frame construction built over a high brick basement. The gable roof was pierced by two front dormers and an interior central chimney. Windows were located in the gable ends. An entrance door and hall were situated on the western bay of the south facade, which had

Meadow Garden.

three bays. Two rooms on the first floor opened off the east of the hall, and the basement contained two more finished rooms.

Sometime after 1800 the house was enlarged and converted into a central hall type by a major three-bay wide extension to the west of the side hall, which became the central hall. The gable roof of the original building was extended over the new portion, which was also equipped with an interior chimney. About 1903 a single dormer was added to the extension. The two first-floor rooms in the addition, which lacks a cellar, are about two steps lower than the two in the original structure. The second floor of the present house contains four bedrooms. A one-story porch, probably not original, extends across the front, or south, side. Its Doric columns rest on square pedestals and are linked by a light balustrade. About 1903 a one-story kitchen was added to the rear northwest corner of the house.

Many interior features are intact, but the plaster walls are covered with paper. The southwest room, or library, located in the 1800 addition and restored in 1969, contains an excellent late Georgian mantel and overmantel. The building has been roofed with modern material.

The National Society of the Daughters of the American Revolution acquired the residence in 1900, and the following year opened it to visitors. In 1960 the National Society presented it to the State Society. It is currently operated as a historic house museum by the Augusta Chapter. A caretaker's residence is located on the grounds.

Tabby Cottage, Georgia ⊗

Location: Liberty County, on St. Catherines Island, which is located about 10 miles off the Georgia coast southeast of Midway between St. Catherines and Sapelo Sounds.

The original portion of this structure, today an eight-bedroom house and the main building on St. Catherines Island, may have been built by Button Gwinnett in 1765 when he purchased the island, on which he resided until his death in 1777 at Savannah. In 1929 the owner of the island extensively remodeled the gable-roofed building. He retained its basic shape and preserved many of its features, including mantels, stair rail, and wide-board, hand-pegged floors. To the rear at a right angle on one side he added a 1½-story wing, also with gable roof, which more than doubled the floor space. The original, or front, section of the house, also 1½ stories in height, was constructed of "tabby," a mixture of lime, ground from burned oyster shells, with sand, shells, and water. The wing is of frame with a stucco finish. Both parts of the residence are now roofed with Ludowici tile and feature dormers, interior chimneys, and shuttered exterior windows.

Other tabby structures on the island include seven guest cottages and about a dozen slave quarters, all probably dating from the early 19th century. Many of them are in ruins but some are in good condition. Elsewhere are four present employee residences, as well as several barns and maintenance buildings. Boundaries of old cotton and tobacco fields are discernible, as well as dozens of Indian burial mounds. Of special interest, between Persimmon Point and Wamassee Head, is the undisturbed site of the Mission of Santa Catalina (1566-ca. 1684), a Spanish mission. None of the buildings remain, but potsherds and other surface debris are plentiful.

When this volume went to press, the National Survey of Historic Sites and Buildings was making a further study of Tabby Cottage to determine the exact degree of its authenticity in relation to Gwinnett. Privately owned St. Catherines Island, not accessible to the public, has already been accorded National Historic Landmark status because of its associations with Spanish exploration and settlement.

Whipple Birthplace, Maine   ⊗

Location: York County, 88 Whipple Street, Kittery.

William Whipple, a signer from New Hampshire, was a native of Kittery, now in Maine but then in Massachusetts. Born in this house in 1730, he probably lived in it until, like many boys of the locality, he went to sea. About 1760 he abandoned his life as a seaman and took up residence in Portsmouth, N.H.

This handsome frame residence, the only one extant associated with a signer in Maine, occupies a picturesque setting on a small cove along the Piscataqua River. The two-story building has been considerably altered and enlarged over the years, but it is in excel-

Whipple Birthplace.

lent condition and rests on original foundations. It has been painted red since at least 1873.

In its present form the house is Georgian in style with a central hall plan. The exterior walls are clapboarded. On the east, or front, elevation a round arch window on the second story sits over a pedimented center door. The ell at the rear is a 20th-century addition. A slight overhang on the south end of the house indicates that it may once have been a garrison house, and that the upper story projected over the first. This portion of the house was constructed of hemlock, square-dovetailed at the corners. At some later date, the structure was enlarged, and in the mid-19th century the exterior was completely renovated.

The residence originally featured a center chimney floor plan. In the 19th century the central chimney was removed and a center hall with stairway added, as well as two small interior chimneys with fireplaces, one at each side of the hall. On the first floor, to the south of the hall, is the bedroom where Whipple was born; to the north, a large parlor. The original kitchen is located to the rear, or west, of the center hall and parlor.

Privately occupied, the house is not open to the public.

Carroll Mansion, Maryland ⊗

Location: Anne Arundel County, Duke of Gloucester Street, between Newman and St. Marys Streets, Annapolis.

Charles Carroll III of Carrollton was born in 1737 at this townhouse, which his father had probably built about 1735. Around the age of 11, young Carroll traveled to Europe for an education and did not return to Maryland until 1765. Thereafter, he lived mainly at Doughoregan Manor but utilized his birthplace, which he inherited from his father, when in Annapolis. In 1804, when he retired from public life, he closed it up. In 1870 one of his granddaughters deeded the house and property to the Redemptionist Fathers of St. Mary's Catholic Church, which had been built in 1858-60 on adjacent lands also donated by the Carrolls.

Carroll Mansion, a brick rectangular structure constructed in Flemish bond, rises 2½ stories over a basement. Belt courses mark the first- and second-floor levels on the north and south sides. Segmental arches head the windows. Two massive chimneys penetrate the slate-covered gable roof. They are located at what may have been the original gable ends. Five gabled dormers protrude from the south side of the roof; four from the north. A wood cornice with

Carroll Mansion.

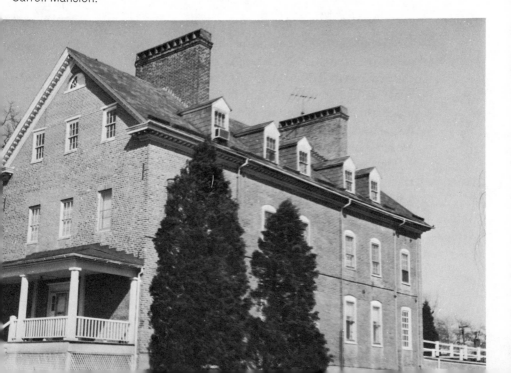

dentils and modillions extends along the sides and up the gables at the ends.

Exterior alterations include the addition of a one-story basement at the east, or present rear, end of the residence and a one-story porch and entrance at the west end. The front entrance, probably dating from the early or mid-19th century, is highlighted by a rectangular transom and sidelights. The original entrance was apparently located in the center of the north side of the house, where a passageway, erected in 1858, now connects it to St. Mary's Church.

Interior alterations have practically obliterated the original floor plan. A stair hall occupies a central compartment at the north side, and the stairs appear to be original. Only two major rooms retain some of their original finish. A large one on the south side of the first floor, now used as a chapel, has walls paneled in plaster and a plaster cornice. Another, at the east end, features a plaster cornice, a ceiling divided by triple panels, and a wooden mantelpiece.

The building, in fair condition, is used as a residence by the Redemptionist Fathers and is not accessible to the public. It is part of Colonial Annapolis Historic District.

Carrollton Manor, Maryland ⊗

Location: Frederick County, on the south side of Manor Wood Road, immediately east of the East Alco Aluminum Company Plant, just west of Buckeystown.

In 1765 Charles Carroll, returning to Maryland after completing his extensive education in Europe, built this home near the mouth of the Monocacy River along Tuscarora Creek on a 10,000-acre tract of land he had acquired from his father. Young Carroll never spent much time at Carrollton Manor. Shortly after he had constructed it, his father died, and he preferred to spend his time at Doughoregan Manor, the ancestral family home in Howard County.

The rectangular manor is constructed of native limestone. It rises 2½ stories above an elevated basement. A pair of chimneys are located at the west end of the gable roof, and a single chimney at the east end. A later one-story addition extends from the east end. The central door, sheltered by a one-story porch on the north, is topped by a rectangular transom and flanked by sidelights, both

Carrollton Manor.

probably dating from the Greek Revival period. Dating from the same time are the two triple windows in the first story at the rear of the house. A one-story porch that once extended across that elevation has been removed.

The house contains four rooms on each floor. East of the front entrance is a stair hall and a spacious dining room; to the west, a library and living room. Large double doors connect the living and dining rooms. The second floor contains four bedrooms; the attic, four more.

Upon Carroll's death, his descendants inherited the manor. In 1968 an aluminum company bought the property and erected a large office and plant buildings and a spur railroad track to the west of the house. In excellent condition, though never restored, it is today used as a company residence and is not open to visitors. A nearby chapel, erected by Carroll, is still used as a parish church.

Chase-Lloyd House, Maryland ⚠

Location: Anne Arundel County, 22 Maryland Avenue, Annapolis.

Although Samuel Chase began building this house in 1769 while he was a young lawyer, he never resided in it, for he sold it unfinished in 1771 to Edward Lloyd IV, a wealthy Maryland planter and politician. Lloyd immediately engaged architect William Buckland, newly

Chase-Lloyd House.

arrived in Annapolis, to continue construction, completed 3 years later with the aid of local architect William Noke.

The structure, one of the first three-story Georgian townhouses erected in the American Colonies, ranks among the finest of its type in the United States and is one of the major attractions in Colonial Annapolis Historic District. The house rises three full stories over a high basement. Two massive interior chimneys protrude through the broad, low, hip-on-hip roof. The brick walls are laid in Flemish bond and adorned by belt courses of rubbed brick at the second- and third-floor levels. An enriched cornice embellishes the roofline. At the front, or east, facade the axial line features a tall, projecting central pavilion and entranceway, an arched window on the third floor, and crowning pediment with a small bull's-eye window.

Of particular note is the entranceway, in essentially a Palladian motif. The three-section composition was rarely used in Georgian houses before the Revolution. The door is topped by a fanlight and flanked by two panels of sidelights. The three openings are framed by two engaged Ionic columns and two Ionic pilasters which support an entablature that becomes an open pediment over the door. The triple windows on the second floor over the entrance door and the arched windows in the center of the three on the third are also unusual.

The sides of the house lack architectural distinction, but in the rear a large Palladian window within a brick arch ornaments and lights the interior stair landing. The only exterior alterations are a three-story wooden screened porch and adjoining steel fire escape on the south side of the structure near the west corner.

The floor plan is typical of the center hall type of house, with four rooms on each floor, except that lateral halls divide the front and rear rooms. The unusually large center hall is dominated by a magnificent stairway and a pair of free-standing Ionic columns bearing a full entablature. A parlor, large dining room, sitting room, and breakfast room are located on the first floor, which has been only slightly altered. A small back stairway is adjacent to the breakfast room. Ornamentation of the plaster ceilings and doorways is outstanding. The dining room, the most elaborate room, contains an imported Italian mantelpiece that is richly decorated. The second floor is also exquisitely ornamented.

The Lloyd family owned the house until 1847, when Chase's descendants acquired it. In 1888 one of them bequeathed it to the Protestant Episcopal Church for use as a home for elderly women. It is in excellent condition and is well maintained. The first floor is open to visitors and contains some items that belonged to the Lloyds or to the later Chase owners. The upper two floors are utilized for the ladies' home.

Deshon-Caton-Carroll House, Maryland ⊗

Location: 800 East Lombard Street, Baltimore.

This was the winter home of Charles Carroll of Carrollton during his twilight years and the site of his death in 1832. Christopher Deshon, a Baltimore merchant, built it in 1811-12, and in 1818 sold it to Richard Caton, husband of Carroll's youngest daughter, Mary. Carroll spent the winters there with the couple until his demise. The rest of the time, he resided at Doughoregan Manor in Howard County.

The Deshon-Caton-Carroll House, a good example of Classic Revival architecture, is constructed of brick laid in Flemish bond. It

Deshon-Caton-Carroll House.

stands 3½ stories high. Six pedimented dormers—three each at the south (front) and north elevations—as well as a central chimney and two end chimneys pierce the low gable roof. A belt course at the second-floor line and dentil cornice at roof level, both of sandstone, extend across the north and south elevations. Recessed rectangular panels of wood are inserted between the second- and third-story windows of the south and west elevations. A large semicircular window is located in the west gable of the attic story. The wide-paneled center door at the main entrance to the house is sheltered by an Ionic marble portico surmounted by an iron railing.

The central hall plan provides for four large rooms, two on each side of the hallway on each of the first three floors. The front entrance opens into a stair hall, in which an elegant spiral stairway rises in an open well up through the three stories. A counting room for business purposes, family dining room, breakfast room, and study occupy the first floor. The second floor, once used primarily for recreation and formal entertainment, contains a large parlor, formal dining room, music room, and library. Bedrooms occupy the third floor, and the attic at one time contained slave quarters.

The house remained in the Caton family until 1856. During the last quarter of that century, a furniture store occupied the first floor, and the owner divided the upper floors into apartments. In 1914 the city of Baltimore acquired the building, and 3 years later put it to use as the "Carroll Vocational School." From about 1930 until 1956 the structure served as a recreation center. Subsequently the house faced the threat of demolition, prevented by the efforts of the Charles Carroll American Heritage Association, Inc. In 1963 the mayor of Baltimore decided that the residence should be preserved. Upon completion of restoration and renovation, in 1967, it was placed under the Municipal Museum, a nonprofit corporation. This organization operates it today for the city as a historic house museum.

Doughoregan Manor, Maryland ⚠

Location: Howard County, on the west side of Manor Lane, about 1 mile south of Md. 144 and 8 miles west of Ellicott City.

Charles Carroll III of Carrollton preferred this manor, the ancestral family home, over his other residences. He lived in it for most of the period 1766-1832 rather than at Carrollton Manor or his Annapolis townhouse. In 1717 Charles Carroll I had acquired the 10,000 acres that originally comprised the estate. His son Charles II probably built the main section of the mansion about a decade later. In the 1760's Charles III inherited it. In the 1830's, after his death in 1832, it was greatly enlarged. It is still owned and occupied by the Carroll family.

Much changed over the years, Doughoregan Manor is now an architecturally distinguished complex of buildings united into one long structure, about 300 feet in extent. The original manor was a Georgian, 1½-story, brick structure with gambrel roof and two

Doughoregan Manor.

pairs of end chimneys. A kitchen-servants' quarters and a chapel, both probably one-story and constructed of brick about 1780, stood detached from the house, on the south and north respectively.

In the 1830's Charles Carroll V undertook a comprehensive expansion in the Greek Revival style that converted the manor to its present five-part composition. He raised the main house to two stories and cut off the gable roof to form a flat deck, which was balustraded and surmounted by an octagonal cupola. At the front (east) center door he added a one-story portico with four Doric columns. To the rear of the residence, he attached another portico, over which he erected a room. Along both sides of the rear portico, he constructed a covered, one-story veranda with iron columns that extended the length of the main house. The heights of the kitchen-servants' quarters and the chapel were raised and they were connected to the main house by two-story wings, topped by unifying wooden walkways.

Inside the central part of the mansion, an oak-paneled central hall extends from front to rear. The principal stairway is located in a small side hall adjacent to the front of the main hall. On one side of the main hall in the 1727 portion of the house are library and large parlor; on the other, small parlor and dining room. The second-floor bedrooms, remodeled in the 1830's, were completely renovated and redecorated about 1915. The chapel, refurbished in the 1830's and again after the Civil War, is in good condition and is still used as a parish church. It is one of the few surviving private chapels in the United States dating from the 18th century. The grave of Charles Carroll III is located next to the altar.

The estate, comprising 2,800 acres, and mansion are well maintained. They are not open to the public.

Habre-de-Venture, Maryland ⚠

Location: Charles County, on the west side of Rose Hill Road, which connects Md. 6 and Md. 225, about 1 mile north of Port Tobacco.

In 1771 Thomas Stone built this plantation house near the busy riverport town of Port Tobacco, Md. He lived in it during his most politically active years, and on his death in 1787 was buried in the adjacent family graveyard.

Habre-de-Venture.

A Georgian structure of brick and frame, Habre-de-Venture consists of five parts: a central house connected to two wings by two covered passageways, or "hyphens." The hyphens and wings extend southward to form a semicircle. The main building is a 1½-story structure over an elevated basement. It has a dormered gambrel roof flanked by external end chimneys. The brick walls are laid in Flemish bond with glazed headers. Center doors and full-length, one-story porches are located at the front and rear of the house.

A center hall, with stairs set against its west wall, divides the central unit into dining and living rooms. In 1928 the Baltimore Museum of Art removed the elaborate hand-carved paneling in the living room; it was subsequently replaced with a replica. The fireplace wall in the dining room protrudes out into the room, and the flue curves back to the wall and up to the ceiling.

To the west of the central house is the kitchen wing, a low, two-story, gable-roofed structure with brick ends and frame sides. Its second story, added about 1820, contains two bedrooms. The connecting hyphen, originally gabled roof and one story in height and containing a breakfast room, was increased to 1½ stories by the addition of a gambrel roof with dormers to provide bathrooms for the second floor of the main house. The east wing, a gambrel-roofed, low, 1½-story frame structure that has one room on each floor, served as Stone's law office. A one-story gabled brick hyphen connects it to the main house.

Except for the alterations mentioned above, Habre-de-Venture has changed but slightly through the years. In excellent condition and carefully restored, it now serves as a private residence and is not shown publicly.

Paca House, Maryland

Location: Anne Arundel County, 186 Prince George Street, Annapolis.

William Paca, a young, newly married lawyer, built this townhouse in the years 1763-65 as his principal residence and occupied it until 1780. At that time, a few months after the death of his second wife, he sold the house and moved to Wye Plantation, a country estate in Queen Annes County he had acquired about 1760.

The Paca House is a large, five-part Georgian structure, today part of Colonial Annapolis Historic District. Two brick wings (kitchen and office) sit at right angles to the main axis of the central house, to which they are connected by brick passageways, or hyphens. The central unit is a gable-roofed brick structure of 2½ stories over an elevated basement. The front facade is laid in all-header bond, and the ends in Flemish bond. The window arches, of rubbed brick,

Paca House.

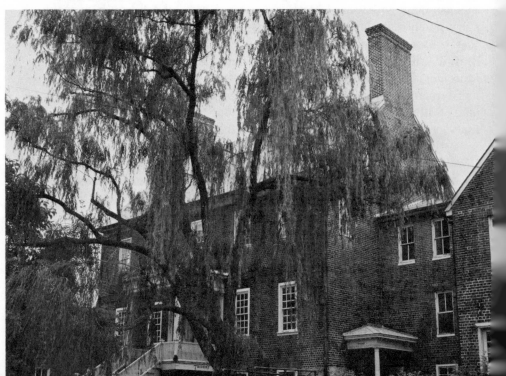

are flat. A small, one-story frame porch, which is pedimented and done in modified Roman Doric style, provides access to the central entrance.

Large brick chimneys rise from both ends of the central house, and smaller ones from the wings. Three gabled dormers are situated in the front of the main roof and two in the rear. The 1½-story wings are also gable-roofed. The west wing and both of the hyphens had been raised to two stories in the 19th century, but were recently lowered to their original height.

On each side of the center hall in the main house are two rooms. The interior has been greatly altered over the years, and portions of the original wood and plaster finish remain only in the center hall, the stair hall behind it, and the parlor. The main stairway is equipped with the original Chinese Chippendale balustrade.

In 1899 the Paca House became the Carvel Hall Hotel, enlarged in 1906 by rear additions that completely hid the back of the original house. In 1964, when the structure faced demolition, Historic Annapolis, Inc., purchased the Paca House portion. The next year, the State of Maryland acquired the entire property. In 1967-69 it razed the 1906 hotel additions and restored the gardens. Presently, the Maryland Historical Trust, a public agency, holds title to the house, but Historic Annapolis, Inc., retains all the responsibilities and rights of ownership and administration. When this volume went to press, the residence was undergoing an extensive restoration program and was not accessible to the public. Historic Annapolis, Inc., plans to utilize it as a guesthouse for visiting dignitaries, though the first floor will be open to visitors.

Peggy Stewart House, Maryland ⊗
Location: Anne Arundel County, 207 Hanover Street, Annapolis.

Thomas Stone purchased this Georgian residence in 1783 and until his death 4 years later occupied it while in Annapolis, though he maintained his home at Habre-de-Venture in Charles County. The Peggy Stewart House was built sometime between 1761 and 1764 by Thomas Rutland. Its owner in the period 1772-79 was Anthony Stewart, an Annapolis merchant. In 1774 Revolutionaries forced him to burn his ship, the *Peggy Stewart*, when he attempted to land a

Peggy Stewart House.

cargo of tea on which he had paid taxes. Five years later, he fled to England.

Over the years, the rectangular brick house has been substantially modified on both the exterior and interior. Its 2½ stories rest on an elevated basement. At the time of a major alteration in 1894, the gable roof was replaced by the present hip roof, which has a cutoff deck and balustrade, and the chimneys were rebuilt in their current form. Two gabled dormers are located at the front of the roof and one at each side. Highlighting the ends of the house are central pavilions, which have triangular pediments with round center windows. The chimneys cut through the front corners of the pediments. A wooden box cornice with frieze board below extends around the eaves. A large wing at the rear is a later addition.

The front facade of the house is comprised of all-header bond and the sides of English bond. The basement and first-story windows are topped by segmental arches, but the second-story windows have flat ones. The sills are of stone, and louvered shutters flank the first- and second-floor windows. The front entranceway, sheltered by a small wooden porch with a triangular broken pediment, has a paneled door that is surmounted by a rectangular glazed transom.

In 1837 the house had 12 rooms, eight of which were equipped with fireplaces. The original portion of the house, excluding the rear addition, has a center hall floor plan. The stairs are set against the east wall, beyond which is a large living room. A parlor and dining room are situated to the west of the hall. Five bedrooms are located upstairs. The interior of the house has been extensively remodeled in recent times. Only one fireplace, in the southeast front room on the second floor, retains its original mantel.

The Peggy Stewart House, also known as the Rutland-Peggy Stewart House and the Rutland-Stewart-Stone House, is privately owned and is not open to the public. It is part of Colonial Annapolis Historic District.

Adams (John) Birthplace, Massachusetts △

Location: Norfolk County, 133 Franklin Street, Quincy.

This was the original homestead of the Adams family and the birthplace of John Adams. Although not architectually impressive, it is historically notable as the place where John Adams grew to manhood. It is adjacent to the John Quincy Adams Birthplace.

The original house, a typical New England saltbox structure of frame construction with a massive central chimney, was probably built about 1681. It consisted of two lower and two upper rooms. Extensive alterations were made over the years. The rear lean-to, built at some unknown date in the 18th century, added two downstairs rooms and two small upper ones, separated by a large attic.

In 1720 John Adams' father, "Deacon" John Adams, purchased the house, where in 1735 young John was born. He lived there until

John Adams and John Quincy Adams Birthplaces.

his marriage in 1764. He and his bride moved into a residence next
door that he had inherited from his father in 1761 and 6 years later
was to be the birthplace of his son John Quincy. In 1774 John
bought his birthplace home from his brother. His public duties and
legal business kept him away most of the time. By 1783, when he
and his family were in Europe, tenants resided in both the John
Adams Birthplace and the John Quincy Adams Birthplace. In 1788,
when John Adams sailed home, he settled at "Peacefield," or the
"Old House," now Adams National Historic Site, in another part
of Quincy. In 1803 he sold both birthplaces to his son John Quincy.

The John Adams Birthplace remained in the possession of the
Adams family until 1940, when they deeded it to the city of Quincy.
In 1896 they had given the Adams Chapter, Daughters of the American Revolution, permission to restore the residence, which the next
year was made accessible to the public. When the Adams Chapter
dissolved in 1950, the Quincy Historical Society took over the administration. In excellent condition and still owned by the city, the
house is open to the public.

Adams (John Quincy) Birthplace, Massachusetts △
Location: Norfolk County, 141 Franklin Street, Quincy.

This frame structure was John Adams' residence and law office
during the War for Independence and the birthplace of his son John

Quincy. In 1744 "Deacon" John Adams had acquired the residence, the oldest part of which may date from 1663. In 1761 he bequeathed it to young John. At the time of the latter's marriage 3 years later, he moved into it from his neighboring birthplace so that he could better accommodate his library and set up a law office. In 1767 John Quincy was born in the house.

Shortly thereafter, John's growing law practice and role in public affairs made it convenient for him to live in Boston most of the time, but his wife and son remained in the Quincy home until after the War for Independence. By 1783, when the family was in Europe, tenants were occupying it. After coming back to the United States in 1788, John Adams took up residence at "Peacefield," or the "Old House," now Adams National Historic Site. In 1803 John Quincy purchased both birthplaces from his father, and from 1805 to 1807 lived in his own birthplace.

The John Quincy Adams Birthplace is well preserved. Like the John Adams Birthplace, it is of typical New England saltbox design, originally comprised of two upper and two lower rooms arranged around a huge central chimney, and has been extensively altered. John Adams added a lean-to of two rooms at the back for use as a new kitchen during the time he used the original kitchen as a law office-library.

In 1897 the Quincy Historical Society, aided by Adams heirs, restored and opened the John Quincy Adams Birthplace to the public. In 1940 the Adams family turned it over to the city of Quincy. Administered by the Quincy Historical Society, it is accessible to the public.

Adams National Historic Site, Massachusetts ★

Location: Norfolk County, bounded by Adams Street, Furnace Brook Parkway, and Newport Avenue, Quincy; address: 135 Adams Street, Quincy, Mass. 02169.

Featuring the Adams Mansion, this site is a memorial to four generations of the distinguished Adams family, who resided in it from 1788 until 1927.

John Adams (1735-1826), signer of the Declaration of Independence, diplomat, the first Vice President, and the second President,

Adams Mansion.

founded a long line of men who were outstanding in politics and intellectual life. John Quincy (1767-1848), his son, won fame as a diplomat, U.S. Congessman, Secretary of State, and sixth President. Charles Francis Adams (1807-86), son of John Quincy, became a U.S. Congressman, diplomat, and author. His four sons—John Quincy II (1833-94), Charles Francis, Jr. (1835-1915), Henry (1838-1918), and Brooks (1848-1927)—made notable marks in politics, literature, and historiography.

The Adams Mansion, named "Peacefield" by John Adams but known to some as the Vassall-Adams House and later to the Adams family as the "Old House," was dear and close to all of them. In 1730-31 Maj. Leonard Vassall, a wealthy West Indian sugar planter who had come to Massachusetts some 8 years before, built the oldest part of the building. Comprising the front western section of the present residence, it was a 2½-story frame structure of Georgian design with clapboarded walls and gambrel roof. The first floor contained two rooms separated by a central stair hall; the second floor, two bedrooms and center hall; and the dormered attic, three smaller chambers. The kitchen and servants' quarters were detached.

John Adams, while still Minister to Great Britain, bought the house in September 1787 from Vassall's grandson, Leonard Vassall Borland, and on his return the next year took possession. At that time, he apparently attached the 2½-story kitchen and servants' quarters to the rear, or northwest, corner of the main structure. In 1800, near the end of his Presidency, he doubled the size of the residence by adding a large, 2½-story, L-shaped wing of frame at the east end. It was constructed in the same Georgian style as the original house and contained on the first floor a second entry hall and staircase and the "Long Room" to the east of the hall. Adams' large study-library was located on the second floor.

Other additions were made in the 19th century. In 1836 John Quincy Adams built the passage along the back, or north, side of the structure connecting the two rear service ells. In 1869 Charles Francis added 30 feet to the kitchen ell for additional servants' quarters; the following year, a detached stone library overlooking the garden; and in 1873, the stone stable. Brooks constructed the present entrance gates in 1906.

After retiring from the Presidency in 1801, John Adams lived in the house year round until his death in 1826. Subsequently, until Brooks' death in 1927, other family members resided in it full time or spent their summers there. The furnishings, to which each generation contributed, reveal the continuity of life in the residence and the tastes of the Adams family.

In 1946 the Adams Memorial Society donated the property to the Federal Government. Consisting of almost 5 acres, it includes the well-maintained house, library, garden, and stables. It may be visited from spring until the fall.

Elmwood, Massachusetts ⚿

Location: Middlesex County, 33 Elmwood Street, Cambridge.

This impressive 18th-century mansion, also known as the Oliver-Gerry-Lowell House, was the residence of three men prominent in American history: Andrew Oliver, royal Lieutenant Governor of Massachusetts (1771-74); Elbridge Gerry, politician, diplomat, Governor of the Commonwealth, signer of the Declaration, U.S. Representative, and Vice President; and James Russell Lowell, author, poet, teacher, and statesman.

In 1767 Andrew Oliver, while serving as royal secretary of Massachusetts, erected the building. An ex-stamp tax collector and a firm Tory, he aroused the hatred of the Whigs, who on at least one occasion attacked his home. He died in 1774 while serving as royal Lieutenant Governor. Some time during the War for Independence, Oliver's estate, including the mansion, was confiscated.

Elmwood.

In 1787 Elbridge Gerry, who the previous year had retired from business in Marblehead, Mass., moved to Cambridge and purchased the estate. He lived there for the rest of his long career in public service. In March 1813 he took the oath of office as Vice President in his home. Because of heavy debts, on his death in Washington, D.C., in 1814, his Cambridge residence remained his sole real estate holding.

The mansion was also the birthplace and lifelong home of James Russell Lowell (1819-91), one of the most distinguished men of letters of his era, as well as a prominent U.S. diplomat. Except during the period 1877-85, when he served as Minister to Spain and Great Britain, he lived at his birthplace, which he named "Elmwood."

Elmwood is a large, square, clapboarded-frame structure in Georgian style with brick-lined walls and two interior chimneys. The first- and second-story windows are topped by cornices. Above the foreshortened third-story windows, typical in three-story Georgian houses, runs a boldly modillioned cornice. A balustrade encloses the low-pitched hip roof. The most striking exterior feature, however, is the entranceway, which is flanked by Tuscan pilasters supporting a classic entablature decorated with a frieze. A large window rests on the entablature parapet motif and is flanked by Ionic pilasters and topped by a triangular pediment.

A one-story porch with balustraded roof deck on the north side of the house, as well as a terrace on the south side, are later additions. Located in the rear, at the northwest corner, is a two-story service wing; in the rear, at the southwest corner, a one-story wing. Both of them are of frame construction. All three floors in the main section are bisected into two rooms on either side by a central hall. Portions of the interior have been altered and modernized.

Donated to Harvard University in 1962 and now used as the presidential residence, Elmwood is not open to the public. The house and grounds are in fine condition.

Gerry Birthplace, Massachusetts ⊗

Location: Essex County, 44 Washington Street, Marblehead.

Elbridge Gerry was born in this framehouse and resided in it until 1787, when he moved to Cambridge, Mass. His father, Thomas, had built it about 1730, and it remained in possession of the Gerry family until 1820.

Architectural evidence strongly suggests that the L-shaped building was originally a two-story Georgian structure. About 1820 the two stories were apparently raised and a third one built underneath. Since that time, changes have been slight. The original interior finish of the first story is entirely 19th century, and the original paneling on the walls of the second story is clearly 18th century.

Gerry Birthplace.

Today, the exterior is clapboarded. The long arm of the ell faces north toward the street. A central hall divides the first floor of the long arm into two rooms, the east and west parlors, both with 19th century mantels, fireplaces, and flanking arched alcoves. The west parlor opens into the short arm of the ell, which extends southward to the rear and contains the dining room. Attached to the rear of the short arm is a small rear service wing containing an L-shaped, one-story kitchen. A one-story open veranda runs around the east and south elevations of the long side of the ell, and a small porch flanks the dining room on its west side. The second story contains three bedrooms, all displaying the original 18th-century paneling on the fireplace walls. The third floor consists of four bedrooms.

The house and grounds, privately owned and not open to the public, are well maintained.

Hancock-Clarke House, Massachusetts

Location: Middlesex County, 35 Hancock Street, Lexington.

The only extant residence associated with John Hancock, this was his boyhood home. In 1744, upon the death of his father at Quincy, the 7-year-old boy came to live at this house with his grandfather,

Hancock-Clarke House.

Rev. John Hancock. In 1750 the lad joined his childless uncle, Thomas Hancock, a wealthy Boston merchant who adopted him.

By the time of the Revolution, Rev. Jonas Clarke, a relative by marriage of the Hancocks, occupied the house, which had been built as a parsonage by Rev. John Hancock. Clarke encouraged Revolutionaries to use his home as a meetingplace and refuge. On the evening of April 18, 1775, patriot leaders Hancock and Samuel Adams were visiting there. Around midnight, after everyone had gone to bed, Paul Revere and later William Dawes, warning the countryside of the approach of British troops, galloped up and informed the household. A few hours later, Hancock and Adams fled northward to Burlington, Mass. They later moved from place to place, staying away from Boston, until they proceeded to Philadelphia to attend the Continental Congress, which convened the next month.

The Hancock-Clarke House consists of two frame sections, erected by Rev. John Hancock at different times. The original one, built in 1698, presently forms the small rear ell, 1½ stories high with gambrel roof. A living room-kitchen and tiny study are located downstairs and two low-studded chambers upstairs. The 2½-story front, or main, section of the house dates from 1734 and was financed by Thomas Hancock for his father. It has a large central chimney and contains a short center hall and two rooms on each of the two floors.

In 1896, when the building faced demolition, the Lexington Historical Society acquired it and moved it from across the street to its present location. In 1902 the society constructed a rear brick addition containing a fireproof vault to protect its more valuable possessions. Restored to its 18th-century appearance and well maintained, the Hancock-Clarke House is open to the public and serves as headquarters of the society. Recently the society purchased the original site of the house, where foundations are visible.

Bartlett House, New Hampshire △

Location: Rockingham County, on the west side of N.H. 111, opposite the town hall, Kingston.

This is the only extant structure closely associated with Josiah Bartlett. He built it in 1774, after fire consumed his earlier home on the same site, and lived in it until his death in 1795.

Bartlett House.

   The rectangular frame residence is clapboarded and two stories in
height. Two interior chimneys pierce the gabled roof. Exterior
louvered shutters border the windows. Many of the house's existing
features date from the second third of the 19th century, when it
was remodeled in the Greek Revival style. They include the giant
corner pilasters; cornices over the first-story windows; the center
door with cornice, sidelights, and pilasters; and the one-story porch
across the south end of the structure. Another addition, at the
southwest corner, was the two-story frame ell, which gave the
building its present L-shape. This ell contains a summer kitchen and
workroom on the first floor and four bedrooms on the second.
   Center halls bisect the rooms on both stories of the main house into
pairs. The downstairs hall is divided into two sections, each containing a stairway set against the north wall. To the south of the hall on
the first floor are the living room and the dining room, originally the
kitchen. These rooms are equipped with the original chimneys and
fireplaces. North of the hall is a parlor and behind it a bedroom.
Around 1860 the chimney for these rooms and the fireplace in the
parlor were rebuilt, and two closets that flanked the parlor fireplace

were converted into the existing arched alcoves. The second floor contains four bedrooms, two on each side of the central hall. The original wide floor boards are still in place throughout the residence.

The house, in excellent condition, is still in the possession of Bartlett descendants and is not open to the public. It has never been restored, but is furnished with some original Bartlett pieces, including a medical table and instruments.

Moffatt-Ladd House, New Hampshire △

Location: Rockingham County, 154 Market Street, Portsmouth.

An outstanding example of a late Georgian mansion, this impressive three-story structure was the longtime residence of William Whipple. Ship carpenters constructed it in 1763 for John Moffatt, a sea captain and wealthy merchant. He presented it the following year as a wedding gift to his son, Samuel, a merchant-shipowner. In 1768,

Moffatt-Ladd House.

after the latter had failed in business and fled to the West Indies to escape creditors, Captain Moffatt reacquired it and lived in it for the rest of his life. Whipple and his wife, Catherine, Moffatt's daughter, moved into the house the same year as the captain. Whipple resided there until his death in 1785; his wife and apparently his father-in-law, too, survived him.

The square, clapboarded building stands on a slight elevation overlooking old Portsmouth Harbor. Noteworthy features of the elaborate exterior include white corner quoins and richly pedimented first- and second-floor windows. The third-story windows, smaller in size, abut the distinctive cornice. Side windows, like those on the third-floor front, lack pediments. Rear windows on the first two stories have flat arches with lengthened keystones. The hip roof, flanked by three end chimneys, is cut off to form a flat deck, or captain's walk, which is enclosed by an attracive balustrade with urn finials. A delicate fence with large ornamental posts, also topped by urn finials, spans the front of the house, which is approached by a flight of granite steps that lead up to the portico-covered entranceway. Near the front northeast corner of the residence is the countinghouse, or office (1810), a small, square building with a hip roof.

The interior of the house is as highly embellished as the exterior. The outstanding room on the first floor is the unusually spacious entrance hall, one of the finest in New England. Its carved cornice is handsome, and the walls are covered with rare imported French wallpaper of the early 19th century. The beautiful and finely carved flight of stairs is lighted by a roundheaded window in the side wall above the landing. Except for the simple detail in the drawing room, that in other first-floor rooms—dining room and pantry—is rich. Four bedrooms are located on the second floor, and five additional chambers on the third. Three of the second-floor bedrooms have richly carved overmantels.

The carefully restored house and grounds were owned by the Ladd family, descendants of the Moffatts through marriage, until 1969. From 1913 until 1969, they leased the house to the Colonial Dames of America, which maintained it for public display. In 1969 the Colonial Dames acquired full title to the property. The first two floors of the house are furnished in period pieces, and the third floor is not open.

Thornton House, New Hampshire ⚠

Location: Rockingham County, 2 Thornton Street, Derry Village.

Matthew Thornton lived in this residence, which has since been considerably altered, during his medical and most of his political career. He probably acquired it in 1740, the year he moved from Worcester, Mass., to present Derry Village (then a part of Londonderry) to set up his medical practice. He resided in it until about 1780, when he retired as a doctor and moved to a farm near Merrimack, N.H.

The gable roof of the two-story frame structure, of the saltbox type, slopes steeply to the rear, or north, and forms a one-story lean-to. Two interior chimneys sit behind the ridge of the roof. The exterior, remodeled in the Greek Revival style probably in the mid-19th century, features giant pilasters on the front corners and a one-story portico over the center door. The clapboarding is a replacement of the original. All windows, including those in the gable ends, have exterior louvered shutters, and flat cornices surmount those on the first floor. A one-story frame service ell, extending from the northwest corner and giving the house its present L-shape, contains the modernized kitchen and what were once workrooms for servants.

Thornton House.

Inside the house, a center hall bisects the rooms into two pairs and is divided into two sections, each with its own stairway on the east wall. To the east of the hall are the living room and modern laundry room; to the west, dining room and present family room. The two chimneys, built between the pairs of rooms to provide four fireplaces, one for each room, were rebuilt on a smaller scale in the early 19th century for use with Franklin stoves. Thus none of the original fireplaces and mantels exist any longer, but a 19th-century mantel remains in the dining room. The opposite fireplace in the family room, however, is modern. Features dating from the 18th century include the framing and wide floorboards, visible in all rooms except the family room where they are covered. The second floor contains three bedrooms.

The Thornton House, in fair condition, is used as a private residence and is not open to the public. Its present owner hopes to restore it.

Hopkinson House, New Jersey ⬠

Location: Burlington County, 101 Farnsworth Avenue, Bordentown.

Owned by the Hopkinson family for several generations, this house was the residence of signer Francis Hopkinson from 1774 until his death in 1791. It was built in 1750 by merchant John Imlay (Emley), who used part of it as a store. Sometime before 1768 Joseph Borden, a prominent New Jersey citizen, acquired it. Hopkinson married his daughter at Philadelphia in 1768, and, after a tour as customs collector at New Castle, Del. (1772-74), moved to Bordentown and took up residence with his father-in-law.

Upon Hopkinson's death, his eldest son, Joseph (1770-1842), inherited the house. He achieved fame as composer, lawyer, judge, and politician. Among his distinguished guests were Irish poet Thomas Moore, Thomas Paine, and Joseph Bonaparte, Napoleon's brother. The Hopkinson family retained possession of the property until 1915; since then, it has been owned by the Wells family.

The Hopkinson House is an L-shaped, brick and frame structure with a gambrel, dormered roof. The main 2½-story section is constructed of brick. The center door is topped by a rectangular transom, flanked by sidelights, and sheltered by a segmental hood. A central

Hopkinson House.

hall, divided into two sections by means of a wide folding door with an arched fanlight above, bisects the first floor into two large rooms, living room and library. Both of these are currently used by the Bordentown Chamber of Commerce as an office and museum, open to the public. The front portion of the central hall serves as an entrance hall; the rear section, as the stair hall. A narrow hall extends from the stair hall south across the rear of the main house. The second and third floors, each containing four bedrooms, are used as apartments.

A two-story brick wing extends to the rear from the northeast corner of the main section. Its first-floor dining room and the two bedrooms comprising the second floor form an apartment unit. Attached to this wing at the rear of the brick arm is a two-story frame wing that once contained the kitchen and servant's bedroom.

The exterior of the house, except for the metal roof, appears to be little altered. Interior features are plastered walls, wide floorboards, and 19th-century mantels. Much of the original woodwork and trim has apparently been replaced, but the basic floor plan has not been greatly changed. The residence is in good condition.

Maybury Hill, New Jersey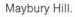

Location: Mercer County, 346 Snowden Lane, Princeton.

Maybury Hill, built about 1725, was the birthplace and boyhood home of North Carolina signer Joseph Hewes. His father leased it from 1730 until 1755.

The house provides a fine example of Georgian architecture. It was originally a small, two-story stone structure with gable roof. A short distance away, at the northeast corner, stood a detached kitchen building. In 1735, following a fire, the main house was rebuilt. In 1753 a major addition was made on the north side connecting it with the kitchen building. This resulted in an L-shaped, two-story structure with gabled roof and three end chimneys. The only alteration of consequence since that time occurred about 1900, when the fieldstone exterior walls were covered with concrete.

Flat brick arches top the windows. Second-story windows have exterior louvered shutters; those on the first, paneled shutters. Today the house has a center hall floor plan. To the south of the hall is the large parlor, which dates from 1725. To the north are the dining and living rooms, added in 1753. Both of them have paneled walls, shell cabinets, and exposed ceiling beams. The kitchen, dating from 1725, is still in the northeast corner of the building. The dining room fireplace is faced with tile. Four bedrooms occupy the upstairs. All the floors are constructed of wide boards.

Little-altered Maybury Hill was renovated in 1920, and is still in excellent condition. A private residence, it is not open to visitors.

Maybury Hill.

Morven, New Jersey 🔺

Location: Mercer County, 55 Stockton Street, Princeton.

Morven was the birthplace and lifelong home of Richard Stockton (1730-81). In the summer of 1783 it was also the official residence of his brother-in-law Elias Boudinot, President of the Continental Congress, which was then meeting in Princeton. That same year, many Revolutionary leaders gathered at the mansion to celebrate the signing of the Treaty of Paris, which ended the War for Independence.

Between 1701 and 1709 Stockton's grandfather, also named Richard, built the earliest section of Morven. It grew in a series of stages until about 1775, when its exterior appearance approximated that of today. Because fires in 1776, set by the British during the War for Independence, and 1821 necessitated extensive repairs, the interior dates from the late 18th or early 19th century.

A large Georgian mansion of brick, Morven consists of three sections: a main central, two-story section over a raised basement and two lower, attached, two-story wings. The facade of the main section, although basically early Georgian in style, was altered in the 19th century by the addition of a wide, one-story, Greek Revival porch. A central hall divides the section into a large dining room and the Gold Room. Fireplace walls in these rooms are fully paneled. The central hall intersects a stair hall, which runs across the rear of the main portion of the house and connects with the two wings. On the first floor of the east wing are two large family rooms, the Red Room and library. This wing was partially burned

Morven.

by the British. The west service wing includes the kitchen. The only recent change, in 1945-54, was the addition of a solarium, or Green Room, at the rear of the main section; a one-story porch was enclosed to form the new room.

Morven remained in possession of the Stockton family until 1945, when Gov. and Mrs. Walter E. Edge acquired it. Nine years later, they donated it to the State of New Jersey. Since that time, it has been the official residence of the Governor. It is not accessible to the public.

President's House, New Jersey ⬠

Location: Mercer County, on Nassau Street just northwest of Nassau Hall, on the Princeton University campus, Princeton.

From 1756 until 1879 this house was the official residence of the president of the College of New Jersey (Princeton University after 1896). In 1768, when John Witherspoon emigrated from Scotland to America to assume the presidency, he occupied it. While living there, he represented New Jersey in the Continental Congress and signed the Declaration. In 1779 he moved to his nearby farm, Tusculum. From then until 1794 his son-in-law Samuel S. Smith, vice president of the college, resided in the President's House. From 1879 until 1968 it was the home of the Dean of the Faculty and was known as the "Dean's House." Since 1968, it has been called the Maclean House and has been used by the Princeton Alumni Council.

President's House.

The Georgian building was designed and constructed in 1756 by Robert Smith, a master carpenter of Philadelphia. Both on the exterior and the interior, it has changed only slightly throughout the years. It was originally a two-story brick structure, rectangular in shape, with gable roof. A one-story polygonal bay extends westward from the rear southwest corner. Near the same corner, a two-story service wing of brick and stone runs southward. Above the windows of the main facade are flat stone winged arches with keystones. Over the center door is a fanlight surmounted by a triangular pediment. The exterior has retained its original appearance and arrangement except that small double dormers were later inserted in the center of the front and rear roofs to create a third level. Additions in 1868 were a wide one-story frame porch on the front of the residence and a one-story frame, polygonal bay on the east side near the northeast front corner.

The center door opens into a central hall that extends through the house to rear stairs, against the east wall. To the east of the hall are a library and study. The fireplace wall in the library is fully paneled. To the west of the hall are a parlor and dining room. The second floor of the main house contains four bedrooms; the third floor, three additional rooms. Two bedrooms are located on the second floor of the service wing. In excellent condition, the house is open to the public.

Tusculum, New Jersey   ⊗

Location: Mercer County, 166 Cherry Hill Road, Princeton.

John Witherspoon made this his home from 1779 until his death in 1794. In 1773, while serving as president of the College of New Jersey (later Princeton University), he acquired some farmland near Princeton and built Tusculum. For several years he leased out the house and farm, but in 1779 he moved from the President's House to Tusculum.

The two-story Georgian structure of fieldstone with gabled roof and two pairs of end chimneys originally had only one extension, a lower, two-story, stone and frame wing attached to the west end of the house along its main axis. First-story windows of both sections have exterior paneled shutters; second-story windows, louvered

Tusculum.

shutters. In later years, two additional wings, both of frame and two stories in height, were added to the east and west ends of the structure. Designed in the same style as the rest of the house, they do not seriously alter the original appearance of the front elevation.

The stairway is located in an ell at the rear portion of the center hall along the east wall. To the east of the hall lie the living room and study; to the west, a large dining room, which occupies the entire west half of the main house. Four bedrooms are upstairs. The finish in two of them date from about 1825. The original service wing, on the west side, contains a kitchen on the first floor and two bedrooms on the second.

Tusculum has never undergone any major alterations and it is in excellent condition. In 1924 the present owner acquired it. Under his supervision, a Philadelphia firm restored it to its 18th-century appearance. The major changes were the removal of 19th-century porches at the front, or south, and elimination of a partition wall in the dining room. The structure continues to serve as a private residence and is not shown to visitors.

Floyd Birthplace (Fire Island National Seashore), New York ★

Location: Suffolk County, 20 Washington Avenue, Mastic, Long Island; address: Fire Island National Seashore, P.O. Box 229, Patchogue, N.Y. 11772.

This farmhouse, which stood on a large estate the Floyd family had acquired in 1718, was the birthplace in 1734 of William Floyd and

Floyd Birthplace.

his residence for the greater part of his life—though he and his family were forced to abandon it in the period 1776-83 and flee to Middletown, Conn. During that time, British troops and Loyalists considerably damaged the estate. In 1803 Floyd presented the house to his son Nicoll and moved to present Westernville, N.Y.

The earliest section of the large, frame Georgian building, which was enlarged several times along its west side during the 18th century, dates from about 1724. The structure now consists of a two-story main section and three wings. The former, entered through a Dutch door, is laid out in central hall fashion. To the west of the hall are a parlor and back of that an office; to the east, a dining room, behind which are a gunroom and pantry side by side. Interesting features on the first floor are exposed ceiling beams and wide floorboards. Seven bedrooms occupy the second floor.

Extending from the rear of the central hall is a two-story north service wing, probably added about 1900. A 1½-story east service wing, with a dormered, gable roof, dates from the 18th century. At the rear, or to the north, of this wing, is a third service wing, 1½ stories high. It contained the original kitchen and was once located at the west end of the main house. Except for this relocation and the addition of the north wing, the main house and east wing are basically unchanged from their 18th-century appearance. The overall structure is in good condition and is furnished with many original pieces belonging to the Floyd family.

In 1965 Floyd descendants donated 613 acres of the estate to the U.S. Government for inclusion in Fire Island National Seashore, but retained use and occupational rights to 43 acres and the house for a period of 25 years. Thus the residence will not be open to the public until 1990.

General Floyd House, New York ⚠

Location: Oneida County, on the west side of Main Street opposite Gilford Hill Road, Westernville.

William Floyd lived in this home from 1803 until his death in 1821. In 1784 he had begun purchasing frontier land near present Rome in western New York, and 3 years later the State granted him 10,240 acres in the same area. During the summers, he visited and developed his tracts. In 1803, nearly 70 years of age, he deeded his residence at present Mastic, on Long Island, N.Y., to his son Nicoll and moved the rest of his family to present Westernville, where he constructed this farmhouse. He spent the remainder of his life farming and improving his wilderness lands.

Constructed of frame, the Georgian-style residence consists of a large, two-story main section with gable roof and a lower, two-story service wing attached to the west end. A center door, flanked by a pair of small windows, opens into a central hall that extends through the house to another door on the north side. The stairs are set against the west wall of the hall. To the east of the hall are

General Floyd House.

two large parlors containing cupboards and paneled fireplace walls. To the west of the hall is a dining room and behind that a study. The rooms have plastered walls and ceilings and wide floorboards. Four bedrooms occupy the second floor, and the attic is unfinished. The service wing, which includes the kitchen, is located to the west of the dining room.

The structure, unaltered except for metal roofs and modern plumbing, is in excellent condition. It remained in the possession of Floyd descendants until 1956. Still privately owned, it is not open to the public.

Iredell House, North Carolina

Location: Chowan County, 107 East Church Street, Edenton.

Early in 1798, in a state of extreme mental anguish because of mounting debts brought on by unwise speculation in lands, James Wilson, probably while visiting North Carolina on Federal circuit court matters, took refuge in this house. It was the home of his friend and fellow U.S. Supreme Court Justice James Iredell. Within a few months, Wilson died there.

Iredell House.

The little-altered Iredell House is a large L-shaped structure. It is constructed of frame and is two stories in height with gable roof. Two-story verandas span the front, or south, and rear elevations of the long arm of the ell. The building was erected in three stages. The earliest, the present short, or east, arm of the ell, was built in 1759 by John Wilkins, with its narrow gable end fronting on the street. In 1776 Joseph Whedbee enlarged the structure by adding to its west side the two easternmost bays of the present five-bay long arm. In 1810 Iredell's widow extended the arm by three bays to its present size and added the verandas.

The original section of the house contains a living room and one other room on the first floor and two bedrooms on the second. The first floor of the 1776 section consists of the dining room; the second floor, a large bedroom. These two sections are furnished as a historic house museum and are open to the public. The remaining section of the long arm, dating from 1810, serves as the caretaker's quarters. The State owns and administers the residence.

Nash-Hooper House, North Carolina ⚠

Location: Orange County, 118 West Tryon Street, Hillsborough.

The Nash-Hooper House is the only extant residence that can be associated with William Hooper and is the only surviving home of a signer in the State. It was built in 1772 by Francis Nash, who later attained the rank of brigadier general in the Continental Army and lost his life in the War for Independence. In 1782, after the British had driven Hooper into hiding and destroyed his estate Finian near Wilmington, he moved to Hillsborough, where his family had fled. He purchased the Nash-Hooper House and resided in it until his death in 1790. Subsequently, from 1869 until 1875, it was the home of William A. Graham, former Governor of North Carolina.

The original portion of the rectangular, two-story house was constructed with a braced oak frame that was held together by pegs and pins. It rests on shale foundations over an elevated basement, in which are located two rooms and a center hall. The roof is gabled with a chimney at each end. A one-story, frame, "sitting room" (later dining room) wing, added in 1819 on a log base, extends from the rear, or north, of the house and creates its present L-shape

Nash-Hooper House.

Weatherboarded siding covers both sides of the wing and the front of the main section. All the windows are flanked with exterior louvered shutters. The one-story porch spanning the front of the house dates from the late 19th century. A detached kitchen, erected in 1819 just east of the house adjacent to the storeroom and dining room in the north wing, was demolished in 1908. Sometime during the period 1939-59, the dining room in the north wing was converted into the present kitchen, and bathrooms were installed in the residence.

The center hall of the main house is divided into two sections by means of an arch near the rear. West of the hall are a large library and a small study or bedroom; to the east, a large parlor and in the rear corner a narrow, lateral stair hall, with the stairs set against the north wall. Three bedrooms are located on the second floor, and the attic is unfinished. Wide floorboards are exposed throughout most of the main house. An original pine mantel remains in the dining room.

Although the little-altered Nash-Hooper House is structurally sound, it has never been restored, and extensive painting and plastering will be required to return it to good condition. It is privately owned and is not open to the public.

Hooper was buried to the east of his home in the garden. That part of the garden was later absorbed by the town cemetery, behind the Presbyterian Church. In 1894 Hooper's remains were reinterred at Guilford Courthouse National Military Park, N.C., though his original gravestone remains in the Hillsborough cemetery.

Independence National Historical Park, Pennsylvania ★

Location: Philadelphia County, in downtown Philadelphia; address: 313 Walnut Street, Philadelphia, Pa. 19106.

This park in the old part of Philadelphia is not only preeminent among the sites associated with the signers of the Declaration of Independence, but also notably commemorates other major aspects

Independence Hall.

of the Nation's founding and initial growth and many momentous national events. These include meetings of the First and Second Continental Congresses; adoption and signing of the Declaration, which marked the creation of the United States; and the labors of the Constitutional Convention of 1787, which perpetuated it. As historian Carl Van Doren has said: "On account of the Declaration of Independence, [Independence Hall] is a shrine honored wherever the rights of man are honored. On account of the Constitution, it is a shrine cherished wherever the principles of self-government on a federal scale are cherished."

Independence Hall was originally the State House for the Province of Pennsylvania. In 1729 the provincial assembly set aside funds for the building, designed by lawyer Andrew Hamilton. Three years later, construction began under the supervision of master carpenter Edmund Wooley. In 1736 the assembly moved into the statehouse, which was not fully completed until 1756.

As American opposition to British colonial policies mounted, Philadelphia became a center of organized protest. To decide on a unified course of action, in 1774 the First Continental Congress met in newly finished Carpenters' Hall, whose erection the Carpenters' Company of Philadelphia had begun 4 years earlier. In 1775 the Second Continental Congress, taking over the east room of the ground floor of the statehouse from the Pennsylvania assembly, moved from protest to resistance. Warfare had already begun in Massachusetts. Congress created an Army and appointed George Washington as commander in chief. Yet the final break with the Crown had not come; not until a year later would independence be declared.

On July 2, 1776, Congress passed Richard Henry Lee's resolution of June 7 recommending independence. The Delegates then turned their attention to Thomas Jefferson's draft of the Declaration, which had been submitted on June 28. After modification, it was adopted on July 4. Four days later, in Independence Square, the document was first read publicly, to the citizens of Philadelphia. In a formal ceremony on August 2, about 50 of the 56 signers affixed their signatures to the Declaration; the others apparently did so later.

Long, hard years of war ensued. In the late autumn and winter of 1776-77, the British threatened Philadelphia and Congress moved to Baltimore. Again in the fall of 1777 it departed, this time for

York, Pa. During the British occupation of Philadelphia that winter and the next spring, the redcoats used Independence Hall as a barracks and as a hospital for American prisoners. In the summer of 1778, the Government returned. On November 3, 1781, Congress officially received news of Cornwallis' surrender at Yorktown. Independence practically had been won.

Earlier that same year, the Articles of Confederation and Perpetual Union had gone into effect. Under the Confederation, Congress stayed in Philadelphia until 1783, and later met in other cities. In 1787 the Constitutional Convention also held its highly secret sessions in Independence Hall, in the same chamber in which the Declaration had been adopted.

About the same time that Philadelphia became the second Capital (1790-1800) under the Constitution, after the Government had moved from New York City, Independence Hall acquired three new neighbors in Independence Square: City Hall (1791), on the east; County Court House (1789), on the west; and American Philosophical Society Hall, on the southeast. Beginning in 1790, Congress met in the County Court House (subsequently known as Congress Hall). The following year, after sitting for a few days in Independence Hall, the U.S. Supreme Court moved to City Hall. In 1793 George Washington was inaugurated for his second term as President in Congress Hall, and 4 years later President Adams also took his oath of office there.

In 1799 the State government vacated Independence Hall and moved to Lancaster. The next year, the Federal Government relocated to Washington, D.C. The city of Philadelphia then used City Hall and Congress Hall, and various tenants occupied Independence Hall until the city acquired it in 1818. For example, during the period 1802-27 artist Charles Willson Peale operated a museum there. He and his son painted many of the signers and heroes of the War for Independence. These portraits form the nucleus of the park's present collection, which is exhibited in the Second Bank of the United States Building; a special room is devoted to the signers.

Stately and symmetrical Independence Hall, a 2½-story red brick structure that has been carefully restored, is the most beautiful 18th-century public building of Georgian style in the United States. The tall belltower, reconstructed along the original lines in 1828 by architect William Strickland, dominates the south facade. Smaller

Independence Hall in 1778.

two-story, hip-roofed, brick wings, erected in 1736 and 1739 and restored in 1897-98, one of which serves as a park information center, are connected to the main building by arcades.

The interior focus of interest in Independence Hall is the Assembly Room, the eastern one on the first floor. Probably no other room in the United States has been the scene of such political courage and wisdom. In this chamber, members of the Continental Congress and the Constitutional Convention formulated and signed the Declaration of Independence and Constitution. The room is about 40 feet square and 20 feet high. Twin segmental-arched fireplaces along the east wall flank the speaker's dais. Massive fluted pilasters raised on pedestals adorn the paneled east wall. The other three walls are plastered. A heavy Roman Doric entablature borders the plaster ceiling. The furniture arrangement at the time of the Continental Congress has been duplicated. The only original furnishings are the "Rising Sun" chair and the silver inkstand with quill box and shaker used by the signers of the Declaration and the Constitution.

The other large room on the ground floor, where the U.S. Supreme Court held sessions for a few days in 1791 and again in August 1796, housed the Supreme Court of Pennsylvania and later other State and

Restored Assembly Room, Independence Hall, where Members of the Continental Congress adopted and signed the Declaration of Independence.

local courts. The paneled walls are decorated with massive fluted pilasters of the Roman Doric order. The central hall between this room and the Assembly Room is richly adorned with a Roman Doric order of columns and entablature, fully membered. On the second floor are the Long Room, Governor's Council Chamber, and Committee Room. These are furnished to represent the activities of the Pennsylvania legislature and government prior to 1775.

The Liberty Bell, a worldwide emblem of freedom, is displayed in the tower stair hall on the south end of the first floor. [When this volume went to press, the bell was scheduled to be moved in the near future to a newly constructed belltower, part of the park visitor center, located 2 blocks from Independence Hall.] The source of the 2,080-pound bell's name is the "Proclaim Liberty" inscription, engraved on it to commemorate the 50th anniversary of William Penn's Charter of Privileges (1701). In 1750 the Pennsylvania assembly authorized erection of the Independence Hall belltower, and the next year ordered a bell from England. After it arrived in 1752, it was cracked during testing and was twice recast by local workmen. As the official statehouse bell, it was rung on public occasions. In 1777, before the British occupied Philadelphia, the Government moved it temporarily to Allentown, Pa. Traditionally the bell cracked once again, in 1835, while tolling the death of Chief Justice John Marshall. The exterior appearances of City Hall and Congress Hall have changed little since the 1790's, when many of the signers served in the Government. The interior of Congress Hall has been restored and refurnished as the meeting-place of Congress in the 1790's. Exhibits in City Hall describe the activities of the U.S. Supreme Court during the same period of time, and portray Philadelphia life during the late 18th century. Carpenters' Hall, a block east of Independence Square, is still owned and operated by the Carpenters' Company of Philadelphia. The hall memorializes the First Continental Congress and possesses architectural significance.

The American Philosophical Society, founded in 1743 by Benjamin Franklin and the oldest learned society in the United States, still maintains its headquarters in Philosophical Hall. Its distinguished membership once included 15 of the signers. The society's collections also contain furniture and documents associated with them.

In the years 1789-91, the Library Company of Philadelphia (organized in 1731), one of the first public libraries in the United States, erected Library Hall, across from Independence Square on the corner of Library and Fifth Streets. Numbering among the members were 11 signers, including company founder Franklin. Library Hall, reconstructed by the American Philosophical Society, now serves as its library. The Library Company is quartered elsewhere in the city.

In addition to the preceding buildings, numerous sites associated with the signers have also been identified within the park. Many of them have been marked. On some, later buildings now stand. In a few instances, the National Park Service has excavated and stabilized foundations. Outstanding among the sites is that of the Jacob Graff, Jr., House, two blocks from Independence Hall on the southwest corner of Seventh and Market Streets. Jefferson was occupying the second floor of the 3½-story brick house when he wrote the Declaration in June 1776. His rented quarters consisted of a bedroom and parlor. He likely did much of his writing on a portable writing desk of his own design. In 1791 the Graff House was also the residence of signer James Wilson. It was demolished in 1883.

Other sites include those of the home (1766-90) and other structures associated with Franklin, on Franklin Court in the block south of Market Street between Third and Fourth Streets; two adjoining homes (1785-90 and 1790-95) of Robert Morris, on the southeast corner of Market and Sixth Streets, one of which was the unofficial Presidential Mansion (1790-1800), where John Adams resided (1797-1800) while President; Clarke Hall, on the southwest corner of Chestnut and Third Streets, the residence of Samuel Huntington (1779-81) and Thomas McKean (1781); Benjamin Rush's home (1791-93), on the northwest corner of Walnut and Third Streets; the James Wilson home ("Fort Wilson") (1778-90), on the southwest corner of the same intersection; and City Tavern, near Walnut and Second Streets, a gathering place for members of the Continental Congress and Constitutional Convention, as well as other Government officials.

In connection with the U.S. Bicentennial commemoration, the National Park Service plans to reconstruct the Graff House and the City Tavern.

The graves and tombs of seven signers are also located in the

Congress Hall, seat of the U.S. Congress from 1790 until 1800.

Carpenters' Hall, meetingplace in 1774-75 of the First
Continental Congress.

park. Five (Franklin, Hewes, Hopkinson, Ross, and Rush) are in
Christ Church Burial Ground, at the southeast corner of Fifth and
Arch Streets; and two (Wilson and Robert Morris) in the yard of
Christ Church, on Second Street between Church and Filbert Streets.
The graves of Hewes and Ross are unmarked. A rose garden,
dedicated in January 1971 to the memory of the signers of the
Declaration by the Daughters of the American Revolution, is
situated in a plot in the area between Walnut and Locust and Fourth
and Fifth Streets.

Buildings and sites in the park that are mainly of interest in other
themes of history than that treated in this volume include: the First
Bank of the United States; the Second Bank of the United States
(Old Custom House); New Hall (Marine Corps Museum); the
Pemberton House (Army-Navy Museum); the Philadelphia (Mer-
chants') Exchange; the Bishop White House; the Deshler-Morris
House, in Germantown; the Todd House; St. George's Church; St.

The Graff House about 1855. By this time, alterations had rendered it almost completely unrecognizable from its original appearance. Among other changes, it had been joined to an adjacent building and raised a story higher, more than doubling its size.

Joseph's Church; St. Mary's Church; Mikveh Israel Cemetery; and Gloria Dei (Old Swede's) Church National Historic Site.

The structures and properties in 22-acre Independence National Historical Park, most of which are open to the public, include those owned by the city of Philadelphia, but administered by the National Park Service. These consist of Independence Hall, Congress Hall, City Hall, and Independence Square. In recent years, to enhance the setting of the area, the Commonwealth of Pennsylvania has created Independence Mall in the three blocks directly north of Independence Hall. Federally owned buildings include the First and Second Banks of the United States; the Deshler-Morris House, administered by the Germantown Historical Society; Todd House; Bishop White House; New Hall; Pemberton House; and the Philadelphia Exchange.

Among those privately owned buildings whose owners have co-operative agreements with the National Park Service are Carpenters' Hall and Christ Church, both National Historic Landmarks. The American Philosophical Society owns Philosophical Hall, another Landmark and the only privately owned building on the square, but also operates Library Hall, on federally owned land.

In 1948, upon recommendation of the Philadelphia National Shrines Park Commission, Congress created Independence National Historical Park. This act specified the Federal Government's role in the commemoration of existing historic sites and buildings and the acquisition and management of others. The entire undertaking is guided by an advisory commission of distinguished citizens. Many individuals and private and civic organizations have contributed to the preservation and beautification of the park.

Parsons-Taylor House, Pennsylvania ⊗

Location: Northampton County, northeast corner of Fourth and Ferry Streets, Easton.

This house, built by William Parsons in 1757, was leased by George Taylor during the last year of his life and was the site of his death in February 1781. His health failing and his iron business declining, he had moved there the previous April from Greenwich Township, N.J.

Parsons-Taylor House.

The residence, a small, two-story Georgian structure constructed of fieldstone, has a steep gable roof and a pent roof extending along the front at the second-floor level. A single chimney is located in the north sidewall. The front door is surmounted by a rectangular transom; the center door, in the south side, is sheltered by a hood. A frame attachment to the house, probably existing in 1780, no longer stands.

A single large room containing stairs and a fireplace on the north wall make up the first floor. The walls are plastered, and the joists are supported by heavy, exposed beams. Bedrooms occupy the second floor and attic. Restored about 1906, the structure is in fine condition and is owned by the George Taylor Chapter, Daughters of the American Revolution, which uses it as a meetingplace. It is not usually open to visitors.

Shippen-Wistar House, Pennsylvania ⊗

Location: Philadelphia County, southwest corner of Fourth and Locust Streets, Philadelphia.

Meetingplace of medical and political dignitaries, this townhouse was the residence of three eminent doctors and was visited by some of the signers and other key governmental officials. It was erected about 1750 by Dr. William Shippen, Sr. (1712-1802). A prominent medical man of his day, he also served in the Continental Congress and contributed to Philadelphia's cultural life. His son, Dr. William Shippen, Jr. (1736-1808), won distinction as a teacher as well as a practitioner, helped found the University of Pennsylvania Medical School, and in the period 1777-81 directed medical services in the Continental Army. He and his father apparently shared the residence part of the time during their careers. Like the Shippens, Dr. Caspar Wistar (1761-1818), who acquired the house in 1798, was distinguished in medical and intellectual circles.

Various signers and other Delegates to the Continental Congress paid visits to the home. Richard Henry Lee, brother-in-law of young Shippen, stayed there. Francis Lightfoot and Arthur Lee likely often made calls. On occasion John Adams and John Witherspoon stopped by. Other notables who did so later were George Washington, while presiding over the Constitutional Convention (1787); Benjamin Rush, before his clash with Shippen, Jr., over medical conditions in the Continental Army; Robert R. Livingston, who had served on the Declaration drafting committee, in the 1780's; John Adams, while Vice President; and Jefferson, as Secretary of State.

The exterior of the house is in good condition, but the interior has been extensively altered. A 3½-story building in the colonial Philadelphia architectural style, it is constructed in Flemish bond with red bricks and black headers. The windows are shuttered. Notable are a high gable on the Fourth Street side and brick parapet walls on the roof joining the two end chimneys, one on each side of the roof near the peak of the ridge. A garden extends along the Locust Street side at the original rear of the house, which is now entered from that side rather than from Fourth Street. The building is owned and occupied by an insurance company, which has built a passageway between it and the adjacent Cadwalader House on the south. Access to the two structures is limited to the company's customers.

Summerseat, Pennsylvania ⚠

Location: Bucks County, on Clymer Street in the block bounded by Morris and Hillcrest Avenues, Morrisville.

Summerseat was erected in the 1770's by Thomas Barclay, a Philadelphia merchant. In 1806 George Clymer acquired it and resided in it until his death in 1813. It is a two-story, brick and stone Georgian structure over an elevated basement. The roof is gabled and slate-covered. The wall of the front, or east, facade is brick; the end walls, probably also of brick, are covered with cement; the rear wall is of fieldstone. Front first- and second-story windows are topped by flat arches of gauged brick; rear windows on both levels and all the basement windows, by segmental arches, also of gauged brick. Exterior solid shutters flank the first- and second-story windows.

A rectangular transom and triangular pediment surmount the front center door. Central halls divide the four rooms on each floor into pairs. Each of the rooms is equipped with a fireplace. The stairs, located at the rear of the hall along the south wall, are lighted by a large window over the landing. The walls, floors, and some of the woodwork appear to be original. Restored in 1931 and renovated 4 years later, the house is owned by the Morrisville School District and is used for educational purposes. It is open to the public only on a restricted basis.

Summerseat.

Taylor House, Pennsylvania ⚠

Location: Lehigh County, on Front Street, Catasauqua.

In 1768 George Taylor employed Philadelphia carpenters to build this stone residence on the east bank of the Lehigh River, about 15 miles west of Easton at the site of present Catasauqua. The structure was located on a 331-acre tract of land, known as the "Manor of Chawton," which he had acquired the previous year. In 1771 he leased out most of the manor as a farm, and 5 years later sold the house and land to Philadelphia merchant John Benezet.

The rectangular residence is Georgian in style and consists of two stories over an elevated basement. The thick walls are built of stone masonry rubble faced with a whitish, slaked-lime stucco. Over the windows are flat arches of gauged brick. First-floor windows have exterior solid-panel shutters; those on the second floor, louvered. A heavy, overhanging cornice surrounds the truncated hip roof. The brick chimneys at both ends are symmetrically paired. A two-story stone kitchen wing, dating from about 1800, adjoins the house at the south end.

At the center of the front, or west, facade, a flight of marble pyramidal steps lead up to a double door, over which are a rectangular transom and triangular pediment. The central hall, which extends to the rear of the house toward the stairway, is divided by an archway, with fluted pilasters. Situated to the north of the hall are living room and parlor; to the south, dining room and reception, or service, room. Of special interest in the dining room, parlor, and living room

Taylor House.

are the finely executed door pediments and fully paneled fireplace walls. Other walls in these rooms have paneled wainscots and finely detailed chair rails. The fireplace paneling and mantel in the dining room date from the 19th century and represent the Greek Revival style, but the rest of the first-floor paneling and mantels are original, as are also the wide pine floorboards and iron hardware.

The second floor consists of four bedrooms and two small dressing rooms. The fireplace paneling in the two bedrooms on the front side of the house is almost as elaborate as that downstairs. A 1½-story, brick summer kitchen, near the rear of the house, dates from about 1850.

The slightly altered Taylor House, acquired in 1945 by the Lehigh County Historical Society and restored in 1966-68, is in excellent condition and is open to the public.

Governor Hopkins House, Rhode Island ⚠

Location: Providence County, 15 Hopkins Street, Providence.

Stephen Hopkins bought this framehouse in 1742 and resided in it until his death in 1785. It is the only extant structure closely associated with him. The oldest section, the lower level of the present southwest rear ell, dates from about 1707, when the small dwelling comprised two first-floor rooms and an attic. As soon as he acquired the building, Hopkins enlarged and remodeled it into its present L-shaped, two-story form.

The Georgian building, which has a gabled roof and two chimneys, is clapboarded. Cornices decorate the first-story windows. In 1928, during a major restoration, a reconstructed door, with triangular pediment and pilasters typical of the 18th century, was inserted in place of one of the four windows along the present front elevation. This door, the only major alteration in the house, became the main entrance. It replaced a door on the west side, which opens into the original kitchen and is still extant.

The central hall, along the east wall of which is the main stairway, divides the front of the residence into two rooms, study and parlor. The recessed parlor bookshelves, set in paneling above the hearth, are distinctive. The paneling of the two fireplaces in the study and ell is simpler. A passageway leads from the parlor to the southwest ell,

Governor Hopkins House.

which consists of the original kitchen and in the southeast corner a small bedroom. Five bedrooms, two of which are equipped with fireplaces, are located upstairs. The interior of the house, including stairs, woodwork, floors, and fireplaces, is largely original. The fine garden was designed by a descendant of Stephen Hopkins, the late Alden Hopkins, prominent landscape architect.

The Governor Hopkins House, first located on the northeast corner of Hopkins and South Main Streets, was moved eastward in 1804 along the north side of and about halfway up Hopkins Street. In 1927, to make way for the construction of a new courthouse, the building was again relocated eastward along the same street, to its present site, and the next year was restored. Since that time, the State of Rhode Island has owned the house and maintained the exterior and grounds. The Society of Colonial Dames in the State of Rhode Island maintains and administers the interior as a historic house museum.

Heyward-Washington House, South Carolina

Location: Charleston County, 87 Church Street, Charleston.

From 1778 until 1794 this townhouse was the principal residence of Thomas Heyward, Jr. During this period, however, he also spent considerable time at White Hall, his country estate near that of his father about 25 miles northeast of Savannah, and in 1780-81 was imprisoned by the British at St. Augustine. In 1770 his father, Daniel, a rice planter, had purchased the lot and a two-story house standing on it. Within 2 years, he probably demolished it and erected the present one. Thomas inherited it in 1777, and moved in the following year, upon completion of his tour in the Continental Congress. In 1780, when the British took Charleston, they captured him and forced his family to flee from the townhouse. For a week in 1791 the city rented it for use of President Washington, who was visiting Charleston while touring the Southern States. Three years later, Heyward sold the property and retired to White Hall.

A slightly altered Georgian structure, the residence is a superb example of a Charleston "double house." The floor plan is the typical Georgian center hall type, with four rooms on each floor. Two

Heyward-Washington House.

interior chimneys allow for two fireplaces in pairs set back to back on all floors. The first-floor rooms are simple; those on the second, elaborate, for entertaining. The downstairs hall, divided by an arch at midpoint, extends to a rear door. A Palladian window lights the stairway, located at the rear of the hall against the north wall.

The large second-floor drawing room, the most elaborate room in the house, features paneled walls, pedimented doors, interior paneled shutters, an elaborate ceiling cornice, and a fireplace with a magnificent carved mantel. In addition to the drawing room, the second floor contains a smaller parlor and two bedrooms, each of which has a paneled fireplace wall. Four more rooms are located on both the first and third floors. Except for reconstruction in 1929 of one front room and the front of the hall on the first floor, the structure is largely original.

The brick house is square and rises three stories. The hipped roof is pierced by a single front dormer and ornamented by a narrow, denticulated cornice. Brick flat arches head the windows. The upper windows have louvered shutters; those on the first floor, paneled shutters. The center entrance, a reconstruction, consists of a fanlighted door surmounted by a pediment and flanked by Roman Doric columns. A rear courtyard contains a brick kitchen-laundry with slave quarters above, a carriage house, wood and tool sheds, a necessary, and garden.

Subsequent to Heyward's ownership, the house passed through several hands until rescued from the threat of demolition in 1929 by the Charleston Museum. After restoration and furnishing with period pieces, it was opened to the public. A collection of china once owned by Heyward is on display, as well as portraits of the Heyward family.

Hopsewee-on-the-Santee, South Carolina ⌂

Location: Georgetown County, on an unimproved road just west of U.S. 17, about 13 miles southwest of Georgetown.

Erected by his father during the 1740's, this house on the north bank of the North Santee River was the birthplace in 1749 and the boyhood home of Thomas Lynch, Jr. He lived in it until his father sold it in 1763, the year before young Lynch sailed to Europe to

Hopsewee-on-the-Santee.

continue his education. It is the only surviving residence closely associated with him.

The 2½-story framehouse rests on a brick foundation, which is covered with scored tabby. Two front dormers and two interior chimneys protrude from the hip roof. A broad, two-story porch, or piazza, with square columns extends across the front of the building. The frame, comprised of black cypress, is of mortise-and-tenon construction, and the walls are clapboarded. Exterior paneled shutters flank the first- and second-story windows. Except for the present metal roof and the screening of the front porch, the outside of the structure has not been appreciably altered.

The central hall arrangement divides four rooms into pairs on the first two floors. All the rooms are equipped with fireplaces. Throughout, the mantels, wainscoting, cornice mold, and heart pine floors are original and excellently crafted. The full cellar is constructed of brick and divided into rooms. Two one-story, cypress, shingled outbuildings, located to the northeast and northwest of the main house, probably once served as kitchens. About 1948, by which time the house had fallen into decay and the grounds were overgrown, the present owner acquired the property, restored the garden, and repaired the residence. In fine condition, it is privately occupied, but is shown to the public part of the week.

Middleton Place, South Carolina ⚠

> *Location: Dorchester County, on an unimproved road just east of S.C. 61, about 13 miles northwest of Charleston.*

This mansion, of which only the south wing stands today, was the birthplace and lifelong home of Arthur Middleton (1742-87). About 1738 his grandfather had built a 3½-story brick house at the site. Some 3 years later, Arthur's father began laying out the surrounding gardens that have since won international fame as Middleton Place Gardens. More than 100 slaves labored for a decade to complete the 45-acre gardens and 16-acre lawn. In 1755 the mansion was enlarged by the addition of two two-story brick flankers, or detached wings, on the north and south sides of the original structure, for use respectively as a library-conservatory and guest quarters.

During the War for Independence, British troops pillaged the residence and despoiled the plantation. In 1865, as Union soldiers approached during the Civil War, the slaves set the mansion to the torch, which left only the walls standing. In 1868 William Middleton erected a roof over the south wing, the least damaged section of the three, and reoccupied it. In 1886 an earthquake felled the ruined walls of the north wing and central section.

The south wing (1755) of Middleton Place, the only 18th-century section of the mansion that has survived.

In the 1930's the two-story, brick south wing was renovated and enlarged. The major additions, both two-story brick and executed in an 18th-century manner, were a service wing along the main axis of the wing at the south end; and, on the west side, a right-angled entrance wing, containing a vestibule and stairway, and constructed with a stepped and curvilinear gable roof to match those on the ends of the original south wing. A third addition in the 1930's was a one-story brick porch on the east, or river, elevation. All the brickwork is Flemish bond, the shutters are paneled, and a louvered circular window decorates the gable end of the new entrance wing. The interior chimneys are three in number. A parlor, dining room, and living room are located on the first floor of the original south wing and three bedrooms on the second. The interior finish dates from the mid-19th century, but many of the furnishings are original 18th-century Middleton pieces.

To the east and north of the present house and ruins of the central block and north wing are the famous gardens, which have been enlarged and perfected over the years. They extend from the Ashley River and the paired butterfly lakes at their foot west toward the residence and beyond in sweeping terraces. To the northwest of the house, in another 18th-century formal garden, is the family graveyard, containing the mausoleum of Arthur Middleton.

The estate comprises 7,000 acres and is still owned by Middleton descendants. They occupy the south wing, which is not open to the public, unlike the gardens. According to present plans, about 110 acres, embracing the gardens, burial plot, plantation house, and reconstructed outbuildings, will be donated to a nonprofit organization that will preserve them and keep them open to the public.

Rutledge House, South Carolina △

Location: Charleston County, 117 Broad Street, Charleston.

The residence of Edward Rutledge during his later years, this building is the only existing one that can be identified with him. Unfortunately the construction date and the exact years of his residence cannot be determined, though he was definitely the occupant in 1787.

The large, rectilinear, clapboarded, frame structure is two stories high over a basement. The roof is hipped. A bilevel porch, supported

Rutledge House.

by columns, extends across the west side and around the south, or rear, side of the house. A central modillioned pediment with circular window fronts the main roof and is "supported" by consoles. Exterior louvered shutters flank the corniced windows. The center doorway, once crowned by a cornice, now has a triangular pediment. A small, two-story clapboard wing, added to the front of the east end along the main axis in the late 19th century, is the only definite major exterior alteration. Behind it, runs a two-story porch.

A center hall extends about halfway through the house. On one side are two rooms with fireplaces; on the other, a front stair hall containing a curved stairway. Behind this is a large room, accessible only from the entrance hall. The kitchen, possibly another later addition, is located in a wing that projects from the rear of the house at the southeast corner. The interior woodwork appears to date from the 1880's, and partition walls now subdivide the large original rooms into smaller ones.

The Rutledge House, known in modern times as the Carter-May House, is now a Roman Catholic home for elderly women. Portions of the first floor may be visited upon request. A large garden is located at the rear of the building.

Berkeley, Virginia

Location: Charles City County, on the south side of Va. 5, about 8 miles west of Charles City.

In historical interest this fine mansion has few rivals among the James River plantations. It was the birthplace and lifelong home of Benjamin Harrison V (1726-91), signer of the Declaration and three-term Governor of Virginia, as well as the birthplace and boyhood residence of his son, William Henry (1773-1841), ninth President of the United States and grandfather of Benjamin (1833-1901), the 23rd President. William Henry probably wrote his 1841 inaugural address at Berkeley in the room in which he had been born.

Benjamin Harrison IV, the signer's father, built the structure in 1726. In 1781 British troops under Benedict Arnold plundered the plantation, but did not seriously harm the mansion. In the 1790's one of the Harrisons, probably Benjamin VI, made some architectural alterations and redecorated the interior in the Adam style. By the time of the Civil War, the plantation was known as Harrison's Landing. In 1862 it served as a supply base and camp for the Union Army of the Potomac following its retreat from the Battle of Malvern Hill, Va., which ended the Peninsular Campaign. Gen. George B.

Berkeley.

McClellan utilized the mansion as his headquarters. While quartered nearby, Gen. Daniel Butterfield composed the famous bugle call "Taps."

The early Georgian mansion has been altered somewhat over the years, but retains much of the original structure and character. It is 2½ stories high and has a dormered, gable roof with two tall interior ridge chimneys, and distinctive pedimented gable ends, including modillioned cornice. The brick walls are laid in Flemish bond. Gauged brick is employed in the flat window arches, the belt course, and door pediments. The broad-piered central doors on the north and south elevations, with pediments in gauged brick, are reconstructions. Two detached, two-story, brick dependencies, set slightly south of the house on the river side, were built in the 1840's to replace similar structures that had been erected sometime before 1800.

The center hall plan has been slightly modified. The hall bisects the four rooms on the first floor into pairs. A small stairs in the northwest corner was probaby inserted about 1800. Most of the interior finish clearly reflects the Adam alterations of the 1790's.

By 1915 the mansion was in poor condition. Subsequent owners have reconstructed and restored it to its 18th-century appearance. This included removal of a 19th-century porch on all four sides, replacement of the window sash and exterior door framings, and reconstruction of the center stairs. The upper floors are used as a private residence, but the basement and first floor may be visited. The unmarked grave of signer Benjamin Harrison is located in the family cemetery, a quarter of a mile southeast of the plantation house.

Elsing Green, Virginia △

Location: King William County, on a private road about 1 mile southwest of Va. 632, some 10 miles southwest of King William Court House.

In 1758, while Carter Braxton was visiting in England, his brother George probably built for him this impressive plantation home on a high bluff overlooking the Pamunkey River. Upon his return in 1760, Carter took up residence in it and lived there until 1767. He then moved to a new residence, Chericoke, a few miles to the northwest.

Elsing Green.

The exterior is original, but about 1800 a fire destroyed the interior. The present 18th-century style woodwork is a 20th-century reconstruction. The Georgian structure of brick, laid in Flemish bond, is U-shaped. Two wings project to the north, or rear, of the central section. The large building is two stories in height and has a hip roof and four tall chimneys. Side doors are centered in each wing, and there are also central doors in the front and rear facades of the main house. The door on the front, or river, facade, with gauged brick triangular pediment, is a reconstruction.

The flat window arches are constructed of splayed brick. The second-floor level is marked by a strong course of gauged brick, unmolded and four courses high. Two old, detached, brick dependencies, 1½ stories high, flank the mansion. The eastern one may date from 1719; the western contains a restored kitchen. A reconstructed smokehouse and dairy rest on their original, symmetrically located, foundations.

An off-center hall extends northward halfway through the main arm of the U from the south, or front, entrance and intersects with an east-west lateral hall running the length of the main mansion. The ends of this long cross hall each contain a stairway set against the south wall. The southeast corner of the residence is occupied by a large parlor; the southwest corner, by a smaller living room; and each of the north wings, by a single large room. Four bedrooms are upstairs, which has the same general plan as the ground floor.

The carefully restored house and well maintained estate, which now includes about 3,000 acres, are in excellent condition but are privately occupied and not open to visitors.

Menokin, Virginia ⚠

Location: Richmond County, on an unimproved road about 1 mile west of County Route 690, some 4 miles northwest of Warsaw.

Menokin, completed in 1769 by Col. John Tayloe of nearby Mount Airy as a wedding gift for his daughter and her husband, Francis Lightfoot Lee, was the home where they spent most of their lives and the one Lee loved best. He died there in 1797.

This late Georgian house, similar in many respects to Mount Airy though much smaller, was likely constructed by the same architect-builder, probably John Ariss. The exterior possesses the qualities of a large mansion, though the actual dimensions are rather modest.

Ruins of Menokin.

The residence, constructed of local brown sandstone, is two stories high with hip-on-hip roof and two large interior chimneys. Its exterior walls are covered with plaster. The stone trim—quoins, belt courses, and window and door trim—is elaborate. Two stone belt courses, one at the second-floor line and the other at the sill level of the upper windows, divide the main, or north, facade horizontally. The upper course is eliminated on the other three facades. No longer standing are two two-story, gable-roofed, detached, symmetrical service buildings, a kitchen to the east and office to the west, which once stood in the forecourt at right angles to the main house. They undoubtedly heightened the impression of the mansion's large size.

A center hall extends halfway through the first floor, which contains dining room, living room, kitchen, and bedroom. Four bedrooms, divided into pairs by a central hall, are located on the second floor.

Unoccupied for many years, Menokin is in ruinous condition. The roof and walls on the southeast side have collapsed. The yard and grounds, part of a 590-acre farm, are overgrown with vegetation and small trees. The owner has removed and stored the original interior paneling. Extensive reconstruction would be required to restore the structure to its original condition. It is not open to the public.

Monticello, Virginia ⚠

Location: Albemarle County, just off Va. 53, about 2 miles southeast of Charlottesville.

"Monticello," Italian for "Little Mountain," is an enduring tribute to the genius and versatility of Thomas Jefferson, who personally designed and supervised erection of the splendid mansion. He resided in it for many years of his long life, his spirit lives on in its architectural perfection and the ingenious devices with which he equipped it, and he is buried nearby. Sitting amid pleasant gardens and lawns on a hilltop, the residence overlooks Charlottesville; the University of Virginia, which Jefferson founded and some of whose buildings he designed; and the green rolling hills of the surrounding countryside. Especially after his retirement from public life in 1809 until his death, at the age of 83 on July 4, 1826, the prominent men of his

Monticello.

age made pilgrimages to Monticello. To this day it is visited by the humble, as well as the great—all who admire Jefferson's character and accomplishments.

In 1757 Jefferson's father died and passed on the property, 2,750 acres, to him. Eleven years later, he began leveling the hilltop. To make all parts of it accessible, he built paths, or roundabouts, as he called them, on its slopes at four different levels; remains of these are visible today. In 1770 fire destroyed Jefferson's modest residence, his birthplace Shadwell, and he moved to Monticello, where he had already begun building a mansion. The first part of it completed was the small southwest pavilion, which Jefferson occupied as a bachelor's quarters until January 1772, when he brought his bride, Martha Wayles Skelton, to share it with him. It is still known as "Honeymoon Cottage."

The first Monticello, vastly different from the present one, was probably completed in 1775. Constructed of brick with cut-stone trim, it consisted of a central two-story unit, with pedimented gable roof running from front to rear and one-story gabled wings, set perpendicularly to the central block. The chief architectural accent was the main two-story portico, Doric below and Ionic above. Small polygonal bays projected from the ends of the wings. Jefferson made numerous alterations and major changes after the War for Independence. The present two-wing structure, built between 1793 and 1809, incorporates the rooms of the original house at its rear. It also reflects a shift in architectural preference in the United States from Georgian to Roman Revival—elements of both of which are represented. Jefferson was almost entirely responsible for starting the Roman Revival.

The mansion consists of 2½ stories over a basement and contains 35 rooms. The dominating feature is the central dome, over an octagonal room. The house is furnished largely with Jefferson belongings, including a replica of the small portable desk on which he probably wrote the Declaration of Independence. Some of the clever devices in the residence are a 7-day calendar-clock and a dumbwaiter. One room contains one of the first parquet floors in the United States. The upper levels, accessible only by narrow staircases, are not shown to the public.

Before Jefferson built Monticello, every plantation had a group of small outbuildings such as the laundry, smokehouse, dairy, stable, weaving house, schoolhouse, and kitchen. Jefferson sought to render these as inconspicuous as possible and increase the efficiency of the facilities they provided by constructing two series of rooms for these purposes beneath the outer sides of two long L-shaped terraces extending from the house. Below the south terrace, beyond the angle of the ell, are the kitchen, the cook's room, servants' rooms, room for smoking meat, and the dairy. At the end of this terrace, stands "Honeymoon Cottage." Under the far side of the north terrace are the stables, carriage house, icehouse, and laundry. Jefferson used the small building terminating this terrace, adjacent to which is the paddock, as an office. An underground passageway—containing storage rooms for wine, beer, cider, and rum—connects the basement of the main house with the series of service rooms along the outer sides of the ells. Jefferson is buried in the family graveyard, which is adjacent to the road leading from the house.

Upon Jefferson's death in 1826, his daughter Martha inherited Monticello, but was soon forced to sell it, to the first of a series of private owners. In 1923 the newly organized Thomas Jefferson Memorial Foundation purchased the estate, the following year opened it to the public, and has retained ownership to the present day.

Mount Airy, Virginia △

Location: Richmond County, on the north side of U.S. 360, about 1½ miles west of Warsaw.

Francis Lightfoot Lee resided in this beautiful mansion for a short time in 1769, while its owner, his new father-in-law, Col. John Tayloe completed building Menokin nearby as a residence for him and his bride.

Mount Airy, which sits on a ridge overlooking the Rappahannock Valley, is one of the finest late Georgian mansions to be erected in America. Built in the years 1758-62, it is attributed to noted Virginia architect John Ariss, and is considered to be his best work. It was the first residence in the English Colonies to carry out completely a full five-part Palladian villa plan: a main house connected to two dependencies by quadrant passageways that partially enclose a forecourt. The massive main section, standing over an elevated basement, and the two dependencies are two stories high and of dark brown sandstone construction trimmed in light-colored limestone. The one-story passageways curve from the main house to the dependencies and enclose a semicircular forecourt on the north, or entrance, facade.

Prominent characteristics of the main building are front and rear central projecting pavilions of rusticated limestone, both having loggias, three windows in the second story, and crowning triangular pediments; limestone belt course; rusticated angle quoins; and two pairs of interior chimneys near the ridge of the hip roof, which was

Mount Airy.

rebuilt after a fire in 1844 and may have replaced a hip-on-hip roof. The four square piers gracing the front loggia are faced with Roman Doric pilasters. The rear loggia has three round arches topped with heavy, marked, voussoired keystones.

The two dependencies have hip roofs and central chimneys, and their corner quoins match those of the main house. The connecting passageways, also of stone, are covered with shed roofs concealed from the front. At the point where they connect with the main house, which rests on an elevated basement, they are stepped up to allow entrance to the first floor.

Fire destroyed the probably fine wooden interiors in 1844, but the original floor plan was retained in the reconstruction. A magnificent central hall extends through the house between the front and rear loggias. Full-height windows flank both central entrance doors. The elliptical stairway in the front northwest corner room, in which there is also a pantry, dates from the 19th century, but the original stairs may have been in the present cross hall between the two east drawing rooms, lighted by the central arch of a Palladian window in the east end wall. In the southwest corner is a large dining room.

Mount Airy, in good condition, is still used as a residence by Tayloe descendants and is not open to the public. Francis Lightfoot Lee is buried with his wife in the Tayloe family cemetery, located about 300 yards northwest of the mansion.

Nelson House (Colonial National Historical Park), Virginia ☒

Location: York County, northwest corner of Main and Pearl Streets, Yorktown; address: Colonial National Historical Park, P.O. Box 210, Yorktown, Va. 23490.

Thomas Nelson, Jr., may have been born in this house in 1738, resided fulltime in it from 1767 until 1781, and probably stayed in it on occasion during the following 8 years prior to his death. During the latter period, he was living in partial retirement at his Hanover County estate, Offley Hoo.

The probable builder, between 1732 and 1741, was Thomas ("Scotch Tom") Nelson, Sr., the signer's grandfather. Thomas Jr.'s father, William, lived in the residence until about 1738, the year of his marriage, when he moved to his own house across the street.

Nelson House.

Thomas, Jr., could have been born at either place. After "Scotch Tom" died, in 1745, his widow continued in residence. Upon her death in 1766, Thomas, Jr., who since his marriage 4 years earlier had apparently lived with his father, acquired her home and moved in the next year.

According to family tradition, the Nelson House served as the second headquarters of Gen. Charles Cornwallis during the siege of Yorktown (September-October 1781), and with Nelson's permission American artillery shelled and hit the house. The historical record indicates that both British and French military personnel likely used it, but their identities cannot be definitely ascertained. And the southeast face of the residence does show evidence of damage from cannon fire. The Marquis de Lafayette, who revisited the United States in 1824-25, was quartered there when in the former year he attended the celebration of the anniversary of the Battle of Yorktown, in which he had played a key role.

The Nelson House is an impressive specimen of early Georgian architecture, though the four south and five north dormers added in the 1920's detract from the original design. The broad roof is gabled and pedimented at the ends, with two massive interior chimneys and strongly dentiled cornice. The Flemish bond brickwork includes gauged belt course, water table, and flat window arches with segmental soffits. Corner quoins, as well as the window sills and lintels and their tall keystones, are of stone. The quoins and two levels of tall windows give the house a strong vertical effect. The north center door has simple gauged and molded brick piers that are topped by a brick pediment. Destroying the symmetry of the south facade is the off-center door, enclosed in a vestibule. A more elaborate door on the west side is modern, replacing an original untrimmed service opening.

On one side of the off-center hall are two small rooms, with a lobby and service stairs between them; on the opposite side of the hall, are two larger rooms, divided by a tiny one, probably a pantry. The general plan is repeated upstairs, where there are four bedrooms. Most of the original interior woodwork, highlighted by the first-floor wall-to-ceiling paneling, is still intact. From a decorative standpoint, the most striking chamber is the northeast drawing room. All the fireplaces in the residence are apparently reconstructions, as are also the balusters and handrails of the stairs.

The house remained in possession of the Nelson family until 1914. In 1920-21 its owners rehabilitated and restored it and renamed it York Hall. In 1968 the National Park Service acquired it. When this volume went to press, an extensive research and restoration program was being carried out preparatory to opening the building to the public.

Poplar Forest, Virginia ⚠

Location: Bedford County, on the east side of County Route 661, about 6½ miles west of Lynchburg.

In 1806-19 Thomas Jefferson designed and built this architecturally significant octagonal house on his 4,000-acre Bedford County plantation as a summer home and retreat. He occupied it intermittently until his death in 1826.

The plantation came into the possession of Jefferson through Martha Wayles Skelton, whom he married in 1772. For many years, whenever he visited it to superintend its management, he resided in a two-room cottage, the only dwelling. In June 1781, just after abdi-

Poplar Forest.

cating the governorship and narrowly escaping capture with a group of legislators during a British raid on Charlottesville, he temporarily moved his family to the cottage. Before the month was out, a horse threw and injured him. During his recuperation, he wrote *Notes on the State of Virginia*, a study of social and political life in 18th-century Virginia. In 1806-19 he erected Poplar Forest, whose completion coincided with his retirement from public office. When visitors became too numerous at Monticello or the fancy struck, he took up residence at his retreat for a month or two, usually twice a year. As the years went on, he refined the structure.

In 1845 a fire destroyed the roof and interior, leaving only the four chimneys, the brick walls, and possibly the portico columns. That same year, the present unadorned roof, octagonal and hipped like its predecessor, and dormers were added. Prior to the fire, there was a skylight and balustraded deck at the edge of the roof, with a Tuscan cornice below that extended around the building. The one-story brick building is set over a high basement. Because of the sloping ground on the rear side, the structure is two stories high there. One- and two-story tetrastyle Tuscan porticoes are attached to the front and rear of the house respectively. The front one is pedimented; the unpedimented rear one is built over a one-story arcade.

The original interior plan is unchanged. Four elongated octagonal rooms are grouped symmetrically around the present dining room, a square central room that was once lighted from above by the central skylight, not replaced in 1845. No aboveground traces remain of a flat-roofed office wing, referred to by Jefferson, but a kitchen and smokehouse still stand.

Poplar Forest, in good condition, is a private residence and is not open to the public.

Stratford Hall, Virginia △

> *Location: Westmoreland County, just north of Va. 214, about 1 mile northeast of Lerty.*

This architecturally outstanding mansion along the Potomac River was the ancestral home of the Lee family. It was the birthplace and boyhood home of two signers of the Declaration of Independence, Richard Henry and Francis Lightfoot Lee, as well as their three distinguished brothers, Arthur, William, and Thomas Ludwell. A later resident was Col. Henry "Lighthorse Harry," hero of the War for Independence. His son, Robert E., Confederate leader during the Civil War, was born in the house in 1807.

Thomas Lee—planter, merchant, shipowner, and politician—built the mansion in the years 1725-30 on his 16,000-acre plantation. Upon his death in 1750, the residence passed to his eldest son, Philip Ludwell. Meantime, Richard Henry had been born there in 1732 and Francis Lightfoot 2 years later. They maintained residence until 1757 and 1758 respectively, when they moved to their own estates. In 1782 Philip Ludwell's oldest daughter, Matilda, wife of

Stratford Hall.

"Lighthorse Harry," her cousin, inherited the mansion. In 1790 she died, and 3 years later her husband remarried. One of his sons by that union was Robert E. Lee, who lived in the house only 3 or 4 years, at the end of which his parents moved to Alexandria.

Stratford Hall is a magnificent and rare example of an H-shaped residence and illustrates the transition from the 17th-century William and Mary style of architecture to early Georgian. The mansion is one story high over an elevated basement and has a hip roof. Variations in color and size between the Flemish bond brickwork in the basement and upper story soften the austerity of the bold mass of the house. In the central connecting arm, the flights of stone steps leading up to the north and south entrances, which diminish in width as they ascend to the main floor level and are flanked by ponderous balustrades, are conjectural reconstructions, erected in 1929. Twin sets of four huge chimney stacks are centered over the east and west wings. The stacks are connected by arches and encompass balus- traded roof decks, from which the Lees could view navigation on the Potomac River.

"Lighthorse Harry" Lee made many changes. By 1800 he had altered or replaced the exterior stairs and changed most of the interior trim, except that in the central block's great hall, to the Adam style. The floor plan is unusual in colonial dwellings. The two wings each have four rooms, divided laterally by a central hallway on the main floor. The connecting central block consists of the fully paneled great hall, or salon—one of the most formal and monumen- tal rooms of the early Georgian period in the English Colonies. The basement contains service rooms and some bedrooms; the main floor, living quarters and bedrooms. In the east wing's dining room is a service alcove, common in Virginia mansions. The 18th-century stairway was removed during the 1929 restoration. The only access between floors is now a small stairway in the east wing.

The mansion is built in the center of a square parterre, a service building being located at each corner of the square. Flanking the entrance forecourt are the kitchen and library, 1½-story brick structures with jerkin-head roofs. At the rear corners are a school and office, with hip roofs. Outside the square are balanced brick buildings: a stable on one side and smokehouse on the other. Seven of the 12 original structures that were still standing in 1929 have been restored. They provide an excellent picture of plantation life in the 18th century. Farther removed from the house, near the wharf on the river, is the reconstructed mill.

In 1929 the Robert E. Lee Memorial Foundation, Inc., acquired the mansion and 1,100 acres. Besides reconstructing the exterior stairs, the foundation restored the library and library closet in the west wing, as well as the dining room and service alcove in the east wing, to their 18th-century appearance. The east and west corridors, parlor in the west wing, Robert E. Lee's birthplace room, and an adjoining bedroom in the east wing were left as they appeared about 1800. The formal garden, just east of the mansion, has also been restored. The foundation today operates Stratford Hall as a historic house museum.

Tuckahoe, Virginia

Location: Goochland County, on the south side of Va. 650, about 13 miles west of Richmond.

Tuckahoe, situated along the James River, was the boyhood home of Thomas Jefferson for 7 years and the place where he obtained his elementary education. The mansion, outbuildings, and surrounding

Tuckahoe.

gardens and lands constitute an outstanding example of a Southern colonial plantation.

The land on which Tuckahoe stands was patented in 1695 by William Randolph. His son Thomas inherited the plantation and built the north wing of the mansion about 1712. Sometime between 1730 and 1745, William Randolph II enlarged the residence to its present proportions. When Randolph died in 1745, Peter Jefferson moved his family, including 2-year-old Thomas, from Shadwell to Tuckahoe to fulfill a promise Peter had made to Randolph, his wife's cousin, to act as guardian of his son, Thomas Mann Randolph. In 1752 the Jeffersons returned to Shadwell.

Like Stratford Hall, the house is an outstanding and rare example of an H-shaped structure of early Georgian style in the Colonies. It is a large, two-story frame structure lined with brick nogging and exterior weatherboarded walls, except for the two solid brick ends of the south wing. Two long gabled wings are connected by a broad central block. Tall slender chimneys accentuate the narrow gable ends and the marked verticality of the structure, which is further enhanced by the high brick foundations. The chimneys in the frame ends of the north wing project, but those in the south brick ends are flush with the walls. The second-floor level is marked by a wooden belt course and the roofline by a modillioned cornice.

The central doorways on the north and south sides have low porches with square posts supporting gable roofs. The south porch is approached by a long flight of stone steps, splayed but lacking a balustrade; the north porch is near ground level. The doors in the center block, on the east and west elevations, are sheltered by pedimented hoods. All four exterior doors, one in each wing and two in the central block, are original, as are also the weatherboarding and sash.

On the first floor of each of the wings are two rooms, divided by a center cross hall. The north wing contains two parlors; the south, a dining room and "children's" room. The central connecting block contains one large room, or salon. The second floor repeats the plan of the first floor except that, of the original five bedrooms, the one in the central block has been modernized and subdivided into several rooms.

The interior decoration and trim, of the finest workmanship, is remarkably unaltered and in fine condition. All the walls are covered with simple paneling. The original wide floorboards remain through-out the structure. The hall stairways, especially the north one, with elaborately turned and spiraled balusters, are outstanding examples of early Georgian style. Mantels throughout the house date from the 19th century, but the marble fireplace facing in the west bedroom of the north wing is original.

East of the mansion is the small, one-room, brick, one-story schoolhouse attended by Jefferson, as well as fine boxwood gardens. A short distance to the west of the main house is a plantation street, containing a complex of eight early 18th-century buildings, all in excellent condition and little altered. They include kitchen, tobacco house, three slave quarters, smokehouse, and barn.

Since Tuckahoe passed out of the possession of the Randolph family in 1830, a succession of individuals have owned it. It is still a private residence, not open to the public.

Wythe House, Virginia ⧊

Location: On the west side of the Palace Green, between Duke of Gloucester and Prince George Streets, Williamsburg.

This house in Colonial Williamsburg is a superb example of a Georgian brick house. It was the residence of George Wythe from around 1755 until 1791, a period that spanned some of his most active years in politics and jurisprudence. His father-in-law, the noted Virginia architect Richard Taliaferro, designed and built it for him and his second wife about 1755. When Taliaferro died two decades later, Wythe inherited it and resided in it until 1791, when he moved to Richmond. A decade earlier, the house had served as Gen. George Washington's headquarters prior to the siege of Yorktown.

The outstanding aspects of the little-altered early Georgian structure are its good lines and fine brickwork, in Flemish bond. It is two stories high over a basement and has a hip roof and two interior chimneys. Smaller windows on the upper level create an illusion that the modestly sized house is larger than it actually is. The simple facade is enriched mainly by the broad muntins and wide frames of the windows and a fine paneled double door with rec-

Wythe House.

tangular transom. The flat window arches are constructed of gauged brick. Windows, doors, and house corners have rubbed dressings, and a modillioned cornice decorates the eaveline.

Each floor consists of four rooms bisected into pairs by a central hall. Chimneys between each of the pairs afford fireplaces for all eight rooms. The handsome but unpretentious stairway contains the only elaborate woodwork. Plaster dadoes, however, are found in every room, with chair rails on plasterboard, and single molded cornices. On the first floor are study, parlor, students' room, and dining room; on the second, four bedrooms. The existing mantels are replacements. Furnishings are of the late 18th century or earlier and represent American craftmanship. Extending behind the house is the formal garden; along the north, the kitchen, smokehouse, laundry, lumberhouse, and stable.

In 1926, when Bruton Parish acquired the residence, it was in poor condition. By 1931 the parish had repaired and restored it, and utilized it as a parish house for 6 years. Colonial Williamsburg then acquired it, and in 1939-40 accomplished additional restoration. Today the building is one of the main attractions at Colonial Williamsburg and is part of Williamsburg Historic District, a National Historic Landmark.

Appendix

The Declaration and Its History

Text of the Declaration

The unanimous Declaration of the thirteen united States of America,

When in the Course of human events, it becomes necessary for one people to dissolve the political bands which have connected them with another, and to assume among the powers of the earth, the separate and equal station to which the Laws of Nature and of Nature's God entitle them, a decent respect to the opinions of mankind requires that they should declare the causes which impel them to the separation.

We hold these truths to be self-evident, that all men are created equal, that they are endowed by their Creator with certain unalienable Rights, that among these are Life, Liberty and the pursuit of Happiness.——— That to secure these rights, Governments are instituted among Men, deriving their just powers from the consent of the governed.———That whenever any Form of Government becomes destructive of these ends, it is the Right of the People to alter or to abolish it, and to institute new Government, laying its foundation on such principles and organizing its powers in such form, as to them shall seem most likely to effect their Safety and Happiness. Prudence, indeed, will dictate that Governments long established should not be changed for light and transient causes; and accordingly all experience hath shewn, that mankind are more disposed to suffer, while evils are sufferable, than to right themselves by abolishing the forms to which they are accustomed. But when a long train of abuses and usurpations, pursuing invariably the same Object evinces a design to reduce them under absolute Despotism, it is their right, it is their duty, to throw off such Government, and to provide new Guards for their future security.————Such has been the patient sufferance of these Colonies; and such is now the necessity which constrains them to alter their former Systems of Government. The history of the present King of Great Britain is a history of repeated injuries and usurpations, all having in direct object the establishment of an absolute Tyranny over these States. To prove this, let Facts be submitted to a candid world.

He has refused his Assent to Laws, the most wholesome and necessary for the public good.

He has forbidden his Governors to pass Laws of immediate and pressing importance, unless suspended in their operation till his Assent should be obtained; and when so suspended, he has utterly neglected to attend to them.

He has refused to pass other Laws for the accommodation of large districts of people, unless those people would relinquish the right of Representation in the Legislature, a right inestimable to them and formidable to tyrants only.

He has called together legislative bodies at places unusual, uncomfortable, and distant from the depository of their public Records, for the sole purpose of fatiguing them into compliance with his measures.

He has dissolved Representative Houses repeatedly, for opposing with manly firmness his invasions on the rights of the people.

He has refused for a long time, after such dissolutions, to cause others to be elected; whereby the Legislative powers, incapable of Annihilation, have returned to the People at large for their exercise; the State remaining in the meantime exposed to all the dangers of invasion from without, and convulsions within.

He has endeavoured to prevent the population of these States; for that purpose obstructing the Laws for Naturalization of Foreigners; refusing to pass others to encourage their migrations hither, and raising the conditions of new Appropriations of Lands.

He has obstructed the Administration of Justice, by refusing his Assent to Laws for establishing Judiciary powers.

He has made Judges dependent on his Will alone, for the tenure of their offices, and the amount and payment of their salaries.

He has erected a multitude of New Offices, and sent hither swarms of Officers to harass our people, and eat out their substance.

He has kept among us, in times of peace, Standing Armies without the Consent of our legislatures.

He has affected to render the Military independent of and superior to the Civil power.

He has combined with others to subject us to a jurisdiction foreign to our constitution, and unacknowledged by our laws; giving his Assent to their Acts of pretended Legislation:

For Quartering large bodies of armed troops among us:

For protecting them, by a mock Trial, from punishment for any Murders which they should commit on the Inhabitants of these States:

For cutting off our Trade with all parts of the world:

For imposing Taxes on us without our Consent:

For depriving us in many cases, of the benefits of Trial by Jury:

For transporting us beyond Seas to be tried for pretended offences:

For abolishing the free System of English Laws in a neighbouring Province, establishing therein an Arbitrary government, and enlarging its Boundaries so as to render it at once an example and fit instrument for introducing the same absolute rule into these Colonies:

For taking away our Charters, abolishing our most valuable Laws, and altering fundamentally the Forms of our Governments:

For suspending our own Legislatures and declaring themselves invested with power to legislate for us in all cases whatsoever.

He has abdicated Government here, by declaring us out of his Protection and waging War against us.

He has plundered our seas, ravaged our Coasts, burnt our towns, and destroyed the lives of our people.

He is at this time transporting large Armies of foreign Mercenaries to compleat the works of death, desolation and tyranny, already begun with circumstances of Cruelty & perfidy scarcely paralleled in the most barbarous ages, and totally unworthy the Head of a civilized nation.

He has constrained our fellow Citizens taken Captive on the high Seas to bear Arms against their Country, to become the executioners of their friends and Brethren, or to fall themselves by their Hands.

He has excited domestic insurrections amongst us, and has endeavoured to bring on the inhabitants of our frontiers, the merciless Indian Savages, whose known rule of warfare, is an undistinguished destruction of all ages, sexes and conditions.

In every stage of these Oppressions we have Petitioned for Redress in the most humble terms: our repeated Petitions have been answered only by repeated injury. A Prince, whose character is thus marked by every act which may define a Tyrant, is unfit to be the ruler of a free people.

Nor have we been wanting in attention to our British brethren. We have warned them from time to time of attempts by their legislature to extend an unwarrantable jurisdiction over us. We have reminded them of the circumstances of our emigration and settlement here. We have appealed to their native justice and magnanimity, and we have conjured them by the ties of our common kindred to disavow these usurpations, which, would inevitably interrupt our connections and correspondence. They too have been deaf to the voice of justice and of consanguinity. We must, therefore, acquiesce in the necessity, which denounces our Separa-

tion, and hold them, as we hold the rest of mankind, Enemies in War, in Peace Friends.

We, therefore, the Representatives of the **united States of America.** in General Congress, Assembled, appealing to the Supreme Judge of the world for the rectitude of our intentions, do, in the Name, and by Authority of the good People of these Colonies, solemnly publish and declare, That these United Colonies are, and of Right ought to be **Free and Independent States;** that they are Absolved from all Allegiance to the British Crown, and that all political connection between them and the State of Great Britain, is and ought to be totally dissolved; and that as Free and Independent States, they have full Power to levy War, conclude Peace, contract Alliances, establish Commerce, and to do all other Acts and Things which Independent States may of right do.

And for the support of this Declaration, with a firm reliance on the protection of divine Providence, we mutually pledge to each other our Lives, our Fortunes and our sacred Honor.

History of the Document

The best known of all the copies of the Declaration of Independence is the parchment copy, engrossed by Timothy Matlack. This one, signed by 56 Delegates of the Continental Congress on and after August 2, 1776, is displayed today in Exhibition Hall at the National Archives Building. Jefferson's final draft of the Declaration, known as the "rough draft," cumulatively bearing the corrections, amendments, and deletions of the drafting committee and of Congress as a whole, as well as Jefferson's marginal and textual notes, is preserved among the Jefferson Papers at the Library of Congress. The revised draft, adopted by the Delegates on July 4, 1776, and signed only by John Hancock and Charles Thomson, President and Secretary of the Continental Congress, is known as the broadside copy. It was sent to the printer and has never been located. Sixteen copies of the printed broadside have survived. In addition to the "rough draft," as least six other handwritten contemporary copies of the Declaration, one fragmentary, have survived and are in various archival collections. Five were made by Jefferson and one by John Adams.

The history of the parchment copy of the Declaration is fascinating. From 1776 until 1789, along with other important national papers, it was safeguarded by Secretary of Congress Thomson, who carried it with him as Congress, at first to escape British troops and later for other reasons, convened in various cities: Philadelphia, Baltimore, Lancaster, York, Princeton, Trenton, Annapolis, and New York.

When the Constitution took effect in 1789 and Thomson left office, he relinquished the Declaration to the newly created Department of State, which was under the temporary stewardship of Acting Secretary John Jay. Its offices were in New York's old City Hall (Federal Hall). The next March, Thomas Jefferson became the first Secretary of State and custodian of the instrument he had created. Later that year, Philadelphia became the seat of the Federal Government and the Declaration returned to its birthplace. There it remained for a decade, until 1800, when the Government moved to the new national Capital of Washington.

Secretary of State John Marshall apparently at first stored the Declaration in his Department's temporary offices in the old Treasury Building, at 15th Street and Pennsylvania Avenue NW., and possibly then at Seven Buildings, 19th Street and Pennsylvania Avenue NW. After a few months, likely in 1801, the document was transferred to the War Office Building, at 17th Street and Pennsylvania Avenue NW., where the Department of State moved its offices. The Declaration remained there until the summer of 1814, during the War of 1812, when British troops invaded the Capital. Shortly before they arrived, Secretary of State James Monroe packed the instrument and other state papers in linen sacks and sent them by wagon to a barn on the Virginia side of the Potomac 2 miles above Chain Bridge for one night, and then to a clergyman's home in Leesburg, Va. Within a few weeks, after the British threat had subsided, the documents were brought back to Washington and probably temporarily kept in various structures because of the burning of the War Office Building by the British.

In 1820 the Department of State moved the Declaration to its headquarters at 15th Street and Pennsylvania Avenue NW. Stored for years in scroll fashion, the document had already been damaged by numerous unrollings, other handling, and frequent moves. In the period 1820-23 the use of a "wet" copying process to produce a facsimile apparently divested the parchment of some of its ink, especially that of the signatures.

Subsequently the Declaration remained relatively undisturbed until 1841, when Secretary of State Daniel Webster, concluding that it should be on public view, ordered that it be mounted, framed, and moved to the newly constructed Patent Office, in the block bounded by Seventh, Ninth, F, and G Streets NW. The Patent Office was then part of the Department of State. Placed beside George Washington's commission as commander in chief of the Continental Army in a large frame on a wall of the second floor hall opposite a window, for 35 years the Declaration endured exposure to glare, summer heat, and winter cold. The text retained its legibility, but the parchment faded and yellowed, cracked and warped. Many of the signatures had faded, some becoming blurred or almost invisible.

The Federal Government in 1876 lent the Declaration to the city of Philadelphia, site of the national Centennial Exposition. On July 4 Richard Henry Lee, grandson of the signer, read it publicly. It was then exhibited in a fireproof safe behind a plate glass window and seen by more people than ever before. Philadelphians, deploring its condition, fought to retain it and only reluctantly returned it to Washington. Heeding the outcry of those who had viewed the time-worn parchment, a Government commission studied the possibility of restoration and in time concluded that such an attempt might be damaging.

Meantime, in 1877, as a safeguard the Declaration was moved from the Patent Office to a more fireproof building at 17th Street and Pennsylvania Avenue NW. shared by the State, War, and Navy Departments. It had narrowly escaped destruction, for only a few months later fire gutted the Patent Office. Finally, in 1894, for protection from the light, State Department officials sealed the 118-year-old sheet between two glass plates and locked it in a safe in the basement. There it lay, except for rare occasions, in darkness and unobserved for more than a quarter of a century.

In 1921 the Department of State, responding to the recommendation of a special commission, relinquished custodianship of the Declaration to the Library of Congress. The transfer was made personally by Herbert Putnam, the Librarian, using a library mail truck, a Model T Ford. At first he kept the document in his office. In 1924, however, he placed it together with the Constitution, on public exhibition in a bronze-and-marble shrine on the second floor. At this time, the Declaration was encased between heavy glass panes specially treated to keep out harmful rays of light.

The Declaration and the Constitution remained there until the outbreak of World War II. On December 26, 1941, just 19 days after the Japanese attack on Pearl Harbor, they left Washington under heavy guard by train en route to Fort Knox, Ky., where they arrived the following day. Specialists took advantage of the opportunity and cleaned and restored the Declaration to the maximum degree. In 1944 both it and the Constitution were taken back to the Library of Congress. They remained there until 1952, at which time a tank under military escort carried them to Washington's National Archives Building, repository of the Nation's permanent records, which are under the jurisdiction of the National Archives and Records Service of the U.S. General Services Administration.

Constitution Avenue entrance of the National Archives Building, Washington, D.C.

This marble shrine at the rear center of Exhibition Hall, National Archives Building, contains the Declaration of Independence, the Constitution, and the Bill of Rights.

STILL enshrined there today, along with thousands of other priceless national records, is the parchment copy of the Declaration. The massive bronze doors at the Constitution Avenue entrance to the building lead to the circular Exhibition Hall. At its rear center stands a marble shrine containing the Declaration of Independence, the Constitution, and the Bill of Rights. They are sealed in helium-filled bronze and glass cases, screened from harmful light rays by special filters, and can be lowered within seconds into a large fireproof, shockproof, and bombproof vault.

The hall also features a "Formation of the Union" exhibit, a collection of documents illustrating the evolution of the U.S. Government from 1774 until 1791. They include the Articles of Association (1774), the Articles of Confederation (1777), the Treaty of Paris (1783), and Washington's inaugural address (1789). Above the exhibits are two murals. In one, Jefferson is presenting the Declaration to John Hancock, President of the Continental Congress; in the other, James Madison is submitting the Constitution to George Washington, President of the Constitutional Convention.

Suggested Reading

BECKER, CARL L. *The Declaration of Independence: A Study in the History of Political Ideas*. New York: rev. ed., Harcourt, Brace, 1942. A classic and scholarly study, originally published in 1922, that analyzes the Declaration in terms of its political background, philosophical origins, and literary merit, and discusses subsequent reaction to it.

BOYD, JULIAN P. *The Declaration of Independence: The Evolution of the Text as Shown in Facsimiles of Various Drafts by Its Author, Thomas Jefferson*. Princeton, N.J.: Princeton University Press, 1945. This valuable work is a revised edition of a study published by the Library of Congress in 1943 in connection with the bicentennial celebration of Jefferson's birth. Examines the nature and evolution of the various drafts.

BURNETT, EDMUND C. *The Continental Congress*. New York: Macmillan, 1941. Although written in a cumbersome style, this book remains one of the best on its subject. Includes chapters dealing with the events surrounding adoption of the Declaration.

DUMBAULD, EDWARD. *The Declaration of Independence and What It Means Today*. Norman, Okla.: University of Oklahoma Press, 1950. Phrase-by-phrase study of the contents of the document and differences in the several drafts. Also treats the underlying intellectual and political influences.

MALONE, DUMAS. *The Story of the Declaration of Independence.* New York: Oxford University Press, 1954. Enhancing this readable account of the early phases of the Revolution and biographical sketches of the signers is a fine collection of illustrations assembled by Hirst Milhollen and Milton Kaplan.

McGEE, DOROTHY H. *Famous Signers of the Declaration.* New York: Dodd, Mead, 1955. One of a series oriented to young readers, this volume presents biographies of selected signers.

NATIONAL ARCHIVES. *The Formation of the Union.* Washington: National Archives and Records Service (Pub. No. 70-13), 1970. A handsome but moderately priced brochure that consists of a brief history of the period 1774-91 and facsimiles of key documents.

WHITNEY, DAVID C. *Founders of Freedom in America: Lives of the Men Who Signed the Declaration of Independence and So Helped to Establish the United States of America.* Chicago: J. G. Ferguson, 1964. This superbly illustrated work is one of the best popular versions of the events of the Revolutionary period and those associated with the signing. Includes biographies of the signers and patriots Patrick Henry and James Otis.

Criteria for Selection of Historic Sites of National Significance

A. National significance is ascribed to buildings, sites, objects, or districts which possess exceptional value or quality in illustrating or interpreting the historical (history and archeology) heritage of our Nation, such as:

1. Structures or sites at which events occurred that have made a significant contribution to, and are identified prominently with, or which outstandingly represent, the broad cultural, political, economic, military, or social history of the Nation, and from which an understanding and appreciation of the larger patterns of our American heritage may be gained.

2. Structures or sites associated importantly with the lives of persons nationally significant in the history of the United States.

3. Structures or sites associated significantly with an important event that outstandingly represents some great idea or ideal of the American people.

4. Structures that embody the distinguishing characteristics of an architectural type specimen, exceptionally valuable for a study of a period, style, or method of construction; or a notable structure representing the work of a master builder, designer, or architect.

5. Objects that figured prominently in nationally significant events; or that were prominently associated with nationally significant persons; or that outstandingly represent some great idea or ideal of the American people; or that embody distinguishing characteristics of a type speci-

men, exceptionally valuable for a study of a period, style, or method of construction; or that are notable as representations of the work of master workers or designers.

6. Archeological sites that have produced information of a major scientific importance by revealing new cultures, or by shedding light upon periods of occupation over large areas of the United States. Such sites are those which have produced, or which may reasonably be expected to produce, data affecting theories, concepts, and ideas to a major degree.

7. When preserved or restored as integral parts of the environment, historic buildings not sufficiently significant individually by reason of historical association or architectural merit to warrant recognition may collectively compose a "historic district" that is of historical significance to the Nation in commemorating or illustrating a way of life in its developing culture.

B. To possess national significance, a historic or prehistoric structure, district, site, or object must possess integrity. For a historic or prehistoric *site,* integrity requires original location and intangible elements of feeling and association. The site of a structure no longer standing may possess national significance if the person or event associated with the structure was of transcendent importance in the Nation's history and the association consequential.

For a historic or prehistoric *structure,* integrity is a composite quality derived from original workmanship, original location, and intangible elements of feeling and association. A structure no longer on the original site may possess national significance if the person or event associated with it was of transcendent importance in the Nation's history and the association consequential.

For a historic *district,* integrity is a composite quality derived from original workmanship, original location, and intangible elements of feeling and association inherent in an ensemble of historic buildings having visual architectural unity.

For a historic *object,* integrity requires basic original workmanship.

C. Structures or sites which are primarily of significance in the field of religion or to religious bodies but are not of national importance in other fields of the history of the United States, such as political, military, or architectural history, will not be eligible for consideration.

D. Birthplaces, graves, burials, and cemeteries, as a general rule, are not eligible for consideration and recognition except in cases of historical figures of transcendent importance. Historic sites associated with the actual careers and contributions of outstanding historical personages usually are more important than their birthplaces and burial places.

E. Structures, sites, and objects achieving historical importance within the past 50 years will not as a general rule be considered unless associated with persons or events of transcendent significance.

Acknowledgments

Advisory Board on National Parks, Historic Sites, Buildings, and Monuments (1971)

Durward L. Allen, *Purdue University.*
Hon. E. Y. Berry, *Rapid City, S. Dak.*
Anthony A. Buford, *Clayton, Mo.*
Loren C. Eiseley, *University of Pennsylvania*
Mrs. Lyndon B. Johnson, *Stonewall, Tex.*
Peter C. Murphy, Jr., *Springfield, Oreg.*
Nathaniel A. Owings, *San Francisco, Calif.*
Melvin M. Payne, *National Geographic Society.*
Linden C. Pettys, *Ann Arbor, Mich.*
Steven Rose, *Arcadia, Calif.*
William G. Shade, *Lehigh University.*
Elisha Walker, Jr., *New York, N.Y.*
James W. Whittaker, *Seattle, Wash.*

National Park Service

Edwin C. Bearss, *Historian, Historic Preservation Project (East), Denver Service Center.*
S. Sydney Bradford, *Chief, Plans and Grants, National Register of Historic Places.*

George S. Cattanach, Jr., *Program Coordinator, National Register of Historic Places.*

Henry A. Judd, *Chief, Park Historic Architecture, Division of Historic Architecture.*

Herbert E. Kahler, *Chief (retired), Division of History and Archeology.*

Ronald F. Lee, *Special Assistant to the Director.*

John Luzader, *Historian, Historic Preservation Project (East), Denver Service Center.*

Warren A. McCullough, *Management Assistant, Independence National Historical Park, Pa.*

John D. McDermott, *Assistant Executive Secretary, Advisory Council on Historic Preservation.*

Thomas W. Mullen, *Student Research Assistant (Northeastern University), Division of History.*

Denys Peter Myers, *Architectural Historian, Division of History.*

John D. R. Platt, *Historian, Independence National Historical Park, Pa.*

Charles W. Porter III, *Chief Historian (retired), Division of History.*

Charles W. Snell, *Historian, Division of History.*

Martin I. Yoelson, *Supervisory Interpretive Specialist, Independence National Historical Park, Pa.*

Other Individuals

Roland A. Block, *Regional Director, Taconic State Park Commission, Staatsburg, N.Y.*

Jerry M. Bloomer, *Secretary-Registrar, R. W. Norton Art Gallery, Shreveport.*

Edwin Cox, *President, Virginia Historical Society, Richmond.*

Alonzo T. Dill, *West Point, Va.*

Educational Programs Staff, *National Archives and Records Service, U.S. General Services Administration.*

Ms. Constance M. Greiff, *Vice President, Historical Society of Princeton, N.J.*

Ms. Virginia Gunter, *Curator, New Hampshire Historical Society, Concord.*

Edgar R. Lafferty, Jr., *Elsing Green, King William, Va.*

Charles H. McCormick, *Assistant Professor of History, Fairmont State College, Fairmont, W.Va.*

Ms. Mildred Steinbach, *Librarian, Frick Art Reference Library, New York.*

E. Berkeley Tompkins, *Director, Division of Historical and Cultural Affairs, Department of State, State of Delaware, Dover.*

Art and Picture Credits

The National Park Service gratefully acknowledges the assistance of agencies and individuals furnishing illustrations and granting permission to reproduce them.

Page

ii   Oil (1817) by John Trumbull, after his earlier painting of the same name (1786-95). Color separations courtesy United States Capitol Historical Society and Eastern National Park and Monument Association. Of the 48 individuals in the painting, 44 are signers. The likenesses were the basis for many later portraits by other artists.

4   Oil (date unknown) by Allan Ramsay. Print supplied by Library of Congress.

5   Engraving (1770) by Paul Revere. Library of Congress.

6   Lithograph (1830) by either William or John Pendleton, after a cartoon (1774) published in London. Library of Congress.

7   Lithograph (1846) by Nathaniel Currier. Library of Congress.

8   Engraving (1775) by Amos Doolittle, after a drawing by Ralph Earl (Earle). Print by National Park Service.

9   Detail from broadside, publisher unknown. National Park Service.

10   Engraving (ca. 1776) by an unknown artist. Library of Congress.

11   Library of Congress.

12   Oil (ca. 1858) by Bass Otis, after George Romney. Independence National Historical Park.

13   Mezzotint (1778) by an unknown artist, after Corbutt. Library of Congress.

14   Oil (ca. 1782) by Charles Willson Peale. Independence National Historical Park.

17   Library of Congress.

19   Engraving (1823) by William Stone. Library of Congress.

21   Library of Congress.

22   Engraving (1859) by John C. McRae, after Johannes A. S. Oertel. Library of Congress.

23   Oil (date unknown) by Xavier D. Gratta. Valley Forge (Pa.) Historical Society.

28   Oil (before 1897) by an unknown artist, after Thomas Sully. Independence National Historical Park.

Page

29   Oil (date unknown) by W. Trego. Valley Forge (Pa.) Historical Society.

30   Engraving (ca. 1725-26) by William Burgis. Library of Congress.

33   Oil (ca. 1791-94) by Charles Willson Peale. Independence National Historical Park.

36   Oil (ca. 1770-72) by John Singleton Copley. Museum of Fine Arts, Boston.

39   Oil (1871) by Caroline Weeks, after John Trumbull. Independence National Historical Park.

41   Watercolor on ivory, miniature (date unknown), by an unidentified artist. National Portrait Gallery (Smithsonian Institution); on loan from Mr. and Mrs. Douglas M. Braxton.

43   Oil (1823) by Charles Willson Peale, after Rembrandt Peale. Independence National Historical Park.

45   Oil (1819) by Charles Willson Peale, after his 1773 painting. Independence National Historical Park.

47   Oil (1873) by James R. Lambdin, after John Trumbull. Independence National Historical Park.

48   Wood engraving by an unknown artist, after F. O. C. Darley, from Henry Howe, *Life and Death on the Ocean* (1855). Library of Congress.

49   Oil (1807-10) by Charles Willson Peale. Pennsylvania Academy of Fine Arts, Philadelphia.

50   Pen and ink drawing by an unknown artist, from *Magazine of American History* (September 1880). Library of Congress.

51   Oil (1876) by Samuel B. Waugh, after John Trumbull. Independence National Historical Park.

53   Oil (1793) by Ralph Earl (Earle). Independence National Historical Park.

55   Oil (1767) by David Martin. Pennsylvania Academy of Fine Arts, Philadelphia.

57   Engraving (1859) by Robert Whitechurch, after Christian Schussele. Library of Congress.

59   Oil (1861) by James Bogle, after John Vanderlyn. Independence National Historical Park.

62   Oil (1769) by Jeremiah Theus. Fulton Federal Savings and Loan Association, Atlanta.

63   Lithograph, probably by an artist named Ferris, from William Brotherhead, *The Book of the Signers* (1861). Library of Congress.

65   Detail from the lithograph "Signers of the Declaration of Independence," published in 1876 by Ole Erekson. Library of Congress.

67   Oil (1765) by John Singleton Copley. Museum of Fine Arts, Boston.

70   Oil (1873) by James R. Lambdin, after John Trumbull. Independence National Historical Park.

Page

71 Oil (ca. 1884) by Herman F. Deigendisch, after Henry Bryan, Jr. Independence National Historical Park. Art authorities have never confirmed the existence of a portrait from life of Hart.

73 Watercolor on ivory, miniature (1776), by Charles Willson Peale. United States Naval Academy Museum, Annapolis.

74 Engraving by James B. Longacre, after Charles Willson Peale, from James Herring and James B. Longacre, *The National Portrait Gallery of Distinguished Americans* (1836). Library of Congress.

75 Oil (before 1851) by Charles Fraser, after Jeremiah Theus. Independence National Historical Park.

77 Oil (1873) by James R. Lambdin, after John Trumbull. Independence National Historical Park.

79 Oil (1873) by James R. Lambdin, after John Trumbull. Independence National Historical Park. According to one authority, Trumbull based his likeness on the features of Hopkins' eldest son, Rufus, who bore a close resemblance to his father.

81 Oil (before 1854) by Dubois (probably Samuel T.), after Robert E. Pine. Historical Society of Pennsylvania and Independence National Historical Park.

83 Oil (1783) by Charles Willson Peale. Independence National Historical Park.

85 Oil (1791) by Charles Willson Peale. Independence National Historical Park.

87 Library of Congress.

89 Engraving (1826) by Benjamin Tanner. Library of Congress.

90 Detail from the lithograph "Signers of the Declaration of Independence," published in 1876 by Ole Erekson. Library of Congress.

92 Oil (1784) by Charles Willson Peale. Independence National Historical Park.

94 Oil (1906) by Albert Rosenthal, after an engraving from John Sanderson, *Biography of the Signers to the Declaration of Independence* (1824). Independence National Historical Park.

96 Oil (ca. 1770) probably by Abraham Delanoy, Jr. Frick Art Reference Library, New York City, and Taconic State Park Commission, Staatsburg, N.Y.

97 Pen and ink drawing by an unknown artist, from *Magazine of American History* (December 1885). Library of Congress.

99 Oil (1875) by Anna Lea, after John Trumbull. Independence National Historical Park.

100 Oil (1797) by Charles Willson Peale. Independence National Historical Park.

Page

103 Oil (1872) by Philip F. Wharton, after Benjamin West. Independence National Historical Park.

104 Oil (1873) by Charles N. Flagg, after John Trumbull. Independence National Historical Park. Art authorities have never confirmed the existence of a portrait from life of Morris.

106 Oil (ca. 1782) by Charles Willson Peale. Independence National Historical Park.

107 Engraving by William Birch, from *The City of Philadelphia* (1800). Independence National Historical Park.

109 Watercolor (ca. 1765) by Pierre Eugene Du Simitière. The R. W. Norton Art Gallery, Shreveport, La.

110 Oil (ca. 1876) by William L. Sheppard, after Mason Chamberlin. Independence National Historical Park.

112 Oil (date unknown) by Louis E. Lami. Hangs in the Virginia State Capitol. National Park Service.

113 Oil (date unknown) by Francis B. Mayer, after Charles Willson Peale. Independence National Historical Park.

115 Oil (1876) by Richard M. Staigg, after Edward Savage. Independence National Historical Park.

116 Detail from the lithograph "Signers of the Declaration of Independence," published in 1876 by Ole Erekson. Library of Congress.

118 Oil (1784) by Robert E. Pine. National Portrait Gallery.

120 Detail from the lithograph "Signers of the Declaration of Independence," published in 1876 by Ole Erekson. Library of Congress.

122 Oil (1873) by Philip F. Wharton, after Benjamin West. Independence National Historical Park.

123 Oil (1783) by Charles Willson Peale. The Henry Francis du Pont Winterthur Museum, Winterthur, Del. Gift of Mrs. Julia B. Henry.

125 Engraving (1799) by William Birch & Son. Library of Congress.

127 Oil (date unknown) attributed to James Earl. National Portrait Gallery; on loan from Mr. and Mrs. Edward Rutledge Moore.

129 Oil (1874-75) by Thomas Hicks, after Ralph Earl (Earle). Independence National Historical Park.

130 Lithograph by an unknown artist, from William Brotherhead, *The Book of the Signers* (1861). Library of Congress.

132 Watercolor (ca. 1760) by an unknown artist. The R. W. Norton Art Gallery, Shreveport, La.

133 Oil (1873) by George W. Conarroe, after John Wollaston. Independence National Historical Park.

135 Oil (ca. 1785) by Robert E. Pine. National Portrait Gallery.

Jacket No. 578-084—G.P.O.

Page

137   Oil (1912) by Laura J. Schneider, probably after George T. Pool. Independence National Historical Park.

139   Oil (date unknown) by an unknown artist. New Hampshire Historical Society, Concord.

140   Oil (1874) by Samuel B. Waugh, after Charles Willson Peale. Independence National Historical Park.

142   Oil (1888) by Ulysses D. Tenney, after John Trumbull. Hangs in the Moffatt-Ladd House, Portsmouth, N.H. Photographer, Douglas Armsden, Kittery Point, Maine.

144   Oil (1873) by James J. Sawyer, after John Trumbull. Independence National Historical Park.

145   Watercolor on ivory, miniature (1793), by Jean Pierre Henri Elouis. National Collection of Fine Arts (Smithsonian Institution).

146   Sketch (date unknown) by C. A. Poulson, Historical Society of Pennsylvania and Independence National Historical Park.

149   Oil (ca. 1783) by Charles Willson Peale. Independence National Historical Park.

150   Engraving by Henry Dawkins, after W. Tennant, from *An Account of the College of New Jersey* (1764). Library of Congress.

152   Oil (1796-97) by Ralph Earl (Earle). Connecticut State Library, Hartford. Photographer, Gus Johnson, Windsor, Conn.

154   Engraving by James B. Longacre, after a portrait by William S. Leney in *The American Gleaner* magazine (1807). Print supplied by the National Portrait Gallery.

164   National Park Service (Tony P. Wrenn).

165   National Park Service (Wrenn).

167   National Park Service (Wrenn).

168   National Park Service (Wrenn).

169   National Park Service (Wrenn).

171   National Park Service (Abbie Rowe).

172   Aquatint by an unknown artist, from Charles W. Janson, *The Stranger in America* (1807). Library of Congress.

174   National Park Service (Charles W. Snell).

175   National Park Service (John O. Littleton).

178   National Park Service (Wrenn).

179   National Park Service (Littleton).

181   National Park Service (Snell).

182   National Park Service (Jack E. Boucher).

184   National Park Service (Snell).

Page
185   National Park Service (Snell).

187   Photographer, William L. Klender.

188   National Park Service (Littleton).

190   National Park Service (Boucher).

192   Engraving (date unknown) probably by Stephen A. Schouff. Library of Congress.

194   National Park Service (Cervin Robinson).

196   National Park Service (Wrenn).

197   National Park Service (Wrenn).

198   National Park Service (Snell).

200   National Park Service (Wrenn).

201   National Park Service (Wrenn).

203   National Park Service (Snell).

205   National Park Service (Snell).

206   Historical Society of Princeton, N.J. Photographer, Constance Greiff.

207   National Park Service (Boucher).

208   Department of Public Information, Princeton University, Princeton, N.J.

210   National Park Service (Snell).

211   National Park Service (Snell).

212   National Park Service (Snell).

213   National Park Service (Snell).

215   National Park Service (Boucher).

216   National Park Service (Boucher).

219   Engraving by an unknown artist, from *Columbian Magazine* (July 1787). Library of Congress.

220   National Park Service.

223   National Park Service (Boucher).

224   National Park Service (Boucher).

225   National Park Service.

227   National Park Service (Snell).

229   National Park Service (Snell).

230   National Park Service (Snell).

232   National Park Service (Wrenn).

233   National Park Service.

235   National Park Service (Boucher).

Page

236   Photographer, Jesse Gibbes.

238   National Park Service (Snell).

239   National Park Service (Horace J. Sheely, Jr.).

241   National Park Service (Littleton).

242   National Park Service (Littleton).

244   National Park Service (Snell).

246   National Park Service (Boucher).

248   National Park Service (Snell).

250   National Park Service (Snell).

251   National Park Service (Boucher).

253   National Park Service (Snell).

256   National Park Service (Snell).

265   National Archives.

266   National Archives.

—   FRONT END PAPER: Engraving (ca. 1876) by John C. McRae. Independence National Historical Park.

—   REAR END PAPER: National Park Service sketch.

Index

Vocations of signers, compared, 31. *See also individual signers.*

Wakefield Academy, England, 92
Wales and Welshmen, 53, 62, 118
Wallingford, Conn., 65, 130
Walton, George (signer), career of and sites associated with, 31, 50, 64, 65, 66, 138, *140-142*, 161, *173-176*
Walton, George, Jr., son of signer, 175
Walton, Mrs. George, wife of signer, 141
Walton descendants, 175
Walton-Harper House, Ga., *see* College Hill
Wamassee Head, Ga., 177
War for Independence (U.S.), and Declaration of Independence, 3, 23-24, 217; and Loyalists, *see* Loyalists and Tories; battles and campaigns, land and naval, and course of, 3-156 *passim,* 207-218 *passim,* 228, 233, 236, 239, 248, 263, 264; begins, 12, 38, 42; ends, *see* Treaty of Paris; feared, 134; financed, *see* Continental Congress, fiscal problems and policies of; generated, *see* Independence movement and British-colonial clash; heroes of, 75, 251; heroes of, painted, 218; impact of, on signers and their families, *see* Risks and sacrifices of signers; Iroquois Indians neutral during, 153; peace negotiations during, 35, 58, 98, 128, 136; verge of, 9; won, 24. *See also appropriate topics throughout this index.*
War of *1812,* 172, 173, 263
War Office Building, D.C., 263
Ward, Samuel, politician, 80
Warren (town), R.I., 80
Wars, and historic sites, 159. *See also specific wars.*
Warwick Furnace, Pa., 137
Washington, President George, career of and sites associated with, 14, 23-24, 27, 29, 34, 35, 42, 46, 52, 60, 69, 75, 95, 98, 104, 107, 108, 114, 124, 125, 148, 171, 217, 218, 228, 233, 255, 264, 267
Washington, D.C., history of and historic sites in, 3, 62, 108, 161, 170-173, 218, 263-266 *passim*
Washington College, Md., 114
Watkins, Thomas, and Meadow Garden, 175
Wealth and financial status of signers,

compared, 27, 28-29, 30, 31, 43. *See also* Debts and economic reversals of signers; *and individual signers.*
Weapons, *see* Arms, ammunition, and ordnance
Webster, Daniel, Secretary of State, 264
Welcome (village), Md., 135
Welles, Rev. Samuel, and Williams Birthplace, 166
Welles-Williams House, Conn., *see* Williams Birthplace
Wells family, 204
West, Benjamin, artist, 82
West Indies, 100, 194, 202
West Nottingham Academy, Md., 124, 134
Westchester County, N.Y., 105
Western Reserve (in present Ohio), 153
Western United States, *see* Frontier and frontiersmen
Westernville, N.Y., 54, 211, 212
Westminster School, England, 95
Westmoreland Association (*1766*), 93
Westmoreland County, Va., 91, 92
Westward expansion, *see* Frontier and frontiersmen
Whedbee, Joseph, builder, 214
Whigs (patriots) and Whig Party, *see* Independence movement and British-colonial clash
Whipple, Joseph, brother of signer, 143
Whipple, Mrs. William, wife of signer, 143, 202
Whipple, William (signer), career of and sites associated with, 28, *142-143, 177-178, 201-202*
Whipple Birthplace, Maine, *177-178*
White Hall Plantation, S.C., 76, 233
White (Bishop) House, Pa., 224, 226
White House ("President's House"; "President's Palace"), D.C., 34, 85, *170-173*
White Plains, N.Y., 105
Whitestone, N.Y., 95
Widowers, signers as, 35, 41, 46, 54, 148
Widows of signers, *see* Wives and widows of signers
Wilkins, John, builder, 214
William and Mary, College of, *see* College of William and Mary
William and Mary architectural style, 252
Williams, Mrs. William, wife of signer, 144

☆ U. S. GOVERNMENT PRINTING OFFICE : 1975 O - 578-084 (Rev. Ed.)

𝔗𝔥𝔬𝔪𝔞𝔰 𝔇. 𝔥𝔬𝔬𝔨𝔰